A PEDIATRICIAN'S
BLUEPRINT

A PEDIATRICIAN'S
BLUEPRINT

Raising Happy, Healthy, Moral, and Successful Children

Donald Ian Macdonald, M.D., FAAP

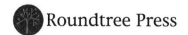

Roundtree Press

Library of Congress Control Number:
2013912875

Printed in the United States of America

10 9 8 7 6 5 4 3 2 1

Book design by Robert Schlofferman

Distributed by
Publishers Group West
1700 Fourth Street, Berkeley, CA 94710
Ph 510.809.3700
pgw.com

Roundtree Press

6 Petaluma Boulevard North, Suite B-6
Petaluma, California 94952
Ph 800.779.5582
roundtreepress.com

ISBN: 978-1937359362

*Dedicated to my wonderful grandchildren
and to the thousands of children and parents
who have entered and enriched my life*

CONTENTS

PREFACE AND OUTLINE

In the challenging world in which we live, it has become increasingly difficult to raise children to be the adults we would like them to be. This book was written to provide an A-to-Z twenty-first-century parenting roadmap, focusing on knowing about and steering your child's normal developmental processes. Strong, active, time-consuming, purpose-driven parenting is emphasized. The failures of the all too common "permissive parenting" will be emphasized. The book is divided into five sections.

1.   What do you want your child to be when she grows up? This, perhaps the most important section in the book, stresses the need to early in the process set goals and develop a plan for their implementation.

2.   Who will nurture your child? In the most important early years, you the parents will, with your home environment, have the principal role. All too soon, however, you will be joined by what I call your child's "other parents"—the media and his peers. The importance of media literacy and of parent peer groups cannot be understated.

3.   What will you have to know? This section presents important information and necessary parenting tools, looking at such subjects as discipline, time management, sleep, and the characteristics of inborn nature.

4.   What are the issues at each age of development? Here we look at the parenting process with an age by age walkthrough of parenting issues from conception through age 24.

5.   What are the potential traps of adolescence and beyond? The final section deals with the all too common but preventable problems of youth that led to the writing of this book.

A Pediatrician's Blueprint may be seen as a tool for pediatricians to recommend to their patients to convey the material that most do not have the time to adequately discuss in their increasingly busy practices.

INTRODUCTION

Why This Book? *This book was written to stress the importance of parents setting appropriate goals for their children and to provide parents with the tools needed to accomplish this mission. This will mean, among other things, developing a plan to help their children avoid the traps into which so many of today's youth are falling. Strong, active, time-consuming, purpose-driven parenting will be stressed. The failures of the all too common "permissive parenting" will be emphasized.*

This book, originally titled *We're Losing Our Kids: A Pediatrician's Guide to Saving Yours*, was written because of my deep concern for what is happening and what is not happening to an increasing majority of today's generation of American children. Large numbers of today's generation of teenagers have fallen into serious health and behavioral traps that are often baited by today's cultural environment, the media, and their peer groups. For me, the book-writing process began with concerns about what I was reading in medical publications and newspapers and what I was seeing in young people around me.

With that in mind, let me begin by telling you about some of the things that worry me. The rate of teenage obesity has tripled in the last twenty years, associated with which there have been predictions that this generation of young people will not live as long as their parents.

Rates of physical fitness are shockingly low. Scholastic Aptitude Test (SAT) scores have reached their lowest levels in forty years, and one study shows that 45% of college students are making no academic gains during their first two years in college. Over 40% of births are to unmarried mothers, many of them teenagers. There are disturbing rates of teenage violence and addiction to nicotine, alcohol, and other drugs. Binge drinking among high school and college students is a major problem. The list of concerns goes on: there are growing numbers of young women who are immodestly dressed; foul language and rude manners have been "normalized;" and an alarming number of young men, mostly African Americans, are spending their most formative years incarcerated. Accidents, suicides, and homicides remain the three leading causes of death in teens and young adults. There is more, much more. Without serious help, a disturbingly high percentage of our children are—or will be—in deep trouble.

Book Goals: To address the problems confronting today's youth and to stress the point that properly motivated, well-informed, and goal-directed parents may be the only ones capable of protecting our children. This book aims to help parents set goals, develop a mission statement to achieve those goals, and move ahead with an implementation strategy. My hope is that what you read will help you guide and assist your children through the traps of childhood, leading them until they emerge from the teenage tunnel as well-directed, well-informed, and properly motivated adults.

What to Do? Greatly concerned about current issues, I called a group of experts from across several disciplines to a meeting at my house, where our mutual concerns were shared. At first we considered that government agencies and schools might be best suited to address these problems. It did not take long, however, for us to realize that because of their overcrowded budgets, government agencies are not likely to take on new programs. In fact, many programs that were helpful in the not-so-distant past have seen cuts in their funding or been eliminated altogether. Children always seem to be low on government budget agenda, especially when polls show that voters have not placed children's issues very high on their list of concerns. Politicians also know that children don't vote.

Recent first ladies of our country are to be saluted for having taken on a number of these issues: Nancy Reagan worried about drug use; the Bush women were concerned about reading and education; and Michelle Obama is tackling the very important issues of fitness and diet. Our group recognized these contributions but thought that rather than tackling the many problems individually, there might be a strategy that would include an attack on all of these as components of basic and related issues.

The group agreed that the most effective approach might be one that focused on strengthening and correctly aiming families. My hope is that the parenting plan described in this book will prove infectious, and will spread from one set of parents to whole groups of parents, and from there to communities of ever-increasing size. It is my belief that successful governmental changes can come only from the bottom up. One member of the group pointed out that because parents have come to value the advice given to them by their pediatricians, a book written by a pediatrician might be the most attractive to them. As the only pediatrician in the room, I realized that I had been volunteered, and I agreed to take on this book project. Prevention is a big part of what pediatricians believe, teach, and practice.

Possible Cultural Causes: New to our culture since the days when families spent their lives in the communities where they grew up, today's families are often far removed from the support of grandparents and extended family, and from the communities, schools, churches and temples who knew parents in their own childhoods. Often lacking in our new society are strong parental support and guidance, which seemingly have been replaced by an increasingly common belief that the best parenting method is to let the child make all of his or her own decisions, unfettered by parental knowledge, wisdom, and experience. Probably related to this, today's youth seem to be in a state of aimless wandering, with an "if it feels good, do it" mentality. Over 80% of mothers now work, so parenting time is reduced. Scarcity of time is one of the biggest issues that we all need to face. Parenting takes time, energy, and study. For these reasons and more, I recommend co-parenting, where both parents are actively involved, a model in which your child can gain from both female and male styles. Knowing that many children grow up with just one active parent, I have included a section on how single parents can best address parenting issues.

The emergence of communications media as a major player in all our lives has resulted in large quantities of time being spent involved with the media at the expense of other important activities, such as sleep, play, exercise, study, and family communication. The need to become media literate, to teach your child media literacy, and the reasons why are stressed in this book.

What This Book Is and Isn't: Unlike Dr. Spock's pediatric masterpiece, this book is not about diagnosis and treatment. When I first began writing, I included topic sections on fears, anxiety, depression, and attention deficit disorder—all important pediatric subjects. But the more I thought about the importance of other topics, such as the autism spectrum disorder and cystic fibrosis, the more I realized that this book was about prevention, and these other important topics were more than I could adequately handle here. A number of these important topics are mentioned, with comments on recognition and management, but if they continue or are especially severe, they should be addressed with your child's healthcare provider.

This book is about prevention and helping your child grow into a healthy future. To save your child from the traps of adolescence that have captured so many of today's youth, you must accept the role of problem preventer and learn how to be most effective in this role. As parents, you should begin this process early, including setting goals and developing a strategy to achieve them.

Aim High: Realize that all children are by nature different, as are all parents, and that you must make adjustments to your plans to better fit your child as you both get to know each other. One-size parenting does not fit all. Over time, and increasingly with your child's input, your initial goals and strategies may need to be modified. Your plan should include helping your child pick his own life goals and strategy so that when you turn him loose he will be purpose-driven. The best prevention comes when your child knows who he is, why he is here, and what is expected of him.

Being a twenty-first-century parent is no easy task, but now more than ever good parenting is vitally important. Time flies. To best prepare your child for the difficult time of adolescence, when the separation process begins in earnest, you should have him well schooled on the lessons that are best taught before he reaches his teen years. Before he separates from you, your schooling should be almost complete. The clock is ticking.

The book is divided into five sections. The first deals with setting goals and making a parenting plan. This is followed by a look at parenting in its many forms, followed by Section III, a section on things every parent should know and an introduction to the concepts of nature and nurture. Section IV explores nurturing at various ages. Finally, the book addresses the problems facing today's teens, which provided the impetus for writing this book.

A Few Caveats Before We Begin:

This book was written for parents with children of all ages, but its goals will be best achieved when the parenting process is begun early. Some readers may prefer to go directly to sections of the book that interest them the most, rather than reading the book from start to finish.

There is repetition and redundancy in this book. I hope not too much. The repetition is necessary so that those who read chapters selectively will not miss some important and related topics. For example, discussions on the importance of sleep and the media appear in many places. The issue of sleep has its own chapter but is relevant in chapters on obesity, learning, media use, and in some of the chapters devoted to specific ages in life. Likewise, the subject of media and obesity show up in many chapters, but each of these subjects has a chapter of its own. If you want to know more about a particular subject, consult the index. You may also consult the acknowledgment and references section at the end of the book.

I have presented data from scientifically reliable sources (see section on references at end of book). In interpreting this information I have given you my personal, experience-based opinions. In the first draft of this book that I submitted for publication, I tried to present material in a way that would appeal to all parents and that would offend none. The publisher suggested that there is no book that will please all audiences, and that I would be better off presenting what I believe in a fashion that will appeal to parents who are sincerely willing to learn and to keep an open mind about what needs to be done to produce the adult they want their child to become. Recognizing that subjects such as homosexuality and the pro-life v. pro-choice debate are often divisive, I nevertheless included them, because in my view they are too important to omit.

My wonderfully helpful and workaholic editor, Joe Garfunkel, M.D., who for years edited the *Journal of Pediatrics*, commented that much of what I say may be seen as old-fashioned and overly idealistic. He then said, "But you are right," to which I responded, "Amen." This book is about many of the new-fashioned ideas that have gotten our children off the track.

I have friends who are Jewish and friends who seem not to claim any God who have successfully raised their children. I am a practicing Christian who knows that my beliefs and my faith offer me strong support in the mission I set for myself as a parent. Although my beliefs are reflected in statements in this book, I have tried to teach lessons that should apply to all parents, not just those who are Christian.

Regarding word usage, I have referred to children using the words she/her in some chapters and he/him in others. I hope that I have achieved gender equity in doing this. I have also most commonly referred to your child rather than your children. This should not be seen as implying that I prefer one-child families, but rather as a suggestion to recognize each child as an individual when setting goals and implementing a plan for success.

Finally, almost daily I come across new information that I would like to use to modify the book. Because of this I realized that almost as soon as this book was written parts of it would be obsolete. But I stress that nothing that I have seen has changed my mind about the importance of setting goals, character development, and strong parental involvement.

Purpose-Driven Parenting:
Laying the Foundation

In his bestselling book, *A Purpose Driven Life*, Rick Warren speaks of making your life count for something. In this book, my purpose is to help you become purpose-driven parents. As I see it (perhaps simplistically), in terms of parenting styles, there are two ways to parent. The first is what we might call the "get out of your child's way" style, which is not unlike the "if it feels good, do it" style. Some variation of this method is probably the most common parenting style today. Actually, I'd call it non-parenting or "let your child be her own parent" style, and it is one that, in my opinion, is basically unsafe. Instead, I recommend the "show your child the way" style, which is not to be confused with the "it's my way or the highway" style. It will be your job as parents to take a major role in deciding who you want your child to be. With your mission set, you must lead and guide your child through the difficult times of adolescence and early adult life, helping her to avoid the many traps described in Section V of this book, and to become the adult you want her to be.

1

Morality and Building Character

Chapter Goals: *To stress the importance of character development as a primary goal for raising your child. Although the book title lists happiness, morality, and success in that order, I believe that unless there is morality in happiness and success they are not going to be fully achieved. The goals of having happy and successful children will be discussed in the next chapter, but here we will try to explain how much better these latter two can be when achieved with a moral, ethical foundation.*

Primary Goals: It has been obvious to me that most parents have given little or no thought to choosing or setting goals for raising their children, much less discussed the issue with their co-parents or planned any implementation strategy. Without such planning, the child's development becomes sort of a leisurely drifting through life a la the following quote:

> *"When you come to a fork in the road, take it."*
>
> —Yogi Berra

You do not have to choose the same goals that I have set here, but you must have goals. Unguided, directionless parenting will increase the risk of your child falling into the traps that we aim to avoid, and/or ending up drifting through a purposeless life. Too many of today's parents neglect this goals-setting responsibility based on

1

their belief that it is better to let the child develop her own goals and implementation strategy with little if any parental supervision. To be successful in life, your child will benefit greatly from your active guidance and encouragement.

Understand that in choosing goals for your child, you are choosing goals for yourself. You and your child are in this together. For any goal that you select, the importance of role-modeling cannot be understated.

When I ask, "What do you want your child to be when she grows up?" the most common response I get is a surprised look, followed by some form of "I don't care, as long as she is happy." The next most common answer, one that was the most popular a generation or two ago, is that the parents want their child to be successful. The third most common response, but much less frequent than the first two, is some variation of wanting their child to grow up with good character. My follow-up question is, "What do you mean by happiness (or success or character)?" and then, "Why did you pick this goal?" In most cases, those who have given this character response add that they want her to believe in God. Actually, I would like my child to meet all three of these targets, but when asked to rate my order of preference, the third—wanting my child to grow up with good character, a child of God—is the one I strongly prefer and will discuss first.

A primary goal is one that takes precedence over other goals. The goals of wanting your child to grow up happy and successful are ones on which we all can probably agree, but I call them secondary because if they are not defined properly and achieved morally and ethically, I do not want them for my child.

A second primary goal that we all should agree on needs little explanation. It is to grow up physically fit and healthy. Some of the problems this book addresses, such as obesity-shortened life span in the current generation of children, are caused by failure to adequately address fitness and health issues. Failure in the fitness and health areas can also interfere with the secondary goals of being happy and successful.

"To prevail, a species must have a spirit capable of compassion, sacrifice, and endurance."

—William Faulkner

According to a newspaper column by Peggy Noonan entitled "America's Crisis of Character," only 24% of Americans feel that we are on the right track as a nation. In her article, she addressed events of corruption and other immoral behaviors that are in the news daily. I want my children to be moral, ethical, virtuous, and value-driven—knowing right from wrong. This primary goal sets the tone and lays the foundation for any other goals that you may later wish to add. On the other hand, I have known many people who do not share my belief in God who have raised "good" children. But for me, my belief in God has provided incredible help and very useful guidelines for developing children with character. Whether you believe in God or not, and whether you are Jewish, Muslim, Christian, or practice a different religion, the advice that follows should apply, except perhaps for my comments regarding church or temple attendance and teachings.

What Do We Mean By Moral? Let's consider the Girl Scout Law, which requires scouts to pledge that they will be honest and fair, friendly and helpful, considerate and caring, courageous and strong, responsible for what they say and do, that they will respect themselves and others, respect authority, use resources wisely, make the world a better place, and be a sister to every Girl Scout. Can we agree on some or all of these? How about the Boy Scout Oath, which says, "On my honor, I will do my best to do my duty to God and my country and to obey the Scout Law; to help other people at all times; to keep myself physically strong, mentally awake, and morally straight." Not bad either.

How about conscience, manners, modesty, goodness, empathy, honesty, decency, forgiveness, and idealism? And should we include principled, protective of others, respectful, responsible, and against various injustices and prejudices? Can you think of any more moral objectives?

It is said that every night before he went to bed, Benjamin Franklin would look at his day and rate how he had done on following the ten moral goals that he had assigned to himself for the day. On a really good day he might rate the first nine as well done, but on these days he knew that he would have to rate himself as a failure on the tenth—"be not vain."

3

What Is Your Role? In addition to assessing your child's moral behavior, you also must regularly assess your own moral behavior, as Benjamin Franklin did. Realize that you, like your child, are on a walk through life and have not yet reached the endpoint of your moral development. None of us is a finished product. We all have great potential for moral growth but we also have the potential to backslide. Realizing that none of us is perfect, shouldn't we as parents, the principal role models for our children, practice what we will be preaching to them, and work to bring ourselves closer to the role model that we should strive to be? At some time in your teaching, it may be useful if you point out to your child areas where you have had trouble and what you did or are doing to try to improve. You might also tell her about character-related problems that you are currently working on (she probably already knows about these)—but be cautious if you do. By admitting that you are not perfect and that you are working to improve, you hope that she will learn from your example. Of course, you should not overdo this exercise, nor take on a "woe is me" tone. Always remember that you are the parent and your child needs to respect you if you are to be her prime adviser in matters of life.

Caring and Sharing: Making a Contribution

Recently, when I asked a Marine captain with two young children what he wanted them to be when they grew up, he responded, "That's a really interesting question." He was then called away, but when he returned in about twenty minutes, he told me that as he thought through my question, his first response would have been that he wanted them to be happy (no surprise there), but he then added that after further thought, he had decided that he wanted them to make a contribution—to learn to share. When I asked him how he would pull this off, he had no ready answer.

Caring and sharing are behaviors that are outgrowths of a good moral foundation. For me, part of the joy of living is knowing that I have been and am being of use to others. There have been many days in my life, while driving home from my pediatric office, when I reflected on the fact that I had been playing with children all day and even gotten paid for doing it. This might be called "job joy," a condition which makes going to work something that I have (almost) always looked forward to. With professions such as teaching, social work, and medicine, it is easy to know that you are making a difference in the lives of others, but these are not the only careers in which this goal can be realized. Policemen, firemen, soldiers, mechanics, and many others can also feel the rewards that come from helping others. Volunteer work and charitable efforts are other ways of making a difference. We in this country have been blessed in so many ways that whether we choose to help others should not be a question.

"It is better to give than to receive."

—Acts 20:35, Bible

Help your child to know the joys of giving and of living a purpose-driven life. Have her learn by experience that it is better to give than to receive in terms of her own true satisfaction.

A neighbor knows that it is difficult for her children to choose gifts for their grandparents because they believe the grandparents have all of the things they really need. Knowing this, she takes her children out on an annual pre-Christmas shopping trip to buy clothing and other useful articles for a family in need. She then prepares a photo gift for her parents of the shopping and giving. Her children are being taught sharing and caring. The grandparents are given a very meaningful gift, and the grandchildren are the beneficiaries as well as the givers.

Religion: The Shortcut to Morality. It may not be necessary for you to believe in God, but it sure helps. Knowing right from wrong and the teaching of morality, ethics, values, and compassion are all integrally tied to the basic tenets of all organized religions. The rules set forth in documents such as the Ten Commandments and the great commandment that says to "love your neighbor" can provide the basics of a purpose-driven life. It is my belief that God has put us all here for a purpose.

5

When founders of Alcoholics Anonymous (AA) realized that they were in serious trouble and, for them, seemingly impossible situations, they were able to turn their lives around only after deciding to turn their lives over to God. There is a strong message here for all of us. The first three steps of AA's Twelve Step program are: 1) Admit that you are powerless over alcohol (or substitute your own problem issue) and that your life seems unmanageable; 2) Come to believe that only God (or a power greater than yourself) can restore you to sanity; and 3) Make a decision to turn your will and yourself over to the care of God as you understand him.

In addition to the beneficial teaching that is obtained in religious settings, attending church or similar services and classes can also be of great value because it provides a chance to associate with adults and children with similar beliefs. With these people you have the opportunity to form healthy, moral adult and child peer groups. Maximum benefit to children comes when their parents believe, attend worship services, pray and teach prayer, and live a life that demonstrates their faith and belief. Later on, when your child leaves home to work or to attend college, similarly believing youth groups can be very supportive.

There has been a significant increase in the number of religion-driven parents who are sending their children to church schools or homeschooling, based in great part on these parents' desire to spare their children exposure to the currently disastrous "I just want to be happy" philosophy and to the cursing, immodesty, smoking, and more that have become so common in public schools.

Chapter Summary: *It is essential that you set goals for your child and develop a strategy to see that they are achieved. Character building and being healthy and fit are my primary goals. The importance of parental role-modeling is stressed.*

2

Chapter Two

Happiness and Success

Chapter Goals: *To define what we mean by happiness and success and to develop a mission statement to achieve these goals. Although not my primary goals, I have attempted to define them in ways that can make them both very desirable.*

I Want My Child to Be Happy: As stated in the previous chapter, by far the most common answer to my question, "What do you want your child to be when he grows up?" is some variation of "I don't really care as long as he is happy." Even after reading this book, there may be some of you who, instead of adopting morality as your primary goal, will opt to place one of the currently "popular" goals—being happy or being successful—at the top of your lists. Neither of these is a bad goal, but unless your child is of good character, you may not get what you really want. The door may be left open to immoral (but temporary and too often destructive) happiness that can be found in being stoned, watching pornography, or other inappropriate, immoral activity. The happiness goal may also stand in the way of study and practice because of the "happier" times spent playing video games or texting. Likewise, the goal of maximizing one's potential is a great goal, but not if it is done immorally. Examples of successful (for a time) cheaters are Bernard Madoff, who swindled his clients, cyclist Lance Armstrong, and the many other professional athletes who succeeded at their sports by breaking rules. Unlike being happy and successful, living morally is always the right thing to do.

Defining Happiness: Whether you pick character, happiness, or success as your goal, a good follow-up question is, "What do you mean by character (or happiness or success)?" Happiness has been defined as a mental or emotional state of joy—a state of well-being and contentment with an emphasis on pleasure. Happiness for many people means living a life of positive emotions and ebullience, having multiple friends, and later developing a good romantic relationship. Pleasure is often emphasized. This type of pleasure can be found in your work, in parenting, in your hobby, and in your friendships. As great as this type of happiness can be, there may be issues that can come with it. First, the ability to feel this way seems to be DNA-based and fully expressed in only about 50% of us. Extroverts, who are happy by genetic nature, find this kind of happiness easier to achieve than do introverts, but even for them it is not a certainty at any given time. There may be times when doing the right thing, such as studying, exercising, or sleeping, should take precedence over the pursuit of happiness or relaxing in front of the television. Another issue with this style of happiness is that it tends to habituate, meaning that although a new feeling may be great at the beginning it will tend to become old fairly quickly and require bigger and bigger doses. For example, the first time you win a game may make you happier than regularly winning does.

After a parent responds to the follow-up question, "How do you define happiness?" I might ask, "Are having fun and being happy the same thing?" By my definition, they are not. A good way to separate these two states is to see fun as temporary and real happiness as longer lasting. Activities such as drinking to intoxication or overdosing on fast foods can be enjoyable, but their aftereffects can lead to unhappiness. Do you believe the song that says, "If you're happy and you know it, then your face will surely show it"? I don't. I never saw Martin Luther King Jr. smiling, chuckling, or laughing. Would you say that he was happy? There are people who have a lot of fun who are not really very happy, and there are others who don't seem to have a lot of what most would call fun but are very happy. What makes one child happy may not please another child. When a book tells us at the end that the principal characters will live happily ever after, does this mean that they will continually be having fun or continually finding pleasure or contentment?

*"The happiest people don't necessarily have the best of everything;
they just make the best of everything they have."*

—Anonymous

Expanding the Happiness Definition: Happiness comes in different types, styles, and depths. What psychologist Martin Seligman calls the pleasant life is happiness or pleasure of the type just described. He and others have introduced a field they call positive psychology that expands the happiness definition to include two other types of happiness: the happiness of engagement and the happiness of a meaningful life. A person who finds happiness in engagement is someone who begins a project and finds pleasure in the flow of what they are doing. Time seems to stop for this person in their period of intense focus, and the flow does not cease until it is time to quit for the day, the game is over, or the task is completed.

A third type of happiness described by Seligman comes from leading a meaningful life, one in which you know what your strengths are and apply them to the service of others. To answer the earlier question regarding Martin Luther King Jr., I would say that he was very happy and satisfied in the sense of the very meaningful life he was able to lead. Of the three types of happiness, the meaningful life is the strongest determinant of self-satisfaction, with a life of engagement not far behind. In contrast, emotional satisfactions of the pleasant life are relatively short-lived. A goal of the positive psychologist is not only to make those who feel miserable feel better, but to make untroubled people happier—in the best ways, more fulfilled and more productive. In many senses, happiness can be seen as a close cousin of satisfaction, which has been defined as the fulfillment of one's wishes, expectations, and needs. Seligman points out that having all three types of happiness will bring the most satisfaction, but qualifies this by stating that this feat may not be possible for everyone.

Being Unhappy, Sad, or Depressed: Being unhappy can come in many forms. Losing a game, doing poorly on a test, or having arguments with friends can make us all unhappy, but if we are able to learn from our failures and put them behind us, this unhappiness should go away fairly quickly. Sadness from the grief of losing a pet or a friend or being lonely can last longer. I have always been impressed by the way children handle the loss of a pet. Typically they sob and sob, but by the second day or so they are over their grief. This is resilience in action and a great tool for life. Adult grief, on the other hand, often lasts six months and longer. Children grieve more rapidly because they are most often unencumbered by many of the factors that go into adult grief, such as guilt and anger. Clinical depression is much more serious and longer lasting than the unhappiness we address in this book, and should, when suspected, be addressed with professional assessment and treatment.

Success as a Goal:

> *"Strive not to be a success but rather to be of value."*
>
> —Albert Einstein

In the chapter on self-discipline and success, we emphasize that the popular idea that you can increase your child's self-esteem by praise of accomplishment, such as high grades on report cards, is often counterproductive. Loving parental praise has been shown to lead children to a position where they become afraid of taking on challenges that they feel they may not do well in, for fear of disappointing their parents and missing out on praise. To prevent failure they may fill their school schedule with easy and lightly graded subjects. Additionally, telling children that they are great at everything they do can lead to narcissism. Learning self-respect—very different from becoming narcissistic, especially when coupled with humility—can lay a good foundation for success. We are learning that self-esteem and real achievement are best facilitated by praising your child's effort, time, and study—if indeed he does work hard, spend time, and study hard and effectively. Parents who quickly jump to the rescue when their children show signs of anxiety, unhappiness, and anything negative may produce children who are unable to cope later on with the realities of a world where there is pain, death, and despair. Rather than rescuing your child, you will do him a service by helping him understand his anxiety or unhappiness and helping him deal with it. If it is beyond your ability to do so, you should seek professional help.

A pediatrician friend once told me that the three careers sought by men were careers for joy, careers for wealth, and careers for power. Some people, but not many, are able to achieve all three. Please note that my friend did not include character, an omission I would not make.

My thoughts are that a job for joy is one where you are paid for doing something you love (such as being a pediatrician and seeing children all day) and that at the same time gives you a chance to make a contribution and to provide help to others. Wealth and power-based careers can bring you the joy of material riches. They can also bring you character-based joy if you use your wealth and power to help others. Your aim should be to do well by doing good. It should go without saying that these goals should be achieved without cheating and trampling on the rights of others. Wealth and power without character are not to be recommended.

The Importance of Balance: Working to maximize one's potential in one area must not come at the expense of neglecting obligations in another area. For instance, there must be a balance between committing time and interest to a job or a hobby at the expense of a marriage or the very important job of being a good parent. Too often I have seen young adults so driven to achieve success that they haven't considered marriage until they were too old to have the children they always wanted. Not infrequently, these are parents who are so committed to great career success that their marriage partner and child suffer.

Beware of Setting Too Many Goals: If you set too many goals for your child, you may end up achieving success in none of them. Many of today's parents spend their lives driving their child from one activity to another, allowing no time for other important activities such as practicing the activity they like and are good at, or making time for relaxation, conversation, play, reading, and sleep.

And finally, I would love to have my children be all of these things—good, happy, successful, and, of course, healthy—as defined in this chapter.

3

Communicating

Chapter Goals: *With our objectives in mind, we will address the preparations needed for the implementation of a plan to reach those goals and to avoid all the traps that may be in your child's way. In the process of setting and implementing goals, there must be communication on many levels. In this chapter, we will look at some of the times and ways when there is need for communication. There is some redundancy with other chapters because I believe it is especially important to emphasize certain points.*

Before we start, let me confess that I have put a lot of time into obtaining suggestions for this chapter (and subsequent chapters). It will be up to you to decide how many of these suggestions you will adopt into your family routine, but I believe that every one of them can be helpful. I also realize that none of us is perfect, and that attaining the goal of being a perfect parent is beyond any of us.

Mission Selection:
"If you don't know where you're going, any road will get you there."
—*Alice in Wonderland,* Lewis Carroll

Your mission and the plan for its achievement will be understandably vague during the prenatal and newborn periods, but it is not a bad idea to begin your thinking even then. Begin by remembering that even at birth all children are different and have different temperaments, traits, and talents. Along the way they will develop different likes and dislikes. Parents should know that adjustments will almost certainly be made to their parenting goals and their approach to them as they discover more about who their child really is. Your job is to impart to her values, training, guidance, encouragement, and a push in the direction of maximizing her potential. As your child develops, she should be included in your conversations and eventually become the key player in them. When the time comes, it will be your job to let her go. By then, if you have done your job well, you will be able to release her into her adult life with a pretty good idea of where she is heading and how she intends to get there. This does not mean that she won't change direction more than once in her lifetime, as I have done, but she will be much better able to focus if she has a destination in mind. Unfortunately, many, if not most, of today's children go off to college and/or the workplace with no idea of why they are there or where they are headed.

Communicating comes in many forms—it is much more than just talking. Some of the many ways of communicating, in addition to talking face to face, are with body language, empathetic expressions, touch, smell, appearance, discipline, punishment, rewards, social media, and text messages.

Communicating to Prepare: Before you and your partner or partner-to-be begin your role as parents, perhaps even when seriously dating, you should sit down together and ask yourselves important questions on a number of topics. Know that the adventure of child-rearing will change your life and may be the most important thing that you ever do. The Boy Scout Motto, "Be Prepared," should become your motto. Develop a healthy parental dialogue that will, among other things, involve getting to know your partner and perhaps yourself better. When you have areas on which you disagree, the goal should not be winning arguments but finding ways to solve them, perhaps with compromise. In these discussions you may learn, hopefully before it is too late, that there are important issues on which you will never agree. Although you may both change your answers to a lot of the questions that follow, do not find out after you are married that one of you does not want to have any children while the other strongly does. Using your persuasive skills to badger your partner into agreeing with you on an issue does not necessarily mean that you have really changed his or her mind. Below are some sample questions:

Do you both want to be parents? Why?

How many children do you each want? Why?

If more than one, how should they be spaced and why? It is understood that asking the latter two questions may be a little premature, but it's not a bad idea to have a starting point for the discussion that will continue soon after child number one arrives.

What do you want your children to be when they grow up?

How will parenting change your lives?

What do each of you want to get out of your parenting?

What are your religious beliefs? If your religions are different, from each other's, how will you raise your child?

Same questions regarding your political feelings.

Will you both continue with outside jobs? If not, which of you will continue?

How will you share the responsibility of parenting (more in the next chapter)?

Will you use a nanny, a babysitter, or a daycare center during those times when both of you need to be elsewhere? How will you decide?

Do you both agree on these questions and other parenting ideas? If not, how will you resolve your differences?

Try to anticipate, as best you can, areas where you and your co-parent might have future differences. Develop a plan, agreed on by both of you, for dealing with any such issues.

From birth on, you will be your child's principal teacher, guide, and counselor. As we discuss in the chapter on pregnancy, your parenting role begins with conception. At birth, do not let the apparent helplessness and size of your new family member fool you into believing that there is little that you can do to shape her future at this age other than feeding, clothing, and bathing her. Your little baby will be gathering and storing information at an incredible rate. Throughout her walk through life, there will be ups and downs, but time will fly, and before you know it she will be out from under your roof. Before she reaches her teenage years, when the painful but necessary process of separation begins in earnest, prepare yourselves and your child for the joy and the sadness of that important event.

Your Mission Statement: After you have settled on your goals for your child, you should put together a mission statement and a plan to implement it. This will take time—time that you may believe you do not have—but because of its importance the task must not be ignored or put on the back burner. Developing and implementing a mission statement and a strategy for its implementation will provide a basis for helping your child acquire the tools she will need. Think of yourself as being much like a college football coach, who puts together plays and provides active, usually very active, guidance from the sidelines. Too many coaches focus on winning and little else. Though often successful at the sport they coach, these coaches seem to ignore the whole person in their athletes and to lack interest in their academic performance and any future plans that do not involve continuation in the sport they coach. In your roles as coaches, you will need to be much more involved. Unlike these "successful" coaches, you must continue to show concern for your child's life after she leaves your home. You must be active, constantly active, in guiding your child until such time as she is ready to guide herself.

Meetings as an Essential Component of Your Teaching/Guiding Plan: In a variety of ways, we will discuss communication methods and styles throughout this book, but here we will focus on the use of meetings as a way of getting the job done. At least three types of regularly scheduled meetings are recommended. You do not have to call them meetings and they can take place in the car, while you are exercising together, or at the dinner table. Failing to have talks with your child, for whatever reason, will send a message, but not always the one you intend. Think of the feelings that a child must have when her parents don't attend her school events or games. As outlined below, it is obvious that these meetings will take time from your already overcrowded schedule. To free up time, look at the recommendations in the chapters on Time Management and Your Child's Other "Parents": The Media.

Daily Conversations: When parents greet their children after school or after play, they often ask such things as "How did your test go today?" or "Did you have fun today?" These are good questions, but they raise two issues. First is the emerging evidence (shared in other chapters) that praising for good grades and winning scores directly is less valuable to the child than is praising her for study, hard work, and practice. So you might want to follow up her answer that she aced the test with a response that says, "Was that because of all the studying that you did?" Secondly, although your first two questions relate to two of your parental goals of happiness and becoming successful, you should also include at least one addressed to your prime goals. For instance, you might ask her if she saw any good deeds today. If so, have her describe what she saw and what she thought about it. Did she have an opportunity to share with or to help anyone? Remember your primary goal.

> *One of my grandchildren has made it her project to speak to someone she does not usually talk with every day. After a recent effort, when the teacher asked children to pick someone to partner with, a very shy girl she had recently spoken to said, "I want Katie."*

Parent Meetings: Parents need to make time to communicate regularly. Questions that we listed earlier in the chapter may be raised again if one parent is having a problem with a decision that was earlier agreed upon, perhaps because the other parent is not following through on it, or perhaps because one parent has changed his or her answer.

> *Jane and Jeff schedule their date nights for every Friday. They usually send their children to another part of the house while they dine. Often the meal is brought in from some takeout spot to minimize cooking and cleanup jobs. Although primarily a social meeting, topics for discussion should regularly include talk of their children's progress, setbacks, and any disciplinary issues. Any points of difference that haven't been settled should be discussed, with the aim of agreeing on one method or in agreeing that each parent will use a different method that is acceptable to the other. Also discussed will be their relationship and other issues that have not been addressed and resolved.*

17

Date nights can be a socially attractive form for parental meetings. Conversation at these regularly scheduled parental meetings should include discussion of your children's behavior, as well as your own personal behaviors as role models and how you might improve on them. Topics you might also cover are the behavior of your child's peers, other parents, and the behaviors that have invaded the media. Look at the goals that you have set and how much progress your child has made toward achieving and adopting them. Do not forget, however, that the primary purpose of date nights is to strengthen your bond with your parenting partner.

In these meetings, you must be careful about not only what you say but how you say it. If the meetings turn into "you shouldn't have done that" or "you really goofed" conversations, not only will they fail as problem-solving discussions but they can put a serious strain on your relationship. Carefully consider or avoid any finger pointing; "you"-based discussions will almost always come across as accusations and put an effective end to any meeting. Better to discuss what concerns you about some of the decisions you have had to make and seek your co-parent's comment. In some controversial areas, you may agree that you do not always have to agree and are willing to accept the fact that you are different and can live with your differences. Remember that males and females are basically different and have genetically induced ways of parenting that are not wrong, just different. For example, women tend to cuddle, whereas men are more apt to wrestle and roughhouse.

Family Communication Meetings: As your child gets older, but not too much older, date-night meetings should be supplemented with regularly scheduled family meetings, perhaps at dinner. These may address the same issues that are covered in parent meetings but should not take their place. The agenda for this and one-on-one meetings with your child should include an opportunity for your child to voice any questions or concerns she may have, including any problems that she feels she is having with you, your behavior, or your role-modeling. Careful listening on your part is very important. As disciplinary issues arise, they should be addressed and any action that is taken or that is anticipated should be talked over. The caveat here is that some problems that a child has should be addressed privately with her and not in the company of siblings or guests. Although the child's vote will not be taken over the parents', you should consider any point that she makes, address it, and possibly accept it. Among other factors, it has been shown that compared to teens who have frequent family dinners (five to seven per week), those who have infrequent family dinners (fewer than three per week) are almost four times likelier to use tobacco; more than twice as likely to use alcohol; two and a half times likelier to use marijuana; and almost four times likelier to say they expect to try drugs in the future.

Regular One-On-One Sessions With Each Child: These should address the things you are seeing that make you proud and issues that concern you or concern your child. These are serious and important meetings aimed at helping your child understand and achieve the goals that you have set for her and want her to adopt.

Family Celebrations: Birthdays, anniversaries, graduations, holidays, and other special occasions should be honored and used as times to bond the family further and to celebrate who you are. I know a woman who has decided that half-birthdays can also be a time of celebration. Her whole family seems to love the idea, even though there is only half a decorated cake and the presents are fewer and less expensive, but just as meaningful.

Reassess and Modify Your Goals: As you get to know more about your child and more about yourself as a parent, the goals you have set may change, and almost certainly will be modified and refined. In your case, modifications may have to be made in relation to jobs, household duties, and more. Address these with your parenting partner. For your child, such things as future careers are not possible to establish at birth, nor are temperaments, traits, skills, likes, and dislikes. Reassessments should be a part of your regularly scheduled family meetings, with the focus on the primary goal. This does not mean that you should ignore secondary or tertiary goals, such as having your child maximize her potential and being happy. It does mean that as your understanding of her true potential emerges you may have to revise your strategy.

Involve Your Child in the Goal-Setting Process: As your child matures, you may realize that your goal of having her become a concert pianist has become unrealistic and needs to change. The child may be disappointed in your decision and see her inability as a failure, but she needs to learn that we all fail at times and need to learn from the lessons of our failures. Explain that many successful people use their failures to help them grow. Be a part of any necessary change and do not make the mistake of letting your child make all of the choices by herself.

With increasing age your child should be more and more involved in the process of reassessments and modifications, and should be encouraged to adopt your goals or goals of her own choosing (with your help) as her direction for life. She will also need an implementation strategy. By the time your child is ready to leave your home at about age eighteen, she should understand and have developed her own set of goals. Do not wait until the last moment to have her reach this plateau.

At some point, or at many points, tell your child what your dreams are for her. Practice the psychiatric technique of asking questions rather than always being the lecturer. When your child asks you a question, ask her why she asks or what she thinks the answer is. This is a better way for her to learn than just hearing you give your opinion. Pay attention to what she says but also make comments. Realize that your dreams and her dreams may not be the same, but whatever they are, discuss with her whether her dreams are ones that will set a moral and healthy direction for life. Tell her why you believe she is on the right track or why not.

Chapter Summary: *Communicate with your co-parent and with your child on a regular basis. It is always better to know how your partner feels about all parenting matters before a crisis occurs, but because that is not always possible, a strategy for conflict resolution should be laid out ahead of time. Goal-setting is once again stressed. All children should end up having a good sense of who they are and of who they are not.*

Your Child's Many "Parents"

An adult's behavior and personality are determined by the temperament with which he was born (his nature) and its interaction with the environmental influences (his nurturing) to which he is exposed. Over the past century there have been many significant changes in lifestyle and culture that have had great and, often, very negative effects on how a child is nurtured.

At one time a child's nurturing was pretty much limited to the influences of his parents, his family, friends in his neighborhood, his school, and his church, temple, or mosque, all of which were in close proximity to his home. In the twenty-first century, families and their nurturing influences have become geographically split; neighborhoods are not generally as close-knit as they once were; the media have exploded in ways that can reach us all; and a child's friends are often not well known by his parents (and those friends' parents even less so).

In this section we will look at and make comments on different parenting styles—their pluses, their minuses, and their problems. We will also look at the media and at peers, and the tremendous influence, good and bad, that both can have.

4

Mothers and Fathers

Chapter Goals*: Effective parenting is the key to raising moral, ethical, healthy, happy, and successful children who are prepared to avoid the traps that are ensnaring so many of today's young people. At the end of this chapter, we look at potential problems that should be anticipated, even in a perfect (if there were such a thing) marriage. We begin the discussion of good parenting in this chapter and move on to parenting in situations that are less than ideal in the next.*

The History of Parenting: Many of the problems facing today's youth are directly related to a tidal wave of change that has made parenting much more difficult and at the same time much more important. Over the past century, great societal and cultural shifts have affected the way we parent. A century ago and for millennia preceding that, "typical" families had a father who worked close to home; a full-time mother; and more children than are the norm today. Most children grew up living, working, worshipping, playing, studying, marrying, and raising their children in the community where they were born. Many whose fathers were farmers became farmers, while others, whose fathers were storekeepers, became storekeepers. College was rarely an option and was less often needed for the careers that most would pursue. In many ways life was tougher, but the parenting responsibility was much more clearly defined and in that way much easier. For children, the grandparents, aunts, uncles, and older siblings were there to help, as was the community.

The Changing Face of Motherhood:

As the world has changed, so have the roles of mothers and fathers. Increasing urbanization plus job-related and retirement moves have separated families from the close support systems that were once available. Now marriages are often to spouses of different cultures, religions, locations, and backgrounds. Divorce, once unusual, has become commonplace.

Less than a century ago, led by strong and courageous leaders, women obtained the right to vote—something that we now take for granted. At that time, women who wanted to have an occupation were generally told by their parents to either stay at home or, if they insisted, to get a job as a nurse, a teacher, or a secretary. At the same time, their brothers were being encouraged to become doctors, lawyers, and bankers. For the first half of the twentieth century and well into the second, women were denied admission to many major colleges and universities, but change was on the way.

During World War II, many women went to work in support of the war effort, replacing men who had gone off to fight. Many of these women found that they liked working and liked the extra income that a job provided. Many did not wish to return to their age-old, full-time jobs as mothers and housekeepers. With the advent of the Women's Movement, more and more women saw outside-the-home work as their right.

Most of today's mothers have an outside job in addition to their mothering role. These women work because of a need for money; the desire to achieve a purpose-driven life (forgetting that being an effective parent is a life purpose); a need for more intellectual stimulation; or for a number of other reasons. Some mothers whose friends all work may be made to feel ashamed, by their comments or by an inference the mother herself makes, that she is not living up to her potential by staying at home. To many, the jobs of baby care and housekeeping are seen as boring. Now more and more mothers are partially able to solve the problem of being functional mothers and functional full-time workers by finding jobs that allow them to telecommute or stay at home at least some of the time. All of these changes have been happening at a time when children are facing ever greater challenges and threats—among them, the often toxic electronic media that has the potential to dominate our worldview.

For women wanting to move up the work ladder, marriage, pregnancy, and mothering are frequently deferred, often until the optimal marrying and birthing periods are over. Wanting to advance for many people has also meant having to move at their employer's wish and, in the process, to deal with the challenge of uprooting their families. Further change has occurred in the growing number of teenage moms who either drop out of school to care for their babies or turn them over to a parent, grandparent, or someone else to be their nanny. A very negative development has been the growing number of fatherless homes, related to such things as work, war, divorce, teen mothering, and incarceration.

Not changed or changing is the fact that a mother's love for her child is like no other. Over time, most children come to know and appreciate this love and the psychological boost that it gives them. Unlike any other person, the mother bonds with her child before birth. Perhaps this occurs at the time of fetal motion or perhaps at another time, but it is real. Early in my pediatric career I was surprised when mothers would seriously grieve the loss of a stillborn baby they had never seen. Now I know better. Other family members also grieve, but none like the mother, who has taken her child into her heart.

The Changing Face of Fatherhood:

"Every known human society rests firmly on the learned nurturing behavior of men."

—Margaret Mead

Traditional Fathers: In previous views of parenting, still unfortunately shared by many if not most, it was the belief that the role of the father during the baby's early years was almost solely limited to his role in supporting the mother. In those times, fathers were the principal earners in most families, but that is no longer universally the case.

Adolescents knew that their mother loved them. In their time with her, they had come to learn this and learned how she felt about many subjects, such as her opinions on smoking, marriage, college, etc. The "traditional" father of a teenager, on the other hand, was often a mystery. Not surprisingly, teenagers often wondered whether this important stranger loved them and valued them. Unfortunately, many people went through life without ever having answers to their important questions: who is he; what does he believe; and what does he think of me?

A friend of mine decided that at the age of thirty-nine that she was going to go to law school. I asked her if part of her reason for doing this was to prove something to her father. Her immediate answer was, "Perhaps." When I asked her how long her father had been dead, she said, "Fifteen years."

Try this on your friends and see how closely their self-esteem and success in life are related to their estimation of how their father valued them. You may be surprised. My friend was an obviously talented and motivated woman, but why had she not gotten what she needed from her father? Did he not know how smart she was and what her interests and talents were? Were his expectations unrealistically high? Perhaps he was from the older school that taught that sons should be doctors, lawyers, and bankers whereas daughter's occupational possibilities should be limited to the fields of nursing, teaching, and clerking. Too many of today's adults go through life believing, in many cases correctly, that their parents are disappointed in who they have become. The importance of such parenting failures cannot be overemphasized. For children of successful fathers, self-esteem may be even harder to obtain. I often wonder how the children of presidents, Nobel Prize winners, Yo-Yo Ma, Bill Gates, and Jack Nicklaus are able to recognize themselves as worthwhile.

For most of our past, fathers did not participate in the birth of their children. They were certainly not allowed in delivery rooms or even labor rooms. In the 1950s and '60s, as a predecessor to more complete change, fathers became involved in childbirth classes and began to coach their wives in labor rooms. Those fathers who were the first to enlist or to be enlisted in this prenatal world often faced the derision of their own fathers, brothers, and peers, who thought of these activities as unmasculine. Later, these men were graduated into delivery rooms. I have always loved the glow that emanates from the faces of mothers upon seeing their newborns.

Seeing this same look of euphoria on the faces of new fathers surprised me, but in light of what I know now, it should not have.

Hormonal Changes: Increasingly we are learning more about ways in which a father's involvement in parenting goes much deeper. There should be much more to fathering than just supporting the mother in the baby's early years. Studies show that during late-stage pregnancy and continuing for a period after birth, biologic changes are taking place in expectant fathers. First-time fathers have a drop in testosterone, the principal male hormone, twice as large as the drop seen in single men of similar age. These lower levels allow fathers to become more nurturing. Higher testosterone levels, found in peers who are not expecting babies, make men more likely to chase women in search of a mate. As testosterone levels are falling, the levels of estrogen (the female hormone) are rising in men during the pregnancy period. Both changes make fathers gentler.

The Value of Fathers: Fathers have a major role to play in child development. When a father is not part of the picture, the child loses. This is true for all of the causes of male absence, whether because of death, divorce, serving time in the army, or being in prison, which is unfortunately very common among inner-city men today. There will always be gender differences, but each parent can make significant and important contributions. The two may bring different feelings, management styles, aptitudes, and perhaps values to the parenting partnership. These differences can result in conflict, but rather than being seen that way, a growing body of evidence shows that, when properly managed, the addition of the male approach can, in addition to benefiting the child, bring great marital reward and bonding.

Children gain from early paternal attention and from early recognition of their father's love and his valuation of them. Children actively involved with fathers are less likely to drop out of school; do better while there; have improved cognitive skills; and eventually have more income. Perhaps surprisingly, fathers tend to be at least as empathetic as mothers. Teens who are fatherless are more apt to be the fathers of fatherless children. With a father's early involvement, there are fewer aggression and behavior problems and juvenile justice issues. Additionally, the age of sexual exploration is deferred and the children tend to be more sociable and popular with other children throughout early childhood. The list of benefits goes on, but I think you get the point.

Fathers Are Different: Fathers hold their babies as if they were footballs; mothers tend to use face-to-face cuddling. Men love to wrestle and roughhouse. These "daddy" activities tend to promote teamwork and toughening of the child. Men tend to respond differently to situations than mothers do. When a child shows signs of distress and looks as if a tantrum may be about to begin, mothers tend to pick up the child, cuddle him, and ask what the problem is. This is a great approach and very helpful for the child. In the same situation, fathers may firmly say, "Stop it," which can also be very helpful and effective. Mothers soothe, fathers distract. Mothers play to educate. Fathers are more interested in delight. Fathers tend to let the child work problems out. Mothers tend to help solve them. Both teach valuable lessons.

The role of the father is to do more than be generally supportive of the mother. It is his job to work with her as a teammate and to use their inherent gender differences to help their child develop better. Realizing that their methods will be different, parents should speak with each other about how they feel about these differences and work to a position where each will support the other. If this agreement does not happen, the marriage will suffer and the child will increasingly work the system. When the child realizes that his mother will not let him do certain things that his father will, he will quickly learn to go to the one that lets him have his way.

To sum up our current understanding of fathers and their babies, if you wish to maximize your child's developmental process, a father figure is needed. Recognizing the value of active fathering, in the next chapter we will discuss why, when there is no birth father in a child's life, it is important to find a substitute father, such as a grandparent, uncle, neighbor, or a stepfather.

Chapter Summary: *The concept of Venus and Mars that refers to the inherent differences of men and women is right on target. Both mothers and fathers can and should provide their inputs into child development early and often.*

5

Co-Parenting and Other Parenting Models

Chapter Goals: *To make you aware, if you are not already, of the concept of co-parenting and to stress the importance of having both maternal and paternal input shaping your child's development from conception onward. We will also look at other parenting models currently in use.*

As I will throughout this book, I may seem to assume unrealistically that your time is limitless even though I know that it is not. None of us seems to have enough time to do all the things that we need and want to do. That said, because of the joy and the importance of parenting please try to do as many of the things that I suggest as you possibly can.

The Need for a Co-Parent: In the rapidly changing world in which we live, there are a number of good reasons for parents to adopt what has been called a co-parenting model. In a co-parenting relationship, the father takes on additional childcare and housekeeping responsibilities. As pointed out by Pruett and Pruett in their book *Partnership Parenting*, this model brings rewards for the child, the mother, the father, and for the marital relationship. In our present culture, with approximately 80% of mothers having jobs outside of the home, the working mother has more home and job responsibilities and more associated stress that goes with them than her stay-at-home counterpart. She could use and would appreciate any extra help that she can get. Both father and child will benefit when the father pitches in. A Pew Research Center study showed that 62% of married adults said that sharing household chores was the third most important ingredient of marriage success (after faithfulness and sex). Even with the traditional model of a stay-at-home mother, this model is recommended: allowing the father time to bond with his child and provide male input.

Preparing to Co-Parent: For co-parenting to work most effectively, there have to be major changes from the way parenting roles have traditionally been addressed. In their excellent book on this subject, the Pruetts ask the question, "How do you create a marriage that feels like home and family to both partners?" The earlier the co-parenting model is discussed, modified as needed to compromise with each other's wishes, and adopted, the more successful will be the process. The best-case scenario would be if these subjects were raised during serious courtship—preceded, of course, by an agreement about whether there are going to be children and, if so, how many, and when. If there are serious issues of disagreement, the postponement of pregnancy should be considered until there is concurrence. It is understood that potential parents' answers regarding how many children and how far apart they will be will more than likely change with time.

The New Baby: With the arrival of your baby, the parents' relationship with each other is sure to change. We always knew that the new mother would love her baby, but more recently we have learned that the father, who also is drawn biologically to this new family member, wants to be more involved than in the traditional parenting model. In that model, the father's principal role was seen as being supportive of the mother, who would take care of the baby. The co-parenting father will want to be closely involved with her everyday care. Understand that for most men, the idea of changing diapers, feeding babies, and providing baby care can be very foreign concepts, but we now know these are ones that they should learn. It should also be anticipated that there may be a somewhat natural tendency of mothers to dislike any paternal invasion of what has traditionally been their territory. The different ways that men and women handle babies and deal with various situations may tend to exaggerate the problem of the mother's natural tendency to exclude the father from territory he now wants to enter. To prevent these feelings from becoming significant issues, they must be jointly addressed, understood, and resolved. Any unresolved conflicting feelings can become strong determinants of marital disharmony.

After the arrival of your baby and your newly gained understanding of parenting, changes may need to be made to any co-parenting plan that you put together in your prenatal naïveté. Maternal fatigue related to the stresses of labor, delivery, and around-the-clock newborn needs will take its toll. In almost no co-parenting family will the time spent by each parent be the same. It's best to agree ahead of time not to set a time clock on each parent and understand that it is not the quantity of time spent on the parenting job, but the quality, that is most important. Beware, though, that any time imbalance, especially when it becomes too great, may result in feelings of unfairness. Parents should modify their plans as circumstances change, work together as a decision-making team, and be willing to compromise. A better way of dividing up responsibilities than letting the clock keep score can be using a division of the necessary jobs between the co-parents. In this model the mother might be responsible for the feeding of the baby while the father was tasked with washing dishes and doing the laundry. In any case flexibility is important as is having regularly scheduled meetings at which any frustrations that either parent feels related to work division should be addressed. As your child grows older, he should be assigned a chore or chores. Always keep in mind that men, women, and children think and feel differently. Learn to remain cool, patient, and understanding. Your child will be the winner when you work as a team.

Everyone Wins with Co-Parenting: Please understand that for all the value this co-parenting method provides, it is not easy. Learning new roles will take time, effort, patience, and perhaps money. The more agreement there is on issues such as discipline, life goals, distribution of duties, and the concept of co-parenting, the more likely you are to be successful. Your thoughts and feelings on a number of related issues will inevitably change and must be addressed lovingly together. Expectant parents who think that parenting will be fun are more likely to find it that way. As reward for the extra time and work that co-parenting involves, there are many pluses. Marriages have more intimacy and are generally happier. Mothers who have a good co-parenting deal report better well-being. Co-parenting fathers live longer and safer lives, are less likely to commit suicide, are more productive on the job, are less aggressive, and less impulsive. Children gain from the advantage of having two active parents with their expanded knowledge and experience, plus the extra patience, stamina, and understanding that come from watching the parental team in action. They will learn to value what they get from each of you. Parenting should not be a competitive deal.

Daycare, Nanny Care, and Babysitters: When both parents work outside the home, some form of daycare, especially for the preschool child, will have to be worked out. Cost can definitely be an issue, but it is not the most important one. Before you make your decision about what form daycare will take, decide together what it is you are looking for and what it is you want to avoid. Will the experience be one that works to promote health and fitness, learning, and character development, or will it be some variation of a situation in which the daycare provider places your child in front of a TV and keeps her happy with a parade of fattening snacks? How will issues of bullying and violence be handled by the caregiver? How about foul language? A loving relative such as an aunt or a grandparent, or a good friend, if they have the time and inclination to take on this responsibility, can provide an excellent solution. Even then, make sure you and the caregiver are in agreement on the standard of care on which you insist.

There are real pluses, especially for the younger child, if you can have her stay in her own house with the nanny coming to her. Eventually you will have to teach her to separate from you, but if early separation from you occurs while she is still in her own environment, it will be easier. Later, when she is moved away, there may be no problem, but if there is, you may need to go slowly, with a procedure of staying with her in her new daycare world for a while and not leaving her there too long at the beginning. As she recovers from any separation and any fears of her new and foreign environment, you may extend the times of your absence.

Other Forms of Parenting:

Stay-At-Home Dads: Often, especially in days of economic downturn when a decreased number of white-collar jobs are available and when women often earn more than their husbands, having the father stay home may make great sense and offer real benefits over placing the child with a nanny or daycare center. Despite the advantages to the baby, who benefits from this form of daycare, there are potential problems for the father who elects to be the one who stays at home. Will his friends think he is some sort of sissy or failure for taking on this traditionally female role? Will the other stay-at-home parents (i.e., mothers) accept him in their peer group? My prediction is that, as we overcome the stigma that is sometimes associated with stay-at-home fathering, more and more men will volunteer for this important job.

Stepparents: Currently, blended families are increasingly common. They can be excellent for all concerned but with some potential limitations. It should go without saying that you should not marry a person who does not like children or one who brings a record of untreated drunkenness, violence, or other disturbed behavior with him or her.

Stepparents can do an excellent job as substitute co-parents and role models, but an agreed-upon parenting plan must be in place before remarriage. The birth parent must decide how much parental authority the new parent will have, discuss this decision with the partner-to-be, and reach an agreement before remarriage. If the stepparent is completely left out of a parenting relationship with his or her stepchild, as so often happens, the chances of the stepparent becoming unhappy with the relationship are likely to increase. Children do benefit from both healthy male and female influences in their lives.

For any children involved in remarriage, the insertion of a new parent into their lives can be traumatic and will almost always take adjustment time. This does not mean that the child should have the final say in a decision to remarry, but it does mean that the birth parent should know how their child feels about the potential new parent and why. When the child's objection is strong, it may be a good idea to gently add the new person to the family and then gently move your new partner into a parenting role.

Cohabitation, in which unmarried couples live together, was illegal in most states a century ago. It is now estimated that more than two-thirds of couples getting married had a period of cohabitation before marriage. Because there is no need to legally register cohabitation and because the definition of cohabitation varies, this is just an estimate. A number of reasons are given for this, including economy and convenience, but it has never been adequately explained to me how they would be more economical or more convenient than a marriage package, except perhaps for the expense of a marriage ceremony. Some say that they cohabit to help them decide if marriage is for them, but statistics show that cohabitation does not decrease divorce rates. Cohabitation is a relationship without full commitment, unlike the traditional marriage "until death do us part." Splits (divorces) before the fifth anniversary are twice as likely to occur with cohabitants.

All that being said, this book is not about marriages and cohabitations but about children. When children enter the picture, the differences in the two methods of partnership become more obvious. As with any marital-type relationship, the cohabitants should be talking about a lot of child-related issues. Do they want children? If they say they do not want children, how will they prevent pregnancy? What will they do if pregnancy does occur? Options might include carrying the baby to term and either keeping her or putting her up for adoption. Abortion is another option, but one that, in our society, is very controversial, with people forming their opinions based on their moral and political beliefs. In any case, will the couple continue their cohabiting relationship, get married, or break up? Not infrequently, pregnancy becomes a time for the father to abandon the relationship, causing multiple problems for their child and the new mother. Among these there are economic issues, as well as problems such as: the new baby is left without an active father; the mother's days of formal education may be over; and the mother may be less attractive to a future mate than she was when there was no child involved.

Single Parenting: The number of unmarried pregnancies has risen dramatically over recent years. In 1960, only 9% of families had single parents. By 1980, that number had risen to 18% and in 2010 reached 27%. In 2007, for girls aged fifteen to seventeen, 93% of births were to unmarried mothers.

The problems of the single parent, usually the mother, are many. If the single parent is an educated adult with a good job, the task will be much easier than if the child is the illegitimate offspring of a teenager. Having a grandmother or aunt willing to become the child's nanny can be a big help. In many cases, this related nanny becomes the child's real parent. Without that kind of support, the teenage mother will often have to cut short any hopes of going to college and instead have to find a job to support herself and her child. All too often, no male role model is a part of the equation—a serious situation, especially for growing boys.

Closely tied to the issue of single parenting is the subject of non-marital births. These pregnancies have more adverse outcomes, including more premature births, lower birth weights, and higher infant mortality. This may be because these mothers tend to be younger, less educated, and poorer than older married couples. The best preventive strategies are for parents with children to stay married if possible, and to avoid pregnancy if they are not married.

Gay Marriage: The incidence of gay marriages, male-male and female-female, is rising and has become increasingly accepted. Because parenting in these relationships is a relatively new phenomenon, reliable statistics on their effectiveness in raising healthy, successful, value-driven children is not yet known. An exception might be that The New Family Structures Study did show that same-sex marriages tended to be shorter in duration and had more children ending up in foster care. In any case, these parents should follow the guidelines set down here for all parents and discuss issues such as what they want their child to be when he grows up and why. I don't know for sure, but I suspect that the addition of a close relationship with an adult of a different gender than the parents would prove beneficial.

Family Size: Just because most of what is written in this book is addressed to families with only one child, do not think that I feel that larger families are not a good idea. In truth, I think they are a better idea. No lifelong friendships can take the place of family togetherness, even though in the early years this possibility, to your children at least, may seem remote.

Shortly after we arrived home from the nursery with our second child, our first asked us, "Why do we need her?"

35

Although most only children do not feel threatened by a new arrival, some will. Either way, there will be an almost inevitable change in family dynamics with each additional child. In larger families, a number of important dynamics come into play. If you don't know it when you come home with your second child, you will quickly learn that all children are different, and often require the use of different parenting techniques. Birth order, time between births, and family size can affect child behavior.

Sharing and caring are more easily taught in a family with more than one child. A child with multiple siblings learns to lose early and often. This can give her a head start on learning to deal with the reality of losing, and learning to use the experience to grow in ability. Although never fun, losing teaches important lessons on what works and what doesn't—among them the adage, "If at first you don't succeed, try and try again." In a family engaged in competitive games and other activities, older children usually have the upper hand, but with adequate supervision, lessons can be learned about moving up the ladder of excellence. In larger families, pecking order battles are to be expected. These should be addressed promptly and consistently, but again, they teach lessons about conflict resolution that will be helpful throughout children's lives. When pecking order becomes bullying, stop it and explain why it concerns you. Ask your bullying child how she thinks her sibling, usually younger, feels when this is going on. Wait for her answer and then ask the bullied if the answer is correct, and if not, why not.

Firstborn children tend to feel superior to their late arriving siblings, and girls especially may take on substitute mother roles. Lastborn children are often family pets. Middle children are usually neither bosses nor pets. An advantage of being an only child is that you do not have to worry about who your parents' favorite child is. Many parents will, if seriously questioned, admit to having favorite children, and siblings may choose favorite siblings. My favorite child is the one who is in my presence. If you do have a favorite, be careful—but even when you think you are being careful, your children, who know you very well, may know or think they know who your favorite is, and may be hurt by what they believe. Some may feel that you are playing favorites even when you are not or think that you are not. Not picking a family favorite is different from knowing that one is the most accomplished, another is the most caring, and another is the happiest.

In line with the goals of having your child grow up to be a moral, ethical, good person, it is a good idea to let all the children know when one of their siblings or someone else exhibits a character-building behavior, such as sharing or helping someone in distress. If you have a child with a disability such as Down syndrome, she will be the one who requires the most parental time and effort. Her siblings may at first be hurt by the extra attention she demands, but they will eventually come to understand why you are doing what you are doing. It has been shown that, over time, siblings of a child with disabilities will usually become more caring and will learn to be more tolerant of others with disabilities.

An obvious drawback to having children is the financial expense each brings—expense that includes the costs of food, clothing, housing, education, transportation, health care, child care, and more. Using the Department of Agriculture's web-based Cost of Raising a Child Calculator, it is estimated that the added cost for each child living in a two-parent home in urban-suburban Northeastern United States with an annual family income of $50,000-$100,000 would average $10,000 per year. This includes only the costs through age eighteen, omitting what can be very hefty college expenses. Despite the extra costs, the joy of children and family can be huge and can far outweigh the time and expense of having them.

Adopted Children: Issues related to adoption vary with the age of the child at adoption and with any health problems, whether physical or mental, that the adopted child brings to the family. Bonding with the mother and father is always easier when the child is an infant, and for that reason alone, early adoption is the best option. In addition to the bonding issues, there are very important lessons that are best taught early (see chapter The Early Years).

Regarding adopted children, I have always shuddered when I hear a mother or father introduce their natural children by name and their adopted child by name prefaced with the word "adopted," as in, "and this is our adopted daughter Nell."

Why not just say "our daughter Nell"? Later, many adopted children will become obsessed with the idea of finding their birth parents. Natural and normal curiosity may be the reason, but in some cases it may be more. Does she seek these parents because she is unhappy and wondering how life would have been if her birth parents had kept her? In my view, the less a child is referred to as an adopted child and the better she has bonded with her adoptive parents, the less likely she will be to actively seek out her birth parents.

Chapter Summary: *Parenting in the twenty-first century is much more difficult and more important than it has ever been because of extensive sociocultural changes. Co-parenting models utilize the strengths of two committed and knowledgeable adults to lead their child safely through adolescence and into a successful release to the adult world. Other parenting models can work but will usually require more time and effort to raise the children we all want.*

6

Chapter Six

Arguments, Disagreements, Disharmony, and Divorce

Chapter Goals: *To anticipate and properly address problems that can lead to marriage dissatisfaction and dissolution. We will stress that both parents should not forget that their prime responsibility is to raise a healthy, fit, moral, ethical, value-driven child—one who should benefit from both of their inputs.*

Arguments:

> *My friend Brad and his family were delayed coming to visit me because of an accident ahead of them on the highway. Brad decided, against his wife's advice, to pass through the crash site and in so doing punctured a tire. I jokingly said that must have triggered a brouhaha, to which his wife replied, "We never argue in front or our baby." She then continued, "But later we will," to which Brad said, "Oh, oh."*

The three most important points in dealing with minor disputes are covered in this vignette. The first is that this family had a pre-established plan for dealing with inevitable arguments. Secondly, that plan included an agreement that they would never argue in front of their child. Thirdly, they knew that arguments are better managed after a cooling-off period. Arguments that take place when there is anger flowing are rarely healthy, sometimes lead to statements that will later be regretted, and rarely get to a mutually agreeable point of settlement. The cooling-off period should not last long and the argument is best handled before bedtime. Showing empathy for your partner's point of view can be a great help. Solving arguments and disagreements should not be about winning; it should be about working to jointly solve a problem with a solution that is in your child's best interests. As your child gets older, it would be wise to not only show him by your behavior how to appropriately deal with anger, but to remind him of this when he becomes angry. Well-controlled arguments between parents can be instructional for children, but make sure they are well controlled.

Disagreements: By my definition, disagreements can last longer and be more serious than arguments, often reflecting long-held differences of opinion that may be culture, gender, or religion-based. Or they may be related to differences in people's inherent natures. For example, an extrovert's approach to issues may be much different from the way an introvert views the same issues. As mentioned in previous chapters, disagreements about the desirability of having children should have been resolved before marriage. Other things, about which you might disagree, such as setting bedtimes and choosing to homeschool, are also important but can usually be resolved by compromise. More serious can be issues such as whether to teach your child how to drink at home in hopes of preventing binge drinking (it won't). If your religions are different, how will you agree on what to tell your child about God? The key to resolving all of these issues is mutual respect and working together to compromise or to agree to be different.

Disharmony: Disharmony, to some degree, occurs in almost all marriages. Its causes are multiple and include fatigue, stress, hormonal factors, and transfer of love, at least partially, to the new family member. The joy that comes with the arrival of a new baby can be life-changing in very good ways. On the other hand, even though most have eagerly looked forward to their baby's arrival, the real possibility of postnatal disharmony, a serious marital issue, is often not anticipated, understood, or discussed ahead of time. It should be.

Marital happiness typically peaks in the third trimester of pregnancy but, with the arrival of the baby, what were previously balanced happy lives will change in many ways, often ones that are very negative. No matter how well these changes were explained in prenatal classes or readings, the emotional effects associated with the new world of parenting can create real problems. In the average marriage, marital happiness starts to erode at birth and continues to slip away until about fourteen years after birth. Without a plan to deal with what some have called "the seven-year itch," the results can be disastrous and part of a slippery slope leading to separation and divorce. Currently, the most common time for divorce is about eight years after the arrival of the first child, a statistic that fits very well with the postnatal disharmony concept. In marriages in which only one of the parents wanted children or wanted children at this time, divorce most commonly occurs five years post-baby. Conversely, when both parents want the child, divorce is much less likely.

Knowing all this, postnatal disharmony should be addressed prior to marriage or at least prior to deciding if and when to have children. It should continue to be regularly addressed in planned co-parent conferences and date nights, stressing the fact that there will be changes in the parents' relationships with each other when a baby arrives.

Maternal Disharmony Factors: The fatigue that follows a strenuous labor and delivery, coupled with the time and effort of childcare, will reduce the amount of time and energy that a mother has to spend with her husband. Babies who wake up at all hours or are colicky will add to this exhaustion. A lack of maternal sleep, much more serious than we once thought, can result in changes in mood, physical performance, and cognition. Gone or minimized may be such welcome social events as the "how's your day been?" times that both enjoyed each evening upon return from the workplace. When the father does not chip in and help with baby care or the mother feels that he is not helping enough, any negative feelings about him she might already have will likely escalate. Additionally, a mother's life-changing and quite natural love for her "perfect" baby can partially displace her love for her less-than-perfect husband.

Paternal Disharmony Factors: Even if the father has bought into the co-parenting concept and is doing his co-parenting job well, he also will miss the time to chat and otherwise socialize with his wife. Moreover, 25% of new fathers experience some degree of depression. The naturally occurring drop in testosterone that occurs in expectant fathers will persist for most of the following year, and with it a gentling of the masculine nature and libido. The gentling is great for baby care but the drops in libido and sexual desire, if not understood and addressed, can seriously weaken the marital relationship. A strong effort must be made to continue regular sexual relations even though the once passionate feelings for each other may have diminished. Anticipating these changes, discussing them, and preparing for them should help to alleviate any feelings of lack of relationship that either partner might feel.

Whoever said that the best things in life are free forgot that the wonderful joy that can come with the birth of a baby will be followed by the realization that it takes time, a lot of it, and money to raise a child.

Separation: If disharmony leads to separation, use the separation wisely. Counseling help is advised even if the counselor's role is only to act as a mediator of your future behavior. With the mediator, you must talk seriously and civilly about the most important player in the separation, your child, and work out a plan you both can agree on regarding what is best for him. Next in order are anger management and serious consideration of steps that will lead to possible reconciliation. You may expect that your counselor will talk about the postnatal disharmony concept and help you to understand its causes and its frequent incidence and seriousness. When there is separation or divorce, the issues of where your child lives and who has what visitation rights must be addressed. Although not a subject parents may want to discuss in their earlier conversations and meetings, all parents should be aware of these issues.

Dealing with Anger: Anger on the part of one or both parents is almost always present in separations and divorces. Although this anger is often understandable, it is important that your child not be caught up in it and be placed in the impossible position of feeling that he must decide which of you he likes better. Leave your explanation of the reasons for separation to something as simple as "We have some issues that we need to work out" or "We no longer believe that we can live together without a timeout." Know that when there are parental arguments and separations, children often blame themselves and believe that by changing their behavior they can fix things. Address this issue with your child and tell him that he is not the problem. Make it clear to your child that you both love him and will continue to work together to be his guides and his role models. It is your job to assure your child that this is your issue and not his.

Anger over the most serious causes of family problems, such as infidelity, alcoholism, serious mental disorder, or violent behavior, is very understandable. Fortunately, most of these more serious issues are amenable to treatment, which, when successful, will benefit the child. Even after treatment, the person who has been the victim of the destructive behavior may find it hard or impossible to forgive the offender. Forgiveness is not an easy thing to do for many people, especially when they are really angry, but children should not be caught in the middle of a long-term battle of angry parents. The angry parent will too often become a victim of his or her own anger. I have known many angry parents whose anger continued and negatively affected their emotional moods for years, while the offender, at whom the anger was aimed, moved on. To forgive is not only divine, but it is also cleansing for the forgiver. Do not become a teacher of angry and violent behavior by your own angry and violent actions.

Reconciliation: The best resolution to any separation, at least from the child's perspective, comes when the parents team up again as a family, but this time with a better plan and a more informed commitment to dealing with any areas of dissatisfaction.

Divorce: Divorce is almost never good for children and can be for them a major emotional setback. Younger children who have had no real relationship with one of their parents may be less affected than older children, who may get angry and/or depressed.

The incidence of American marriages that end in divorce has fallen consistently since 1981 and is now about half of what it was at its peak in the late 1970s. Undoubtedly some of this drop is related to the fact that marriage rates are also falling and that, in cohabitation, separation is not recorded as divorce. Still another possible cause of lower divorce rates may be that, on average, marriages are occurring when the bride and groom are five years older than they were in the 1970s. Whether the added maturity that is gained with these extra five years may account for at least some of the drop in divorces is not known. Fortunately, families with children are less likely than childless couples to divorce. If there is divorce, your goals should include continuing to live as model parents and to put your child's interests ahead of yours.

Settlement: If there seems to be no way around a divorce, plans should be made to work out all of the terms of the divorce agreement and proceed to a settlement represented by one mediator or attorney who represents mother, father, and most importantly, the child. When anger and hostility levels are too high for a jointly mediated solution, both parents should seek attorneys who have expressed interest in placing the rights of the child first.

Unfortunately, parents are often represented by battling attorneys while their child has none to represent his needs and his interests. Too often divorce attorneys pride themselves on how much they can get for the party they represent. For aggressive lawyers, parental custody battles are often more about winning a war than what is best for the child. In these battles, money and child custody are usually the big issues, even when one parent has little or no real interest in being the one most responsible for the child.

An interesting model is provided by the Divorce Hotels that are springing up in other parts of the world. In these, a divorcing couple books a room (or two) for the weekend in a hotel, where they will spend time with a hotel-provided mediator. The goal is to reach agreement on the terms of a settlement. The inclusive cost for the weekend, including the cost of filing divorce papers, is currently about $3,500.

Custody in Divorce: In almost all cases, your child wants to have and needs to have a good relationship with both of his parents. Even if one of the parents has not previously spent much time with the child, it is important that he or she do so now. For younger children, visitation might best take place in the house of the principal caretaker. If the parents are exchanging no civil words with each other, the home parent should leave the room or leave the house altogether while the visiting parent is spending time with the child. When adultery has been an issue, the guilty parent

44

must be very careful about when, how, and if any new partner is allowed to become active in the child's life or even be in his presence.

A good solution in many cases might be what is called "nesting," a relatively recently developed way of handling custody and visitation issues. Rather than making the child shuttle back and forth from one home to another, he stays put and the parents take turns moving out to an apartment or other abode to which both have moved some of their belongings. Among other benefits of this situation, the child can ride on his regular school bus and play with his regular neighborhood friends.

Division of Money: In all cases, there will be a financial cost to separations and divorce. Costs will rise because of counselor and attorney expenses, the need for two homes, and the need for additional childcare if both parents need to work. The co-parent who has or makes the most money, and who has helped accumulate the most money, will too often hire an attorney who will seek to minimize or cut off these funds to the parenting partner who has done "nothing" but stay at home with their child.

Role Models: When there is disharmony, separation, or divorce, male and female role-modeling is still needed. No matter what the cause of one parent leaving the primary relationship, whether it is divorce, death, or military service, all children can gain from healthy mother and father role models as part of their developing lives. Stepparents, grandparents, aunts, and uncles can be very helpful but are never the same as a caring parent.

Chapter Summary: *In dealing with all of the subjects presented here, keep the child's interests first. Learn about and pay particular attention to the common phenomenon of serious marital disharmony that occurs after the birth of your first child, noting that divorce most commonly occurs about eight years after his birth.*

7

Your Child's Other "Parents": The Media

Chapter Goals: *To stress the great importance of being media literate and more aware of what is good about twenty-first-century media and what can be very unhealthy. A list of important recommendations regarding media and media use are presented in the dos and don'ts section at the end of the chapter.*

Media in the Twenty-First Century: Several generations ago, and for millennia preceding that time, children were principally influenced by parents, other family members, schools, churches, temples, mosques, and their community. In this century, many if not most parents have moved away from their roots and from the support and nurturing that were once provided by them. Replacing these traditional companions and teachers, the media have become a principal influencer of our children and, too often, of us.

Currently, the average American child between the ages of eight and eighteen is occupied in media activities for six and a half hours each day. At age two years, the total is almost two hours daily. As newer media, such as the Internet, electronic games, DVDs, texting, and teen-popular radio, have become increasingly appealing, the time spent with them each day has not been taken away from the daily four and a half hours of television watching, but from other important activities. Because our days are still twenty-four hours in duration, the new media time has been subtracted instead from time that used to be spent sleeping, reading, studying, playing, exercising, drawing, and/or communicating with family and friends. By the time the average American child leaves adolescence, he will have seen over half a million ads and spent more time watching TV than he will have spent in the classroom—far more time than will actively be spent with his parents.

In addition to the problem of the time that is spent on these activities, there is more than ample reason to be concerned about the opinion-shaping messages that media programs and advertisements can bring. For a majority of parents, media has become their child's other parent and supplies a major part of his training.

Media History: Some of the components of what we call the media have been around for a long time, but a quick look at history tells us what we already know— that the uses of media as a means of mass communication have skyrocketed in recent years. In chronological order of appearance, the media of which we speak consist of:

- Music: *ageless*
- Books: *tablets from antiquity, first printing press in 1447*
- Newspapers: *1631*
- Magazines: *first modern magazine in 1741*
- Radio: *invented in 1885 by Thomas Edison; first licensed commercial radio station was KDKA in Pittsburgh in 1925*
- Television: *invented in 1925, with first commercial sets in 1928 and first ads in 1941; not a household item until the 1950s*
- Electronic games: *just twenty years ago in 1992*
- DVDs: *1995*
- Internet: *first really user-friendly interface in 1991, Google in 1997, and apps in 1985-90*
- Text messaging: *began in the early 1990s but not widely used until the end of the decade*
- Social networking: *Facebook in 2004*

Media Literacy: This electronic world that we live in is very new and often very attractive—almost magnetic. Unfortunately, the explosion of newer types of media and the modification of media messages have left most parents with insufficient understanding of what is going on. Most have not considered, much less adopted, appropriate guidelines to protect their children from potentially harmful messages and from wasting time watching them. Media literacy is a term that is used to describe the process of learning about the media's many positive and negative effects and providing guidelines for dealing with this huge issue. It includes education on media intent and learning how to critically evaluate what you are viewing, listening to, or reading. An essential part of twenty-first-century parenting should be teaching your children critical viewing skills and having them practice them.

In the twentieth century, literacy referred to expertise in reading, writing, and critical thinking. Although this type of literacy is still very important, a growing number of experts believe that media literacy is even more important. They further believe that media literacy should be taught in American schools, as is now being done in both England and France.

The American Academy of Pediatrics (AAP), an organization representing over 60,000 pediatricians, has developed policy statements on the issue of media literacy. Excellent material may be found on the AAP website and in the book, *Children, Adolescents, and the MEDIA*, whose principal author, Victor C. Strasburger, is an AAP member. Stressed is the importance of setting viewing rules for different developmental ages; for time spent; and for what should and what shouldn't be watched. Because media changes so rapidly, you must stay current in your learning and make changes to your child's media involvement when necessary. Time spent with media most often involves a passive form of learning ("If I say it, it's true") that requires considerably less thinking than active learning. In the process of teaching your child the lessons of media literacy, you will also be teaching her a very important course in critical thinking.

Media Messages: All media messages are constructed for some purpose. The business of advertising is to convince people to buy something, whether that something is a calorie-loaded, sugar- and fat-filled food, a beer, a political candidate, or a style. Media messages, whether they are part of programming or advertising content, can be very effective in presenting attitudes, values, beliefs, and behavior that are contrary to what you believe to be healthy. These messages have shaped and continue to shape our culture. Advertisers have learned how to best construct their material to effectively influence young minds—what messages work and what styles of presentation work best for different ages. Many messages are specifically aimed at children under the age of three years and can be, given their immaturity, very convincing and often unhealthy. The pros know that the younger their target audience, the less likely the watchers are to consider critically what they are being told and sold.

The Good Side of Media: In this chapter, we will focus more on the benefits and potential benefits of media than on their more negative sides. In later chapters dealing with such problems as obesity, school performance, violence, and addiction, we will describe the media's potentially toxic effects. Media does offer many opportunities for your children to learn and to be entertained, but you need to know what they will be learning.

Entertainment: Media shows, including sporting events, dramas, and quiz shows, can all be entertaining and educational. Other shows with little educational value can be fun to watch. Likewise, many ads are designed to be entertaining (but what are they selling?).

Learning: Popular shows such as *Dora the Explorer* and *Blue's Clues* can make your child think and can be effective teachers. Research shows that watching *Sesame Street* can make children more ready to learn and can teach tolerance and understanding. Other studies of *Sesame Street* show that when a parent is watching with the child, or even to a lesser degree when the parent is just in the same room as the child, learning is increased. Shows on the History Channel, Discovery Channel, the National Geographic Channel, and other channels dedicated to teaching history and geography can supplement what is learned in school. Shows on the Food Network, the Travel Channel, and religious channels can also teach good lessons.

The News: As newspaper usage decreases, an increasing number of people get their news primarily from radio and television. The problem here is that broadcast news shows tend to focus on the sensational, and tend to be based on "sound bites," tend toward political bias (as do newspapers, but to a lesser degree), and do not often contain full explanations of the significance of what is happening.

Some of the Not-So-Good Aspects of Media:

Negative Portrayal of Parents: In past generations, parents were regularly portrayed as caring and being actively and positively involved with their children. In today's teen shows, notice how often the message is very different—parents are too often shown as less than smart and helplessly out of touch. Parents just don't seem to get it. Building on this attitude of disrespect, it is often implied that it is not only acceptable but really cool for teenagers to do things behind their parents' backs and to disobey parental rules.

Subliminal Messages: Advertisers and other media production people know things that are not intuitive to most of us. They know that visual images are taken into the brain much more quickly and are retained longer than are written messages. You may have noted in the recent past how often images appear on the screen, especially in advertisements, and are quickly gone before you think you have had a chance to really look at them. Despite what you may think, these snippets, designed for you to get their intended message, have entered your brain and have been recorded. An example of the power that the visual has over the spoken and written could be found in a beer ad that stressed the importance of not driving drunk in its oral and written messages, but at the same time its visual message was of young couples drinking and having a great time. You can be sure there were not pictures of DUI-related car crashes or of friends agreeing to be designated drivers. The advertiser made points with their community service ad showing how responsible the beer company is. They also sold beer with the visual message showing attractive young people partying. For the advertiser, this was a two-fer.

Movie and TV Rating Systems:

Educational Television: In 1996 the Federal Trade Commission (FTC), after years of trying, was finally able to enact enforceable regulations that would require each station to show three hours of educational television at appropriate times each week. The definition of what constitutes educational television is still not clear. When your child is watching a show, take the time to watch with her. Those programs that the network classifies as educational will have the letters E/I circled on the screen. When you see this symbol, pause the show and ask yourself and your child what the educational message is. You may be surprised at what the message really is, or you may have trouble finding it.

Motion Picture Association of America (MPAA) Rating System: The message here is that parents need to better understand the rating system and what the various ratings mean and what they don't mean. The ratings can be helpful by providing a starting point, but they do not relieve you of your responsibility to make the final decision. Ratings do not tell you whether a film is good or bad. When a movie is rated G, meaning that it is rated as appropriate for all audiences, that should mean that it is probably safe, but you should still check to be sure before letting your child watch. Movies are rated on whether, in the rater's opinion, there is one of the following four things: foul language, violence, drug-related content, and age-related sexually appropriate material. The standards that rating people use to judge movies may not be your standards.

Inappropriate sexual behavior, certainly an important issue, seems to be regularly considered by the raters as more damaging than violence, which frequently seems to be ignored or overlooked in evaluation ratings. Smoking and drinking do not seem to be considered at all. Add to this the fact that, over the years, the standards of an already flawed rating system have been loosened, so that many shows that in the past would have been rated R are now rated PG-13, and others that would have earlier earned PG-13 ratings are now rated G. Movie theaters often pay little attention to these ratings when selling tickets. Even those that might restrict tickets to an R-rated show at the box office will usually allow easy entrance to their multiple viewing areas.

A PG-13 rating means just what it says. It does not mean that a PG-13 rated movie is OK for thirteen-year-old children. It means that you should know something about the movie, know why it has a PG rating and how this may be useful in making your final decision about whether the movie is safe for your child. Our advice is to be very careful and to watch movies and TV shows with your child, who should be made aware of the fact and not be surprised if and when you decide to pause or click off the TV or leave a movie. If she does react very negatively when you take such action, in your follow-up discussion, after tempers have cooled, remind her that you have already talked about these things as possibilities. Ask her why she thinks you did what you did and how she feels about that subject. Stress the fact that you love her and tell her again why you do what you do. In the chapter on the adolescent years, emphasis will be placed on the importance of your child understanding that her parents love her and that her parents have good judgment.

Until such time as media rating systems are improved, if they will be, I recommend that you consider subscribing to the Parents Council Newsletter, or better yet that you use the website CommonSenseMedia.org. On that site, each media-related program is reviewed, with a red rating given for ages for which it is inappropriate; an orange rating for ages for which there may be content that is not right for your child; and green for ages when it is appropriate. Using a consistent rating system, this excellent site rates movies, television, games, apps, websites, books, and music. With each movie or other media type, it uses a five-point scale to evaluate educational value, positive messages, positive role models, violence and scariness, sexy stuff, language, consumerism, and drinking, drugs, and smoking. For each of these subjects, you can expand the site to find the reasons for each rating. In addition to the ratings system, the site contains a list of current media offerings that it likes, and has short articles on a variety of subjects, such as the one I just read giving five tips for talking to your child when she hears or uses inappropriate language.

The Good and the Bad News about Social Media: Social media have become very popular and very powerful. Of teenagers, 22% log onto a social media site more than ten times daily and more than 50% log on at least once each day. Of the 75% of teens who own cell phones, 25% use them for social media, 54% use them for texting, and 24% use them for instant messaging. Said another way, social media have become a way of life for the majority of today's youth.

The Good News: Social media can enhance communication, social connections, and even technical skills. Staying connected with friends and family; making new friends, sharing pictures, and the exchange of ideas are all facilitated. Some children use them for jointly working on homework. Frequent exposure can increase English usage, written communication, and social skills. On the other hand, new English is being invented that is much different from the language that I learned, such as the common use of "c u" meaning "see you." Opportunities are provided for learning and showing respect, tolerance, and increased discourse about personal issues.

The Bad News: Too many social media users believe that foul language is "cool." You should know that many teens view cyber-bullying as humorous and show little consideration for how painful and dangerous it can be for its victims. This all too common form of bullying has caused depression, anxiety, isolation, and even suicide. "Facebook depression" is a new phenomenon that can occur in teens who spend too much time using social networks. You should also be aware that researchers have shown that 20% of teens have sent or posted nude or semi-nude photos or videos of themselves. A good piece of news is that shy teens using their social network will communicate more readily and learn to carry relationships formed on the Internet into face-to-face relations. Balance this against the bad news that sexual predators tend to prey more commonly on the shy and lonely.

Your Job: It is your job to become literate in social media to protect your children from some of the risks that they may encounter. No more than you would let your child drive without training, practice, and licensing, you should not allow any use of social media before the age of thirteen, and when you do allow it you should do so carefully. Although it is not legal to have a social network site before the age of thirteen, many younger children have learned that if you lie when asked if you are thirteen years old, you are on. Speak to your child about the issues she should look for and avoid.

One of the reviewers of this book told me that she has no intention of letting her daughters use social media networks at age thirteen. She wants no part of cyber-bullies and sexual predators. She goes even further and says she will allow no social media while they live in her house. Her concerns include not wanting her daughters to learn that they haven't been invited to classmates' parties and to be hurt by that knowledge. She also emphasizes that there are better ways to spend one's time and to communicate than the use of social networks and texting, although she does agree that texting does not have many of the potential predator and bullying issues as Facebook and is an excellent way for distant friends to communicate. She reminded me that the best communication occurs when there is visual as well as voice contact between people, allowing both communicators to use their empathetic techniques to discover if what they are saying is hurtful or useful to the person with whom they are talking. On social networks it is very easy to be misunderstood. She makes very good points.

Before you allow your child to join a social network, consider telling her that you want to become her friend on her site until such time as you have developed trust in the messages that are being sent and received. In the beginning you should pay careful attention to her activities and monitor the messages that are being sent from and received on it until such time as you are comfortable about the activity, which may be never. At your regular meetings, or sooner if there is really dangerous activity, discuss what you are seeing. Eventually she will probably object to what she considers your unfair intrusion into her privacy and will want to "un-friend" you. Before this happens you should have had a discussion of trust—how trust is earned and how it is kept once earned. Even if you trust your child and agree to get off of her social media site, you need to remember that predators and cyber-bullies are a reality. Check out the Microsoft website *http://www.microsoft.com/security/family-safety/kids-social.aspx* for tips on how to safely use social networking.

Media Dos and Don'ts: Most of the dos and don'ts here regard television, but many apply to all media. Many of my recommendations have been adapted from the recommendations made by the American Academy of Pediatrics on its excellent national media education campaign website.

Do not allow any TV before the age of two: A principal reason for this is that infants are not able to distinguish the real from the unreal. This ability will eventually come but will not fully be present until they are almost eight years old.

Even then it will not always be automatically utilized. Because of your infant's inability to separate fact from fantasy, she will react and remember differently than you would any messages that she receives. Advertisers know this. Strong and often very subtle messages can be delivered to your infant's rapidly growing and absorbing brain. If they tell her that a certain brand of sugar-loaded cereal is best, that info will stick.

Allow no TV, electronic games, computer, telephone, or other media in your child's bedroom at any age: An important reason for this should be obvious: bedrooms are for sleeping, and sleep deprivation can be a huge problem in a lot of areas (see chapter on Sleep and Time Management). Allowing children unmonitored use of media is asking for trouble. Beware of the opportunities to view porn, violence, and more. Despite this strong recommendation, 20% of three-year-old children have TVs in their bedrooms, as do 40% of children between the ages of three and six, and 68% from ages eight to eighteen.

Limit your child's TV, computer, and video screen times: I suggest that no more than one to two hours per day or seven to fourteen hours per week be spent on these activities. There will be days when you anticipate more TV will be watched, such as sports-watching time or family movie time; this extra time should be subtracted from the weekly time allowance. At your weekly family meeting, review local TV listings and decide which shows if any will be watched during the week. Choose quality age-appropriate programs and favor those with educational content.

Be a good role model: Monitor how much TV you watch and what you watch, because your child will be noticing your personal approach. By acting as a role model and limiting your own TV watching time, you may find that you can gain time to take on tasks that you were "too busy" to accomplish previously. Consider also what your message is regarding your "bedrooms are for sleeping" advice if you have a TV in your own bedroom.

Do not watch TV or listen to the radio, or talk or text on the phone, during dinner: At this important time for interactive family conversation, you should not be distracted.

Turn off the TV, radio, computer, music devices, and DVDs when no one is listening, using, or watching: Whether the programs are good or bad is not the issue here. These things can all be distracting and have the ability to draw people in.

Put all computers and TVs in common areas: Among other reasons for this recommendation is that it will make it much easier for you to monitor time spent and content viewed. This plan will also save you the money you might have spent by putting TVs in a host of rooms.

Do watch TV with your children at all ages and use the time to educate them: When something comes along that is worth talking about, pause the show. If it is an ad whose message you would like to discuss with your child, have the child describe what the ad is trying to sell or teach, and what she thinks about it. For example, if it is advertising cereal that is loaded with sugar, you may want to ask her whether the product would be good for her. Then ask her why or why not. Look for violence and discuss why or why not this might be appropriate. Look for sexual messages or parent putdowns and seek comment. In any case, when the material is clearly inappropriate, follow this period of pause by turning off the TV and asking the child why you have done so. You may, when possible, want to prerecord what you will be watching together to protect yourself from comments that you are ruining the flow of the show.

While watching shows, look for violence, foul language, inappropriate sex, and drugs. Look for deception, one-upsmanship, selfishness, racism, sexism, violence, instant gratification, and risk-taking. Also watch for honesty, compassion, generosity, tolerance, courage, independence, loyalty, and modesty. When particularly negative or positive messages appear, pause the TV and discuss them.

Music: Take time to listen with your child to the music and radio stations that she listens to. Be aware that the lyrics to music such as hip hop may be in languages and accents very foreign to you. When that is the case, ask your child to explain what she heard. Also check out what she is reading and the games she is playing.

Put blockers on TVs and computers: To prevent normal adolescent curiosity from leading your child into porn and other dangerous sites, put blockers on these devices, such as the V-chip, now standard on new TVs. This device lets you identify and stop programs with violence, sexual content, or other material not suitable for your child. For more information about the V-chip, call 888-CALL-FCC (888-225-5322/voice) or 888-TELL-FCC (888-835-5322/TTY).

On the Internet, it is easy to find a number of computer blockers that you can install on your child's computer and that she cannot remove without your help. Among these are Christian Internet Filters, GetNetWise, and PicBlock, a program that blocks porn images by detecting the amount of flesh tones in images. For additional helpful programs try eHow tech.

And finally, although TV is an easily available babysitter, do not use it as such. If you need quiet time, encourage your child to read, work on a puzzle, play with friends, draw, build something, or study. Reinforce efforts in all of these areas.

Chapter Summar: *Become media literate and put what you learn into action.*

ACKNOWLEDGEMENTS: Thanks to Victor C. Strasburger, Barbara J. Wilson, and Amy B. Jordan for their book, *Children, Adolescents, and the MEDIA*, from which I gained much information and insight.

8

The Importance of Peers

Chapter Goals: *To stress the strong nurturing influence exerted by peers, which, good or bad, cannot be escaped, and to suggest ways for helping your child and yourself select and manage healthy peer relationships.*

Parent Peers: Healthy peer relationships are important for all of us. Our feelings about ourselves, our beliefs, our playtimes, and our work times are all influenced by those around us. It is important that we be aware of cultural and religious diversity, but it is our peer group that will have the most effect on the way we think. For parents this means that having a peer group made up of people with similar beliefs to yours, if they are good beliefs, will help to reinforce your own beliefs. It will always help if you share your ideas about such things as televisions in children's bedrooms, dress codes, dating rules, and much more. Parents who share your beliefs can be found at your church, mosque, or temple, but in many other places as well. Because our goal for our children is to have them grow up with character, it will help if your friends and your children's friends have character also. Another use of peers can be to help you decide if a behavior that concerns you is similar to behavior that their children also have, implying that it is normal for the age. This could include things like childhood fears, shyness, depression, attention deficit and more. Also, your peer group may be able to help you with issue management.

Your Child's Peers: Peer pressure can be a powerful force, especially in adolescence. Earning the respect of their peers is a key goal for every adolescent. The better you understand and accept the fact that your child needs the approval of his peer group, the better you will be able to steer him through the shoals of adolescence. Peers can be wonderful and necessary components of his development, but the wrong choice of peers and peer groups can lead to trouble. You should learn to evaluate his peers and have your son provide you with his impression of them. Stress to him how important it is that his friends be on the same wavelength as you want him to be, especially regarding character development. Your discussion on the subject of peers and peer groups should have begun long before adolescence, with emphasis on what he should be looking for and what he should avoid. Do not be afraid to ask his friends questions on a variety of important subjects, such as, "What do you want to be when you grow up, and why?" Although it may seem a little freaky or intrusive to the young people you question, you may be helping them to consider things they have not looked at and might help them to grow from the knowledge and feelings you impart. I suggest that you make comments to them on the responses they give to you. Your real purpose is to protect your child and help him find friends who will support his search for character. Even when you have learned to trust your child and his peer group, you must be watchful and let him know that trust is not permanent. Trust must always be earned. As Ronald Reagan was fond of saying, "Trust, but verify." Along the way, your child may need to change peer groups to regain your trust.

Asking children about their peers may teach you more about your child's behavior than asking them directly.

> *When asked by parents how they could tell if their child was smoking pot or involved in other inappropriate activities, I tell them that asking their teenager directly if he smokes is unlikely to get an admission of guilt. Rather, I suggest asking him if any of his friends smoke pot. Usually this question is not seen as threatening, and you can learn a lot from his response. If he tells you that pot smoking is very common at his school, be warned. On the other hand, if he tells you that none of his friends smoke, that is a good sign. It may be better still if he seems surprised at your question and perhaps a little offended that you asked.*

Parent Peer Groups: Having a parent peer group to provide guidelines for your children and for others in the group can be a great tool for prevention of many common adolescent problems. Before you let your child spend time in a friend's home, you want to feel comfortable about the house rules and the parental stance on monitoring behavior and reporting bad behavior back to you. Before any visit, you should talk with the person who will be the responsible adult when your child is there. It doesn't have to be a long and snoopy call, but it should be one in which you have enough information to make your "go" or "no go" decision.

Parent peer groups will be most important in the teenage years, but even in the latent period, they can provide real support. To form such a group, you might begin by asking your child who his three to four best friends are, and use that information to call a meeting of the parents most involved in daily care of children in the group. At first, you do not need to tell the others that you have a grand plan, thereby scaring some of them away. Instead, sell it as a social teatime or such. At the group get-togethers, learn how each parent feels about issues that concern you, such as how much time the others set aside for various activities. Are they media literate? Do they regularly go to church or temple? Do they give allowances, and if they do, how much and on what basis? When are bedtimes at their house? How about dress codes, etc.? Look for signs of how others are taking your questions. You do not need to cover everything at one meeting. They do not need to all agree with you on everything, but knowing how they feel will help. Keep the first meeting mostly social and fun so that a second can be scheduled. Remember also that these are busy people with many other demands on their time. Try to continue the meetings over time as social affairs and see how each parent is doing. Finally, let me emphasize that the sort of discussions I envision can be very stressful for some parents, especially ones who have never really thought much about the issues that you find so important. Do not scare them away in your zeal.

Right from birth, parent peer groups can be very helpful in sharing, learning, and receiving support.

In my pediatric office, I organized a parent-peer group for newborn mothers every Friday at noon, led by Ginger, a wonderful nurse friend. Ginger talked some, but she saw her role more as a facilitator of group conversation. The mothers loved it. One of the most interesting communications that was reported to me was a silent one. Most of the mothers were cuddling their babies to their chest, but one was holding hers out in front of her, like a man might do. Ginger noticed this but said nothing. As the meeting progressed, she noted that the arms-length mother had also been watching and, by the time the session was over, she was cuddling her baby as the others did.

Another form of parent peer group that has been very popular is a twins' mother club, formed by women who help each other by sharing their ways of solving problems unique to mothers of twins. In this age of urbanization and migration, many if not most parents are separated from the grandparents, relatives, lifelong friends, and community resources that in times past were able to provide much-needed support. As children enter the teenage years their exposure to increasingly toxic environmental influences will become a major risk factor. Although useful at any age, in these years parent peer groups become almost a necessity. Among other things, without them it is much more difficult to deal with the bombardment of "everyone else does it" messages that are so routinely uttered by young people to get what they want, or what they think they want.

While I was doing my internship, I had a friend whose interest was ophthalmology. He convinced the ophthalmologists on staff that it would be good if they taught him how to do a cataract operation. They did, and he later told me that the procedure fit well into the "watch one, do one, teach one" style of education.

As I was thinking about writing this section of the book, it came to me that forming or joining a parent peer group fits well with the teachings passed on to me by my ophthalmologist friend. The lesson here is that in learning about parent peer principles and possibilities and practicing them, you can teach them to others and spread the word on good parenting to others, the school, the community, and on up. What follows has been adapted from a piece submitted to me by Dr. Thomas Gleaton, who has been a major influence in my life and a pioneer in what has been called "the parent movement." By the time your child is in school, you should start your own parent peer group. The players will probably change over the years, but when your child is a teenager you must even more strongly push to know the parents in your child's peer group, and to know their beliefs and their approaches to adolescent issues.

Step 1: Have a family meeting and decide on the basic rules of behavior that you expect to live by. Discuss rewards and punishments and their application to certain behaviors.

Step 2: Determine your child's three or four best friends and start a parent group based on this friendship circle. Such a circle may already be in place—the scout troop, the Little League team, the chorus, the Sunday school class, or the carpool.

Step 3: Have meeting(s) with the parents of your child's friends. Get to know them and let them get to know you. Do not compete. The more you talk and the more you share the basic rules of behavior, reward, and punishment that your family has adopted, the less likely it is that there will be a misunderstanding regarding important safety and other issues. Share with your group the goals you have set for your children and learn theirs (if they have any).

Step 4: Share information and get a commitment. Tell parents how relieved you feel to know that they have the same concerns. Exchange opinions about everything that might relate to a child's health and safety and the goals that you have set for yours. Share email addresses and/or phone numbers and agree to keep an eye out for each other's kids.

Step 5: Know the circumstances of events at the homes of others. Always call ahead before you give permission to attend, and speak with the responsible adult who will be there and learn their thoughts on tobacco, alcohol, drugs, closed bedroom doors, leaving the party and returning, curfews, and more. If you are in any way uncomfortable, do not let your child attend. If other parents ask, tell them why you have decided against the event.

Step 6: When you drive your child to a party, say hello to the responsible adult and tell them where you can be reached. Let your child know that he is to leave if he is uncomfortable or if any of the prohibited activities are going on. To make your child less uncomfortable about leaving, some families give him a password or phrase, such as, "Did you have to take Misty (your pet's name) to the vet?"

Step 7: Let others know what your group is doing and encourage them to join you or form their own group. A long-range goal is to have the parent peer concept involve entire schools and communities. Bottom-up democracy is always the best.

Chapter Summary: *Peers and their influence are important to all of us. If these peers are happy, successful people of character, their influence will be good. If they are not, they may negatively influence us. For parents, making friends with the parents of your child's friends can provide excellent parenting tools.*

Information and Tools

This section begins with the subjects of sleep, discipline, and success. Although sleep is a subject that might have more appropriately been placed as a chapter in Section V, I have placed it here because the problems of sleep deprivation are often not appreciated and lack of sleep can be associated with obesity, learning problems, physical inactivity, sexual activity, fighting, smoking, and drinking—the problems that this book means to prevent.

The last two chapters in this section are on the subject of the interaction between a person's nature and nurture. These should provide a good lead-in to the next section—a section on specifics of nurturing at various ages.

9

Chapter Nine

Sleep and Time Management

Chapter Goals: *I want to make you aware of the great importance of getting an adequate amount of sleep and suggest approaches to ensure that your family gets the sleep it requires. Problems that come from seeming to forget that there are only twenty-four hours in a day are discussed, and more careful attention to scheduling is advised.*

The Importance of Sleep: Getting an adequate amount of sleep is more than a social issue. Sleep is essential to health and well-being. There are more than seventy different sleeping disorders, many of which affect children. Some of the many problems associated with not getting enough sleep are obvious and well known; others are not. Insufficient sleep can be associated with a variety of health-risk behaviors, including physical inactivity, drinking alcohol, smoking cigarettes, fighting, and being sexually active. Diminished IQ, diabetes, cardiovascular disease, obesity, and depression can all be associated with not getting enough sleep. Lack of sleep is not only associated with the onset of these diseases but may also complicate their outcome. Bedwetting, sleepwalking, retarded growth, other hormonal and metabolic problems, and even failure to thrive can be related to sleep deprivation, as can problems with "executive functioning" of the brain: cognitive flexibility, self-monitoring, planning, organization, self-regulation of affect, and arousal.

As many as 3% of all children have obstructive sleep apnea, a disease many think only affects adults. This is a serious condition requiring medical consultation.

67

As many as 25% of children diagnosed with attention deficit hyperactivity disorder may actually have symptoms of obstructive sleep apnea, and many of their learning difficulties and behavior problems can be the consequences of chronic fragmented sleep.

During sleep, the metabolic rate of most, but not all, organs will slow down. As the rest of the body rests, the brain and endocrine organs remain hard at work. Two of the hormones produced by the endocrine glands during sleep, ghrelin and leptin, are being studied for their possible roles in obesity. What we do know is that ghrelin stimulates appetite and is increased in people who do not sleep properly. Leptin, a hormone that works to decrease appetite, is decreased with lack of sleep.

The brain is also busy all night long, cycling through different stages of sleep during which the brain is involved in a number of important actions including hormonal activity and immune system strengthening. It is in the final stage of the cycle, the REM (rapid eye movement) stage, that the brain shifts what has been learned and temporarily stored during the day to more efficient brain storage areas. The fact that infants spend approximately 50% of their sleep time in REM sleep while adults only spend 20% may be because infants have so much more new information to process. Toward morning, REM sleep occupies a greater percentage of sleep time than it does in the earlier hours, meaning that those who get up too early may be missing the best time for sorting and storing information learned the day before. This failure to properly store information explains why students who study long and hard the night before a test, at the expense of needed sleep, often test less well than students who studied less but slept more.

A professor of pediatrics at Johns Hopkins Medical School told me that he believes that his pre-test routine served him well. On the day before important tests, he studied no later than 6:00 p.m., sometimes saw a movie, and was in bed early.

Adequate amounts of sleep are needed to perform well in school. Two large studies showed that on average, teens who received A grades got about fifteen more minutes of sleep than students who got B's and thirty minutes more than those who got C's. Because of studies such as these, the CDC now recommends that all school districts consider later start times.

Traffic accidents are up when sleep is down. Approximately 100,000 auto crashes each year are caused by drivers who are barely awake or who fall asleep at the wheel. Drowsiness-induced crashes are most common in young male drivers, who account for over 50% of these crashes.

Sleep Requirements: The required hours of sleep given here are those recommended by the National Institutes of Health. Although there are exceptions to these guidelines, everyone would be wise to assume that they are correct and move from the recommended time allotments only with great caution.

Birth–2 months:	**12–18 hours**
3–11 months:	**14–15 hours**
1–3 years:	**12–14 hours**
3–5 years:	**11–13 hours**
5–10 years:	**10–11 hours**
Adolescent years:	**9 hours**
Adults:	**8.5–9.5 hours**

When daily sleep time is less than an individual needs, a "sleep debt" develops. Even relatively modest daily reductions in sleep time can accumulate across days to increase the sleep debt, and those debts must be paid. Although an individual may not realize his sleepiness, the sleep debt can have powerful effects on his daytime performance, thinking, mood, and test scores.

Causes of Sleep Deprivation: Excessive activity and overstimulation in the hours before sleep commonly make it difficult to fall asleep. Causes of this type of overstimulation are many, but high on the list is the attraction to stay awake watching or participating in media activities and/or the stimulation of the messages that they contain. Even after going to sleep, more than a few teens are awakened by the arrival of a text message, a message to which they feel compelled to respond. A knowing parent should not allow the presence of TVs and other media devices in the bedroom, but unfortunately even at ages three to six, 40% of children have television sets in the room designed primarily for sleep. Children sleep best when they do not have TVs, computers, radios, phones, or any other electronic gadgets in their bedroom. Make the time before sleep quiet time. Reading, as long as the reading material is non-stimulating, and quiet conversation are good pre-bed activities.

The use of caffeine, alcohol, and certain medications can cause nighttime waking and insomnia. Other possible causes are not participating in sixty minutes of physical activity on five or more of the past seven days, feeling sad or hopeless, or being depressed.

We all have a "biologic clock" that turns our sleep cycle on and off. Most commonly this clock is synchronized with the onset of darkness and the arrival of daylight. When people change the times they go to bed and wake up, their biologic clock may not always be able to keep up, especially if the changes in timing are great. Children whose bedtimes are not the same every night may be victims of a phenomenon similar to the jet lag that occurs when people fly to different time zones. During the time it takes to reset their biologic clock, those involved may have difficulty staying awake or falling asleep, with resulting sleep deprivation problems. In this regard, it is advised that children do not change their bedtimes and wake-up times on weekends; a worsening of school performance can be the result. Currently there are school districts which, knowing that a teen's biologic clock turns on sleep signals later in the day than it does for most of us, have moved school starting times to later in the morning, allowing teens to sleep in later.

Time Management: One of society's biggest problems is that we are all too busy. Too often, we seem to forget that there are only twenty-four hours in each day. Knowing that we can't do everything we want to do or think we need to do, we must make choices. Too often the choices we make are the wrong ones. Perhaps because of a minimization of its importance, sleep often becomes a victim of our time budgeting. Currently, 70% of high school students are not getting the recommended amount of sleep. Not surprisingly, 60% of high school children say they have extreme sleepiness in daytime, and 33% fall asleep in class at least once a week.

Here we will put together a sleep time schedule for a ninth-grade student. Let's put the proper number hours of sleep, nine hours nightly at this age, at the top of our list. Next we will budget for school. Begin with an estimation of how many hours to allow for class time and transportation to and from school. Factors such as proximity to school may vary, but let's say here that we will allow seven and a half hours daily. Then add in study time requirements. The schools in our area recommend ten minutes of homework time per grade level. For a child in the ninth grade, this would mean that we would add ninety minutes for each school day, bringing our daily school time total to nine hours. Now add the sleep and school totals together and we have used up eighteen hours, leaving just six hours for everything else. If your child is one of those average American adolescents who spend six and one half hours each day on media activities, she will have to cut either sleep or study to fit everything in. This child, with her parents as unresponsive accomplices, has decided to cut time from the recommended sleep and school hours and has left no time for dining, exercise, play, conversation, chores, sports, music, or relaxation.

WEEKDAYS	FIRST TRY	REVISED	FINAL
Sleep time	9 hours		
School time	7.5		
Study time (9th grade)	1.5		
Media time	6.5 (average)	2	0
Exercise time (required)	1		
Chores time	0.5		
Dining time	1.5		
Conversation	0.5		
Sports, music, etc.	2		
Playtime	1		
Reading	1		
Relaxing	0.5		
TOTAL	32.5 hours (Oops!) 28		24

Using the numbers just given, it is obvious that some adjustments will have to be made. Because of the hour overload in the First Try column above, something will have to give, and because all activities are essential except for the media time, it will have to go, at least on most weekdays. Giving up any of the others is not healthy.

A common but inappropriate method of compensating for this time crunch occurs when children rush through their study time, tell you they are done with it, and head for the TV. Your correct response in such situations might be to say, "Let me take a look at what you've done," or "Great," followed by the comment, "now you will have more time to read your library book." The only logical answer that I can see for the time scheduling dilemma is that you will have to go to a weekly schedule. Use the extra time you gain on weekends, when there is no need to allot time for school, except for the church or temple times that I recommend. Weekend activities that can be planned for in your scheduling might include playtimes, yard work, or bike rides, each of which can do the triple duty of parent-child times together, exercise times, and communication times. Television programs, especially sports and movies all by themselves, can often take more than two hours of daily media time allowed, but with proper planning you can convert the two-hour daily allowance to fourteen hours per week and cover movie and sports-watching times.

Each weekend in the Smith home, they have a movie night. With their three children alternating weeks as the selector of movies from a list preapproved by the parents, all five members of the family settle in to watch. With the hand of one of the parents on the clicker, the show may be paused at any time for comment on good deeds and inappropriate scenes. In addition to entertainment, this weekly ritual promotes critical thinking and family bonding—another three-for-one deal.

Other time issues can be related more to your personal scheduling requirements. With little time together, many parents have adopted the phrase "quality time," a phrase not often used by those parents whose privilege it is to be stay-at-homers. Too often, quality time means a time of mutual indulgence at a movie or a fast-food restaurant. Because the parent-child time together is so limited, parents may not want to use it to challenge their child's messy room, personal appearance, or failing report card. My definition of quality time is time when a parent, adhering to a preset schedule, spends time in dialogue, exercise, play, or reading, but also addresses the more difficult issues. Anything that you personally have to do, such as shopping, would be best done when your child is in school. If you are working full time during school hours, you should plan shopping in such a way that you do not have to take your children with you, except perhaps on weekends. Having a participating co-parent can really help.

Chapter Summary: *The importance of sleep is major, and much more important than most people realize. Because we are all busy, it is recommended that there be weekly schedules established ahead of time. Required daily activities should push those less essential, such as media time, to weekends when school time requirements are lessened.*

10

Discipline and Punishment

Chapter Focus: *This chapter deals with helping your child become self-disciplined and the steps needed to get there—a major parenting responsibility. The importance of patience and anger management, yours and your child's, will be stressed.*

Definitions: There are many who think that the words discipline and punishment are synonymous. They are not. **Discipline** is training. As defined by the military, discipline is training to act according to rules. In this book, we will use this military definition. **Punishment**, on the other hand, is the authoritative imposition of something negative or unpleasant on a person in response to a behavior deemed to be wrong. It is a tool for teaching rules but not the only one. On the other side of the balance from punishment is reward. Love should be a motivator for both punishment and reward.

> *"In reading the lives of great men, I found that the first victory they won was over themselves—self-discipline with all of them came first."*
> —Harry Truman

Disciplinary Plan: Your goal should be to raise a child who is morally straight, healthy, happy, and successful. At birth and in the months that follow, it can be assumed that your child has no self-discipline. In her early years, your child's primary disciplinarians (teachers) will be you, your family, and your environment. Later, the

75

media, your child's peers, and the outside culture will join you, but not always with the same endpoint in mind. To achieve the goals you have set for your child, you must have a disciplinary plan that sets rules, rewards, and punishments. In setting rules and punishments, be as specific as you can. Modifications to the plan must be made as your child matures, displays his inborn temperamental responses to you, or when you, for other reasons, feel you are making little progress. Regarding progress, remember that the process of developing self-discipline does not occur overnight. Learning these lessons takes time and patience. Know that many infants are not capable of much rule-learning before the age of three. Do not, however, put off your teaching. If not learned early in life, many of life's lessons can only be learned with great difficulty at later ages.

"We have neglected to discipline our children and called it building self-esteem."

—Billy Graham

Praise can be an important teaching tool but, as implied by Billy Graham, is often overused in the hope that praise alone can build self-esteem. Many parents feel that praise should take precedence over needed disciplinary action. Studies show that it can be helpful to praise good behavior, but consistent enforcement of rules and their consequences leads to greater compliance with the rules you have set. In addition to setting rules, you must set whatever punishments and/or rewards are needed to prepare your child for the time when he will take over as a self-controlled, self-disciplined, moral adult. Early on, your sub-goals will be to have him commit to habit-appropriate behaviors on subjects ranging from hygiene, nutrition, dress codes, and study to practice prayer and religious beliefs. Later on, you will set rules on dating, drinking, using drugs, career preparation, and much more. For every rule obeyed there should be a preset method of reward, and for every rule broken, a preset punishment. As mentioned, these presets may change with time and circumstance. To successfully carry out your plan, you will have to learn to deal with impatience, anger, and mood swings, both yours and his. The key to disciplinary success is having a plan with clear rules followed by swift, predetermined consequences. Be loving but also be strict; not strict in the sense of being severely punitive, but in being consistent in enforcing the rules you have set.

Patience: Before we talk further about punishment and discipline, let's consider the importance of patience. Almost all babies are impatient creatures. They come with inborn survival skills and a tendency to want what they want when they want it, often very loudly proclaimed. There are limits to what can be learned at each of life's developmental stages—be patient and understand this. For example, young infants are not capable of crawling, walking, and talking, and no amount of effort on your part or his part will change this. When you are disappointed by your child's inability to do what he is told to do, be sure you know that he is capable of what you ask. Similarly, at developmental stages along the way, know that not all children develop at the same rates for everything. One child may be very quick with certain physical skills and another an early reader. Accept these differences. The issue of nature-driven likes and dislikes may also come into play and should be recognized and dealt with patiently. For instance, if you have learned that your child is slow to accept new things, do not lose your temper because he doesn't immediately like broccoli. Be patient with him, offer it again in small amounts, and eventually he should come on board. He may never love broccoli, but he will in most cases learn to eat it, unless for some reason it does not agree with him. Perhaps as many as 10% of all children are irregular in body functions, intense in their reactions, negative in mood, slow to adapt to change, and have a tendency to withdraw in the face of new stimuli. If these are traits you see in your child, understand that it may be genetically more difficult for him to learn how to be patient. Knowing your child's natural temperament and your own should help you to individualize a teaching method for him and to be patient as you institute it. Different approaches to discipline are often needed depending on the developmental age of the child and the nature of the offense. What works for one child may not work for another, so be creative.

It is your job to help your child on his road to healthy development. Not only should you be patient in your parenting role, but you should also teach your child to be patient. By the time he reaches school age, he should be able to sit in his seat rather than getting up to explore the room. His natural impatience may show up while waiting in a grocery store line, while waiting for a meal to be ready, or while waiting to go to the park and play. A technique for teaching patience is to provide your child a choice when a treat is to be offered. Tell him that he can either have one treat now or wait five minutes and get two treats. Ask him to choose between these options. As he gets better at waiting five minutes, stretch out the time to six, etc. Not all children are as easy as others to manage.

In the best of us, behaviors take time to learn. So-called "detail men," whose job it is to introduce new products to doctors, are taught that it will take, on average, seven visits before the doctor begins to use their product, if ever. Learning takes time and it takes repetition. Advertisers know this. If it takes a doctor seven visits by a skilled salesman to get the physicians to change their prescribing practices, how long do you think it will take an infant to learn something new? Before you lash out at him, remember this and think to yourself that perhaps you haven't yet convinced him of the need to adopt a new habit, or perhaps he is still not mature enough to learn it. Sometimes it helps to try new things for short periods of time. A few minutes may be all that he can handle. Try to lengthen the time in subsequent trials. Perhaps what you are asking him to do may be beyond his ability. Will you scold him if he crashes when he is learning to ride his bike, or will you accept the crashes as part of his learning experience and not a willful disregard of the lessons you have given? The correct response to a crash is to praise him for trying, tell him you admire his persistence and perhaps bravery, and offer a few tips.

The Tools of Discipline: Punishments may be used as tools of discipline, but they are not the only tools. Love and bonding are also tools of discipline, as are rewards and compensation. These tools come in all sizes and one size does not fit all situations, personalities, or all ages. In many situations you will have to learn what works by trial and error, but in these trials use the least punitive approach first. At one end of the discipline spectrum we have the cuddling, rocking, and reading that helps your child learn to sleep on schedule. On the other end we have the old-fashioned "spare the rod and spoil the child" approach, which we will come to later. Women tend to pick up and cuddle. Men tend to say "Stop!" Both can be effective.

Punishments: In deciding on a fair and effective punishment, remember that the punishment should fit the crime. Knowing that not all rule-breaking is of the same significance, nor is it always willful, try to adjust your rules to reflect the degree of seriousness of the crime. What you will be doing is not unlike what the law has done in separating crimes into misdemeanors and felonies, each of which has its own set of prescribed punishments with variations from mild to severe. Hate crimes such as bullying, especially when repeated, are much more serious than a failure to clean one's room. As you set consequences, let your child know what they are and why you have set them the way you have.

Even very young children can understand and respond to punishments, and they should be told why you have each rule even though they may not yet understand what you are implying. When possible, emphasize what your child should do rather than what he should not do. By the example you set and the instructions you give, you will help him learn that your goals are to keep him safe and healthy and to have him become a successful, moral, ethical, value-driven, self-sufficient adult. Point out things that your child is doing correctly or has done correctly. For example, you might say, "Thank you for cleaning your room." If a sibling or a friend is doing something well, especially something this child is having trouble with, comment on it.

What follows is a description of a variety of ways to deal with dangerous or otherwise inappropriate behavior. To repeat, the least punishment that you can get by with to get the job done is the best.

Empathy: My favorite form of dealing with a misbehaving child, after they have learned the English language, is to be empathetic. Empathy is the ability to identify with and understand somebody else's feelings or difficulties. Usually this comes from understanding your child's situation, his facial expressions, his body language, and correctly interpreting what is bothering him or pleasing him. Armed with this empathetic knowledge, you can say something like, "You look very angry." Just saying this will often get his attention. When you are able to then state what you think might be the problem, such as, "I bet you are angry that I took your toy away," the volume of the tantrum is apt to further diminish. Then you can approach him with love, pick him up, and tell him that you love him but were worried that he might break his sister's new toy. With this method the child gets no reward for his behavior except perhaps for your attention. You might practice your empathetic technique in response to positive emotions. For instance, when you see your child is happy, comment to him on what you see.

While we are on the subject of empathy, using the technique just described can also be an effective way of communicating with older children and adults. You might begin your empathetic career by practicing on your co-partner. In addition to gaining proficiency in the technique, you may get the side benefit of an enhancement of your relationship with each other. The way this works is that you study the face and body language of the person with whom you are dealing and try to read from it their emotional state at the time. Do they appear amused, angry, happy, or something else when you are talking with them? Ask them and learn from their response. When your child is old enough, teach him empathetic technique. Later in life, having empathetic skills and being able to read facial expressions, body language, tone, and general appearance can be a great tool for salesmen—and for all of us.

Restrictions: Restrictions come in many forms and are not always thought of as punishments, but they can be effective preventers of dangerous behaviors. For instance, when you punish a child by pulling him away from a stove top or an electrical outlet and placing him in a playpen, let him know why you are pulling him away and what the danger is even if he is not yet old enough to understand what the word danger means. You may even compliment him on his curiosity about these things but make it clear that they are dangerous. Building a fence to keep your child out of the street can also be a form of restriction—a very important and useful form. This restriction should not be relaxed until the child demonstrates a willingness and ability to play near the street without entering it, or later to walk across the street with caution. Other restrictions can be prohibitions of parties and sleepovers that do not meet the proper adult supervisory criteria as set by you. Such criteria might include knowing that the other parent will monitor behavior and apply reasonable consequences to violations when needed. Legal restrictions for teenagers are in the form of laws regarding allowable driving age and allowable drinking age, the latter a law that is often ignored and very poorly enforced.

"Walk-aways" are a form of restriction or separation of the child from what he wants that occur when a parent walks away from a misbehaving child. Because temper tantrums are often aimed at getting your attention, walking away and seeming to ignore his inappropriate behavior can be very effective. You may also punish by loss of privilege. For a teenager, you might tell him, "If you break curfew you will go to school and certain other prespecified activities but will be restricted to the house at all other times for two weeks."

"Timeouts," another form of punishment, are times when a child is separated from what he was doing. In younger children, timeouts can be very effective, but by school age their effectiveness will usually have declined, and in the teenage years will be considerably less likely to achieve the desired outcome. Separation from others, on the other hand, can be very effective if handled properly.

Michael took great pleasure in teasing and picking on his younger siblings. Requests for him to stop were generally ignored. One day at dinner, when his behavior reached a very unacceptable level, his father asked him to leave the table and come with him. In the minutes that followed, I watched father and son walking around their backyard not once but a number of times, all the while talking with each other. When they returned to the table they were both smiling and the teasing was over (at least for the moment).

Anger Management: Punishments should not be decided upon in anger. If you have not been prepared for an infraction, let the child know how upset you are and that punishment will follow but not until you cool down and think about it, and possibly consult with your co-partner. Teach your child the same technique for managing his own anger. When he is misbehaving, and old enough to give you an answer, allow time for him to cool down and then try asking him why he was doing or not doing something that was in violation of a rule he should know. It is important that you let him know that you will listen to and consider what he says and, if indicated by what he tells you, modify his punishment or at least let him know that you understand his reasoning even though you do not agree with it.

A common but potentially dangerous problem occurs when a parent, so angry about what their child has done, lashes out with violent language or by going for the belt. There has been a decrease in the number of parents who spank their children but the incidence is still too high. Always remember that your mission is to teach rules and to teach what is right from what is wrong. Try never to decide on an appropriate punishment when you are angry. Spanking, a once very popular form of punishment, is currently being used much less often than it once was, for a couple of very good reasons. First, there is no evidence that it is more effective than other less physical forms of punishment and plenty of evidence that, unlike other forms of punishment, it is capable of causing resentment and anger that may be lasting. Secondly, parents who teach their child that it is wrong to hit someone and then spank her, especially if the spanking occurs in a moment of anger, are sending a very mixed message. In an age when violence is an important societal issue (see chapter on violence), be careful that its effectiveness is not taught by you.

Beware of belittling your child in anger or even in jest. Putting your child down verbally can be very dangerous, especially at younger ages, when his brain is so retentive. When you belittle your child or put him down, you may be shaping his self-opinion for a lifetime.

Rewards: Children should be rewarded for good behavior. The rewards can go all the way from hugs to "attaboys" to payment for extra chores. This subject is addressed more fully in the chapters on nurturing that follow.

Rewarding Bad Behavior:

A friend of mine has a dog that never eats food from the table. One day when he came home from work, his son Noah proudly showed him how he had been able to teach the dog to eat from the table by placing small treats there and encouraging the dog with larger and larger treats placed further and further from the table's edge. The father was able to restrain his anger and praised Noah for being so creative in his approach to teaching the dog a new trick. He then said, "Please don't ever do that trick again" and told him why.

This was a double-header: praising creativity and effort and teaching why a given behavior was a no-no.

Chapter Summary: *We have presented a strategy for helping your child become self-disciplined that includes the development of a disciplinary plan, with comments that any punishment should fit the crime and that no punishment should be excessive. The importance of rule-setting, the advertisement of your rules to your child, and the importance of prompt disciplinary action when they have been broken has also been stressed.*

11

Self-Discipline and Success

Chapter Goals: *Building on the previous chapter about self-discipline, we now move on to using that self-discipline as a major tool for reaching one's potential. There are many factors that must work together to achieve maximum success. In this chapter we will focus on the importance of self-discipline but point out that inborn talent, effort, and opportunity are also essential.*

Goal Setting: When parents or expectant parents tell me that they don't care what their child becomes when she grows up as long as she is successful, I then ask them what they mean by success. Success can be defined in many ways and at many levels. It can come from solving a jigsaw puzzle or from marrying the person of your dreams. It can come from learning to ride a bicycle or from becoming a billionaire. How do you define it? Usually when I say maximizing one's potential, I am thinking in terms of a career, but I also know the concept can appropriately be used for success in an avocation such as music, sports, art, or writing and I certainly use it for marriages and parenting. The goals of happiness and character building can and should be intertwined with the goal of attaining a successful career. When "success" is achieved at the expense of doing what is right, it is not appropriate. Were Major League Baseball stars such as Jason Giambi and Jose Canseco, who admitted illegal steroid use, and many others who were implicated, successful? They certainly made a lot of money, but in my view, and I hope yours, they were moral failures.

Traditionally, parents expected that their children would follow in their footsteps—for example, a farmer's child would farm. Today it is not wrong to want your child to succeed you in what you do, but your job may not be where her potential and her interests lie. Once you have decided to make the maximizing of your child's potential a life mission, you should begin the process of looking for what vocation or vocations fit her best. You and your parenting partner have genetically derived characteristics of temperament and ability that might provide a clue.

Don't confuse looking for what is best for her with your own natural desire to have her follow in your footsteps. Do not be a parent who wants your child to be successful and who stubbornly believes that only you are smart enough to define her future career for her. Along the way you will have plenty of opportunities to make your wishes and beliefs known, but there should come a time when the final decision is turned over to your young adult based on her understanding of her abilities, talents, and interests.

An acquaintance of mine was a law student and a really talented piano player. If she had the choice, she would have given up her law studies and pursued a career in music. But her parents were not so inclined, and made sure that piano playing became very secondary to her career in law. Were they right in doing this?

In your child's younger years, there are many important and time-consuming things to be accomplished, but do allow some time to think about her final destination and perhaps about what career or direction best fits. New career categories are developing all the time, so specificity of career choice at a young age may well be impossible.

"With self-discipline most anything is possible."
—Teddy Roosevelt

The Antecedents of Success: If you want your child to be successful you will have to help her build self-confidence, self-control, self-discipline, and the willpower, hard work, and persistence that go with them. To become successful in a moral, value-driven way she must also have character. It has been said that character becomes destiny—one's life must matter. Margaret Thatcher said, "Success used to be about trying to do something. Now it is about trying to be someone." Set your goals high. Ronald Reagan had a plaque on his desk in the Oval Office that said, "It can be done." Unless your child believes this about the tasks ahead, she will not likely be very successful.

Self-Discipline: With self-discipline comes the ability to motivate oneself even when tired or in a negative emotional state. Qualities associated with self-discipline include not only willpower but also hard work and persistence. Teach your child to push the envelope and to aim high. In the preceding chapter, we talked about the steps necessary for your child to reach an adequate level of self-discipline. You should hope that, with your help, your child and eventually your young adult will continue to grow in this essential component of success.

> *"Keep away from people who belittle your ambitions. Small people always do that, but the really great make you feel that you, too, can become great."*
>
> —Mark Twain

Self-Control: Self-control is having the ability to control one's emotions, behaviors, and desires in order to obtain some reward or avoid some punishment. This important component of becoming successful helps us deal with our emotional ups and downs, the stresses we all encounter, our anger, and our frustrations. It will be hard to teach self-control to your child if you do not have it yourself.

The Risk of Over-praising Your Child: Over-praising of a child and of a child's achievements can be harmful to her achievement of success. An exception is when praise is given for good deeds done, for sharing, and for moral acts. Another problem is the use of insincere praise, which at younger ages may not be questioned, but later can result in confusion about what you really mean when you praise her. When children are continually told how smart they are (or athletic, or artistic, etc.), they will naturally love the praise but too often the receiving of praise may become their primary goal. This could make your child so fearful of failure and mediocrity that she will become unwilling to take on challenges at which she believes she might not do well. Dropping subjects or dropping out of school entirely can be part of the downside. Dweck and others emphasize that success is most likely to be achieved when a child is praised more for the effort of trying something difficult than for the achievement of that goal. Another expert, Kohn, says it all in the title of her book, *Punished by Rewards: The Trouble with Gold Stars, Incentive Plans, and Other Bribes,* and in her statement that praise, even for effort, encourages children to be praise junkies dependent on outside feedback rather than cultivating their own judgment and motivation. The bestselling book *Nurture Shock* does an excellent job of making all these same points.

When a child does do well in something, you should shape your praise around this concept. Rather than saying, "Aren't you smart," say something like, "It really looks like all the study time you put in paid off." In sports, the praise might be, "Wow, you really did well against the number-one team—that extra practice may have done the trick." For a time, schools placed the development of self-esteem at the top of their lesson plans and tried to prevent feelings of failure by such maneuvers as not grading tests in an A, B, and C fashion.

> *When our child was in the third grade, we received a report card telling us that she was performing up to expectations. We never learned whose expectations she was performing up to, nor were we allowed to have numerical or alphabetical scores. When asked, the principal told us that the schools had adopted the new system because they feared overreaction by parents whose children were not doing well. Because of this, I decided to run for the school board.*

The approach of a mother who wrote a book called *The Battle Hymn of the Tiger Mother* has been criticized by many for the extent to which she drove her children, often at the expense of sacrificing other important youth activities. To these criticisms she has responded, "For me, it's ultimately not about achievement. It's about teaching your kids that they are capable of much more than they think. If they don't give up, don't make excuses, and hold themselves to high standards, they can do anything they want in life, break through any barrier, and never have to care about what other people think." Fortunately, Tiger Mom was blessed with children who were very talented and able to achieve the lofty goals that were set for them. I am not sure what the outcome would have been if her children did not have the skills she assumed that they did.

Related to the subject of getting A grades in school, it is important to remember that not all A's are the same and should not be rewarded in the same way. Among many factors is the innate ability of the child, whether that is measured by IQ or by developmental age. Other factors can be state of health, state of rest, interest in the subject, and amount of time spent in study. Teachers do not all grade the same way and some are notably stingier with good grades. Getting good grades in magnet schools may be more difficult than in non-magnet schools. Some administrators have altered grades to have their schools look good on standardized tests. Students sometimes cheat.

Olympic scoring recognizes many of these factors, and in sports such as gymnastics a complex scoring system that takes many factors into consideration has been developed. In the case of gymnastic scoring, there are two sets of judges. One gives points for the degree of difficulty on eight different skills, rating them on uniqueness and artistry. Another set of judges measures execution and deducts points for errors such as taking a step after dismount. It is a complicated system that was changed in 2005 and again in 2009 in attempts to make it better. Diving judges try to do the same thing but have a different method. In both cases, natural ability and years of practice and study are assumed. In school, praise is most in order for difficult subjects performed well, both of which criteria require study and practice. If such a system could be devised for schoolchildren, there might be less of a temptation to look for easy courses at the expense of taking courses that the student feared she might fail. The takeaway here is that an A is not an A, is not an A.

Aware that current grading systems leave much to be desired, schools are looking at methods of how best to evaluate and motivate learning. In what is called standards-based or mastery grading, schools are better able to measure student learning. Completion of homework, attitude in class, and teacher impressions are included, but the most important consideration is: are the children learning? The final score is based on test data that is carefully calculated.

Failure as a Key Component of Success: To become truly successful, your child must be able to take on challenges, fail some, get up from her falls and disappointments, and move forward. She must learn by doing and by failing. If at first you don't succeed, try and try again.

> *"The only man who makes no mistakes is the man who never does anything."*
>
> —Teddy Roosevelt

Failure can be a confidence builder when it occurs following a good performance against a competitor known to be superior or when it occurs in an effort to move up the level of one's achievement. Failure teaches valuable lessons that must inevitably be learned. With your help, your child should come to understand that losing is not the end of the world. The lessons learned can help her better prepare for the disappointments that inevitably occur in all of our lives. Encourage trying new and more difficult things, explaining that there is much to be learned by both success and failure. Sara Blakely, the founder of Spanx and the first self-made female billionaire, attributes her success to her father who encouraged her try to harder and harder things. When she failed, he would say, "What did you learn?" and "What will you different next time?"

> *"Ready, fire, aim."*
>
> —Tom Peters

In the Ready, Fire, Aim business model proposed by Peters, the plan was to do what you had to do to get ready. Tinkering and stalling until you are positive that your plan will work is not the way to go. When it seems that your idea is a reasonably good one, try it (fire). Then you should assess the results of your trial and readjust (aim) so that when you fire next, your results might be better. When failure results in an unwillingness or inability to try again, it is a real failure, unless an examination of the results convinces you that it is not worth another try. There are failures and there are failures. Failures from inadequate or no preparation and practice are very different from failures that occur after one has prepared and practiced. The inability to take risks can seriously hold back your child's ability to reach her potential. Risk-takers and experimenters are the ones who have most commonly risen to the top in our society. Most of them have had failures, often multiple failures along the way, but the majority of them were not easily dissuaded from taking other risks.

There are those who do not want to risk their present comfort and security. For many, this is understandable, even though it is limiting. This separates them from those who are willing to put much or all of their money into a startup business, even knowing that seven out of ten businesses fail in the first year. The 30% who do succeed have entered a field of work that they love and have moved to a higher socioeconomic status. The 70% who did not succeed, although discouraged, learn a lesson, and most are eventually glad they tried. Many of them will readjust and try again. These risk-takers are different either because of their inherent nature or because they have been nurtured to shoot for the top.

No-No Risks: Not all risk-taking is to be encouraged. The no-no list of risks includes serious safety risks such as high-speed driving, jeopardizing important relationships with inappropriate behavior, job misbehavior, and more. In line with the problems of today's youth, other unacceptable risks are advertising that you are sexy by dressing immodestly, or eating chicken nuggets and a large container of French fries every time the opportunity arises. Many children, particularly adolescents, do not exercise enough or study enough, and see no harm in trying addictive substances. Teenagers, not really believing that any serious consequences can happen to them, can be by nature dangerous risk-takers. The risk of driving after drinking, often done because of unwillingness to admit one is drunk, is more than stupid, and the consequences can be severe and permanent. Those who agree to ride with a driver who they think might be intoxicated are either intoxicated themselves or just as stupidly immature as the drunk driver. The fact that many teens, especially when drinking, will neglect the safety of a buckled seatbelt adds to their risk. A recent AAA study noted that when there is one passenger in the car with a sixteen or seventeen-year-old driver, whether drinking or not, the risk of a fatal crash doubles. With three or more passengers the rate triples.

Self-Confidence: Self-confidence can be a major factor on the road to success. Confidence can come from excelling and from winning. It can also come from the ability to learn from failure, make adjustments, and improve. Self-confidence in one thing can be transferrable and helpful in many situations. Said another way, winning at sports and thereby developing a sense of value and self-confidence can help a child strive for the same sense of accomplishment in other activities that might be avoided by those who are fearful of not being able to succeed.

Recognize Talent Early and Encourage It: When you set your mission and defined what you wanted your child to be when fully grown, you did so without having much of clue as to what her abilities, talents, likes, and dislikes would be. As she grows and develops, you should be able to get a better handle on who she is and use that information to modify or fine-tune the goals and guidance you will be giving her. Learn as she matures what activities play to her strengths and encourage these pursuits. As her skills grow, so will her self-confidence and self-esteem.

The Peter Principle: There are limits to how far you should push your child and yourself. Failure based on participating in an activity beyond the level of her inherent talent or ability is not good for self-image and self-confidence, but it does teach a lesson, a lesson about what she is good at and what she is not good at. Hard work and persistence should be encouraged, but there may come a time when you and your child realize that this endeavor is not for her.

For activities that your child is not good at, doesn't like, and gets little exercise from, why would you make her participate? If your goal is to raise her confidence, how can this activity help? Rather than building confidence, might it set her up for the bullies? Not all of us are good at sports, but if we want to play that is fine. Music, writing, and drawing can be very rewarding, and there are other forms of exercise. All young children should probably be given the opportunity to try their hand on the chance that they show real talent.

Can There Be Too Many Activities? Sure there can. Too many parents push their children into a great variety of activities that more than fill up the daily time clock of child and parent. Too much time spent on a variety of things may prevent your child from focusing on one or two activities that have the potential to be confidence-builders.

Learning to persist is an important skill to develop. There might be reasons other than skill development for participation, such as making friends and sharing an activity with them, and learning lessons in teamwork, but what real good comes from spending time in an activity that your child does not like, in which she is looked down upon by her peers, and which may be above his Peter Principle line? Before beginning any new activity, talk it over with your child and consult with her regarding her interests. If you have been an over-praising parent, keep that in mind if she says, "No, I think it would be too hard for me." If that is the case, you may need to push her to give it a try anyway and see what time, coaching, and team spirit might do. The rules for new activities should include a setting of time and effort that must be expended before quitting is considered. Quitting is not a behavior that should be encouraged.

Chapter Summary: *Self-discipline is a necessary component of real success when success is defined as being the best that you can be. There are more than a few areas where a person can and should be successful, but for each there should be appropriate temperament, opportunity, talent, ability, and appreciation.*

12

Chapter Twelve

Nature vs. Nurture: From Conception to Birth

Chapter Goals: *In this and the next chapter, we will stress the importance of the interaction between the inborn characteristics that are part of every child (their nature) and the influences (their nurture) that will interact from the time of conception until early adulthood and beyond.*

In this chapter, we will look at nature from the standpoint of its principal director, the human brain, and the genetics and nurture that control brain development in utero. At birth, no two children are the same.

I begin with an introduction to some of the scientific studies that address the subjects included in this chapter—I hope not so much so that you lose your interest in the how-to parts later in the chapter.

The Genetics of Behavior: Wikipedia lists over seven hundred genetic disorders, and more than a few of them affect behavior. Disorders ranging from genetically based mental deficiencies such as Down syndrome; school disorders such as learning disabilities and attention deficit disorder; autism spectrum disorders such as Asperger syndrome; and psychiatric disturbances such as depression, bipolar disease, and schizophrenia can all have profound effects on child behavior, requiring professional assessment and guidance. As important as they are, it is not these disorders that we will discuss in this chapter. Here we will look at the different inherent natures that we all have.

Definitions: Nature, for our purposes here, refers to those physical, behavioral, and emotional constituents that are present at birth in each of us. Merriam-Webster defines **nurture** as training and upbringing—the sum of the environmental factors influencing the behavior and traits expressed by an organism.

Nature and Brain Development in Pregnancy: When you first see your baby, he will be a far different creature than he was when he was first conceived. At no time in his life will his rate of growth and development be as rapid or as complex as it will be during his time in the womb. At birth his brain will contain as many as 100 billion brains cells (neurons).

In its first week, a single fertilized cell will divide into about a hundred new cells, each identical to the original. In the second week, these cells will produce new ones that in the beginning will form three layers: the ectoderm, the mesoderm, and the endoderm. From the cells of the ectodermal layer, a neural plate will be formed that will be the forerunner of the brain and other parts of the central nervous system. In month two, before the mother may even realize that she is pregnant, the genetically controlled fetal brain will be well on its way to becoming a distinguishable organ. The speed of neuron production in the second trimester accelerates so that more than 5,000 new neurons are being produced every second (WOW!). As soon as they are formed, these neurons begin to migrate and aggregate in communities. Approximately 3% of migrating neurons lose their way. To communicate with one another, each neuron develops a projection (axon) that will connect with one of the many receiving projections (dendrites) of another neuron. Each functioning neuron will make many such connections. The spaces where these electrical and chemical connections occur are called synapses, and at birth the synapses will number in the hundreds of trillions (BIGGER WOW!). Less than 20% of these synapses will be hooked up before birth, but even with this relatively limited number, fetuses do develop an ability to remember. Although the rate of brain growth will slow in the third trimester, it will continue at a very rapid rate until almost a child's first birthday.

Sensory Receptors in Pregnancy: By the later months of pregnancy, all of your baby's five senses will have kicked in and his brain will be capable of absorbing

96

and retaining sensory stimuli; he will be able to sense touch, and to hear, see, smell, and taste. Babies who are touched in the womb will often react by pulling away or kicking back. Those exposed to a high-intensity light beam may move or alter their heart rates. With their sense of smell, a sense that develops earlier than most other senses, babies exposed to the odors of the mother's food and surroundings will tend to prefer those smells after they are born. The infant may also prefer the tastes of foods that they have been exposed to in the mother's diet during late pregnancy. Babies can hear their mom's voice as early as the end of the second trimester and will prefer it to the other voices they will hear after birth.

Knowing these things, there are those who suggest that the uterus should be bombarded with stimuli to help the fetus grow in ability. Things like hearing soothing music and their mother's voice may produce benefit, but there is no research-based evidence to support this position. Although it is probably a good idea to communicate with your unborn child, it is important that stimulation not be overdone, especially in the early months. The fetus does need uninterrupted time for sleep and other necessary activities.

The Century of the Brain: In the late twentieth century, the quantity of medical knowledge almost doubled every ten years. In that period we learned much about many body parts and functions, but not a whole lot about the human brain. Now, however, is has been said that we are in the "Century of the Brain"—a time when our knowledge of this organ and its functions will grow rapidly. The amount of current research that is brain-focused seems to point to the truth of this statement. Although we know little about how to best use much of this new information to help mothers prevent and deal with problems of pregnancy and beyond, I have included a few comments about what is being learned to introduce you to a field that will take on increasing significance in the years ahead.

There is a growing understanding of the constitutional basis of nature and how what could be called neurons of temperament are sorted and stored in the brain. From an anatomical basis, behavioral researchers believe that the genes for controlling temperament lay down chemical templates for brain structure; they predict that future research will show how environmental factors (nurturing) make changes and contributions to these brain structures.

The HPA Axis: Although the changes her baby will be making in utero are tremendous, the mother will also be making important changes. She will be doing more, a lot more, than just experiencing morning sickness, growing big in the abdomen and breasts, and perhaps developing facial coloring. The maternal brain is the command center of many of the changes that will affect her and her baby-to-be. A phenomenon called "fetal programming" will deal with the effects, some of which are long lasting, of maternal nutrition, stress, and behavior (her nurturing) on the developing fetus and in her child's later life.

Much of this programming is regulated by what is called the mother's hypothalamic-pituitary-adrenal (HPA) axis, an axis that is always at work, not just during pregnancy. The hypothalamus is the part of the brain that sends signals to the nearby pituitary gland, and the pituitary gland sends signals to the adrenal and other glands to initiate and regulate activities of the mother and her baby. On the good side, the HPA sends the signal to develop a hormone that will lead to milk production and for the necessary increase in appetite that will benefit mother and child. On the bad side, "fetal programming" can also lead to later-life problems with heart disease, type 2 diabetes, obesity, and cancer. The HPA is also involved in the regulation of responses to stress. When mothers are stressed or depressed during pregnancy, their offspring may have increased HPA axis responsiveness to stress later in life. Severe maternal stress during pregnancy can also lead to increased rates of autism, schizophrenia, depression, and lower IQs in the children they bear. How exactly this axis does its job is not yet known, but it will be. The HPA axis can also have an effect on maternal behavior and on post-partum depression.

Nurture in Pregnancy: Healthy moms have the best chance of delivering healthy babies. The best advice for expectant mothers is to stay healthy, avoid infection, eat right, control weight, sleep right, exercise, and avoid frequent or excessive stress. On all of these subjects, the mother-to-be should seek the advice of her physician, especially regarding what and what not to consume and what should be consumed only in moderation. She should talk with her doctor about supplements such as iron, omega-3 oils, B-complex vitamins, and folic acid, all of which are needed for healthy brain development.

Alcohol and drug use can affect the developing fetal brain and other organs. Because many of the negative effects of alcohol and drug use occur in the very early stages of pregnancy, the woman who waits until she knows that she is pregnant may be waiting too long. For those who are planning to get pregnant or who are sexually active and not using effective contraception, all dangerous and potentially dangerous substances should be avoided.

Alcohol: A number of serious medical conditions caused by alcohol ingestion during pregnancy are included in what is called the fetal alcohol spectrum disorder (FASD). Of these the most common and best known is fetal alcohol syndrome (FAS). Drinking and especially drinking a lot are most dangerous during the first trimester, but there is no time during pregnancy when alcohol use is safe; no amount of drinking is without risk. Babies born after being exposed to alcohol may have facial abnormalities, stunted growth, and neurologic problems including attention disorders, learning disorders, poor social skills, vision impairment, and behavior problems.

Nicotine: Smoking makes it more difficult to get pregnant. During pregnancy, tobacco puts your child at risk for premature birth, birth defects, and later sudden infant death syndrome (SIDS). Secondhand smoke has also been implicated.

Illegal Drugs: Cocaine use during pregnancy can disrupt the migration of neurons, a process whose sequence and timing must adhere to a precise schedule if normal development is to occur. Although use is never a good idea, all illicit drugs should be avoided in pregnancy and during the time when you are trying to get pregnant or are at risk of becoming pregnant. The number of babies experiencing opiate withdrawal symptoms in their early days has tripled since the surge in popularity of the illegal use of the narcotics Vicodin and Oxycontin.

Legal Drugs and the Food and Drug Administration (FDA): The FDA classifies all regulated drugs into five categories related to their relative risk to pregnant women, with one of the classes deemed completely risk-free and one deemed never to be used in pregnancy.

Chapter Summary: *The growth and development that occur in a fetus from the time of conception until birth are astounding. In addition to his genetic makeup, your baby will be affected by how you treat your body, in good ways and bad, during this critical time. When fetuses do develop senses, these senses will be used to react to various stimuli, and in many cases the fetus will learn from these experiences.*

13

Chapter Thirteen

Nature vs. Nurture II: Your Child Is Different

Chapter Goals: *In the last chapter we looked at how the interaction between genetic makeup and nurture went into the development of your baby's brain. Now we will look at how that nature will interact with the nurturing that she receives from her parents and environment to produce her adult personality. In addition to her traits and temperament, we will also look at her inborn abilities, talents, and intellect, and how they can be shaped by nurture.*

A study of the inherent nature of infants and its interaction with the nurturing they receive is a complex subject. Although you do not need to become expert in the field, a basic understanding of the concepts involved can be very helpful.

Definitions: Temperament, a complex multidimensional concept, describes each child's fairly fixed characteristic way of responding to external events and her ability to self-regulate the way she thinks, behaves, and reacts. **Personality** is the complex of characteristics that distinguish an individual emotionally and socially.

The Nature/Nurture Pendulum: Speculation and discussion about the relative importance of inborn vs. acquired traits and temperament have been with us for a long time, and the belief that one or the other was predominant has over time swung from one side to the other and back. Socrates, Plato, Aristotle, and Hippocrates all made comments on the subject of inborn nature, with Hippocrates teaching that there are four bodily humors (blood, yellow bile, black bile, and phlegm) that shape our adult temperament and health—a concept that persisted for many centuries and in many cultures. In Greco-Roman times, the physician Galen, like Hippocrates before him, noted that all infants were inherently different from each other.

In the late nineteenth century, the pendulum had swung to a belief that nurture was dominant. The father of psychoanalysis, Sigmund Freud, divided personality into three major components. One of these, which he called the superego, was shaped by the nurturing of parents and other environmental influences. Psychoanalysts were taught that delving into a person's past history could provide a useful basis for the management of psychiatric disorders. This form of psychoanalysis fell from favor when it was discovered that some diseases he was blaming on nurture were actually genetically based.

In the earlier years of the twentieth century, Piaget and others spoke of the importance of both temperament and nurture on personality development. The pendulum was then swinging toward a better understanding of the importance of a person's nurturing while still recognizing the importance of their inborn nature. The debate about which most determines adult personality is still far from settled. Currently, there are first-rate researchers who are stressing the importance of the biologic side, while others, equally first rate, believe that nurture is of prime importance. The position taken in this book is that both nature and nurture are important. As a parent, your job will be to take the building blocks that make up your child and use them to help guide her on her path to becoming a moral, happy, and successful adult. Children must have parental love, direction, and guidance.

Research on Temperament—No Two Babies Are the Same: Perhaps best known of the more modern clinical studies looking at children's inherent temperament is the New York Longitudinal Study (NYLS). In it, the behaviors of babies, as reported by their mothers at age two to three months, were followed for five years to see how much if any their initial patterns had changed. Mothers were asked such questions as, "How active is your baby?" (activity level); "How easily is she distracted when you are feeding her or changing her diapers?" (distractibility); "What is her initial reaction to something new, such as a new food or a different person?"

(approach vs. withdrawal); and "How long is her attention span?" (attention span or persistence). Using these traits, three groups of children were identified: the easy child, the difficult child, and the slow-to-warm-up child. Thomas and Chess used their data to argue that the parents of difficult children can have a much harder job raising their children that those with easy children. Thomas and Chess also introduced the concept of "goodness of fit," recognizing that when infant characteristics are well matched with the temperaments of their caregivers, parenting is easier. For example, an active, athletic family would most welcome a child who is active and fearless.

Over time, only four of the characteristics identified in the NYLS study—the four identified in the preceding paragraph—survived further studies using varied testing environments and conditions. Current researchers building on the NYLS studies now recognize twenty-one different temperamental characteristics that form the basic building blocks of personality, social development, adjustment, and psychopathology. Each factor may vary in intensity from very high to very low.

Patterns of inherent coping also vary, falling into at least four different categories: avoidance, distraction, support seeking, and active coping. A person with negative temperament tends to use avoidance, whereas one with a positive temperament uses active coping. In measuring traits, researchers noted that some traits inhibited others. For example, shyness and fear can inhibit a person who is otherwise an extrovert by nature.

Temperament Types in Children: Based on measures of temperament, a number of studies have identified three types of children and adolescents: resilient, over-controlled, and under-controlled. Here the word controlled does not refer to over-controlling parents but to controls that are inborn. Resilient children tend to be extroverted, self-confident, focused, verbally fluent, and able to adapt easily to change. Over-controlled children are shy, introverted, and lack many social skills. Under-controlled children tend to be impulsive, willful, and disagreeable, showing little concern for others. Not surprisingly, the latter are the most difficult to manage. It is much easier to predict the adult personality when children are at the high or low ends of temperament scales. Those who are confident in their early years tend to be confident and unafraid as adults. On the other hand, children who are irritable and who show little self-regulation at ages three to four tend to be high on negative emotionality at age eighteen. In those children who are high in negative emotionality and socially demanding, the development of behavior problems later in life is more likely.

Stability of Inborn Temperament: Comparing the assessment grading of infants with their later assessments at preschool age, it was realized that not all temperamental traits are present at birth. Traits such as being introverted or extroverted, or being spontaneous rather than reserved, are present early in life and persist. Others emerge over time, such as the ability to detect errors, to delay gratification, and to engage in planning—a very welcome sign for parents. In the first three to four years, the rate and time of developing and/or modifying temperamental characteristics will vary from child to child.

Cognitive aspects of personality (thoughts about self, others, and events) will be added throughout development as children construct mental models of who they are; experience feelings, thoughts, and actions linked to their self-concept; and develop a system for describing themselves and others. These characteristics are influenced by temperament and personality, but nurture is also a major factor.

Putting It All Together as a Parent: As you can see, the study of human nature is a complex subject. The more you learn about the components of what we call inborn nature, and the more you apply what you learn about your child's inborn nature, the easier it will be for you to be an effective parent. Do not fall into the trap of believing that when your child is not doing something you want her to do she needs to be punished, when in truth she may be acting very predictably and naturally. For example, if you know that by nature your child tends to react negatively and reject new things or people, you can use that information. If she rejects a new food, do not treat her as if she is being disobedient. Be patient but also be persistent in offering the foreign food. If you know that by nature she has a long attention span (which will serve her well later in many ways), do not be surprised if she doesn't respond quickly when you ask her to do something, especially if she is actively focused on something else.

Ability, Talent, and Skill: Certain abilities and talents, like traits and temperaments, are inborn. They may develop over time, but for the most part they are there from birth. Skills, on the other hand, are developed with study and practice. When Tiger Woods appeared on national television at age two to demonstrate his putting stroke, he had become skilled because his athletic, golf-loving father had encouraged and worked with him. There is no question in my mind, however, that if my father had done the same for me, I would not have had Tiger's natural ability to reach his skill level. Other examples of great natural talents that were nurtured into great skills abound. Symphony No. 1 in E Flat Major was written in 1764 by Wolfgang Amadeus Mozart, who was just eight years old at the time. He was already notable in Europe as a great performer. 2012 Olympic Gold Medalist Gabby Douglas was able to do vertical cartwheels at age three and by age six was showing great promise in gymnastics.

Intellect: Among the most important of inborn abilities is intellect. A person's intellectual ability will be a strong predictor of their future success. The ability to learn and to reason, like so many other genetically derived characteristics, will be greatly shaped by the way that these inborn abilities are nurtured. Children who are neglected or abused will not be nearly as smart as they would have been if raised in healthier environments. Parents who push their child to learn may have success in an activity, at least temporarily, but these gains will be nowhere as profound as the long-term losses that are experienced by children of neglect.

There is much to be learned about the shaping of intelligence, and researchers are in active pursuit of a better understanding of the subject. The study of intelligence is a complex subject, and its components are many. For instance, in studying the genes involved with intelligence, more than three hundred genes have already been identified as being related to mental retardation.

The two basic components of intelligence are **knowledge,** which researchers call crystallized intelligence, and **reason,** which is also called fluid intelligence. Of the two, reasoning is the more complex, requiring the transfer of information between different areas of the brain. This ability to reason does not usually show up until sometime between the ages of two and three. From that time the ability to reason grows rapidly, but in adolescence it levels off.

Intelligence (IQ) testing is widely used and is a valuable measure of intelligence based on one of many standardized tests. Although determination of IQ levels is an important and useful tool, it must be understood that it is not perfect. For one thing, testing of young children may not be a good predictor of future intelligence because some of the intellectual skills that are being measured do not develop at the same time or order in all children. By the time a child is eight years old there should be more consistency in testing, but until adolescence there may still be developmental timing differences.

There are other problems with IQ testing, such as familiarity with this type of testing; discomfort at the time of testing; or lack of motivation to do well, which may be based on poor prior performance. Being depressed, tired, or sick on test day can all affect results. Additionally, children who are very bright in one subject, such as math, may not have the same amount of cognitive skills in language or other subjects.

We Are All Different and So Are Our Children: It is important that parents understand that there is no one correct way of parenting all children. We are all different and so are our children. At birth we all have our own personal temperament, abilities, and physical characteristics. Only after the birth of their second child did a couple of the researchers cited in this chapter become interested in the study of temperament, realizing that the parenting techniques that had worked so well for child number one were not working so well with their new arrival.

Your temperament and the way that it matches your child's will play a part in your interaction with her. Her behavior will shape your behavior and yours will shape hers. When your natural traits resemble those of your child, it will be easier to understand her. There will be times, however, depending on what those common traits are and what the situation is, when your job will be made more difficult. If you and your child both have high anger and frustration levels, you will have to

106

be especially cautious. If you are both persistent in the sense that you both can be stubborn, be aware that you will need to parent more carefully.

Parental Role: From your child's earliest days, you should be looking for signs of what her personality and talents will become as she grows. This will be very helpful as you work with her on planning a course for her life—one that she likes and that best fits her traits and talents. Certain traits and skills are good fits for some careers, while others are not. Who your child will be when she grows up will be a product of her values, her interests, her personality, and her skills, all of which are products of her nature and her nurture.

In Summary: *A person's nature as contrasted to their nurture is genetically determined and will remain with them (with modifications) throughout life. All of us have different natures. An understanding of the concepts presented in this chapter, should make it easier for parents to adjust their parenting techniques to best fit their child. Know your child and work with her temperament and abilities to guide her safely through our sometimes toxic culture into adolescence and beyond.*

Let the Nurturing Begin

In this section, we will look at your parenting job at four different developmental ages. You might call the sections that precede this one preparation chapters—ones that get you ready to parent upon the arrival of your new family member. Now, armed with the goals you have set for your child, an understanding of who will be nurturing your child, and some of the important tools that will be needed and developed, it is time to look at the nurturing process that begins at birth.

As you read what follows, don't forget your principal parenting goals of raising your child to become a good person who is healthy and fit. The importance of your role as a teacher, guide, leader, and role model will be stressed throughout. Without you, your child runs a great risk of being set adrift in a stormy cultural environment, unable to escape the dangers that are all too present. Effective parenting requires time, patience, effort, and lots of love.

14

Chapter Fourteen

The Early Years I: Knowing Your Child

Chapter Goals: *In this, the first of three chapters on the early years, we will touch on some of the ways that newborns are different from older children and how that information should be used. We will remind you that children have inborn natures that make them different from other children and that you must recognize and deal with those differences. We will look at bonding, growth and development, and the inability at this age to separate fact from fiction. In the next chapter, learning will be the topic, and in the third, potential and expected problems at this age.*

The Very Important Early Years: For more than a few reasons, the early years can be considered the most important time in your child's life—a time when many aspects of his future development and personality will be formed. Lessons not learned in this period may never be. Your baby's brain is a learning engine and, in these early years, you, his parents, are his principal teachers—his nurturers. This little helpless stranger will enter your lives needing you to care for, protect, nourish, and guide him. It will take more than a little work and effort to get your job done, but the rewards can be great.

Bonding: Human bonding is the process by which two people develop a close interpersonal attachment, one that may begin to develop in the prenatal period. The experience of early bonding that occurs in the nursery can be powerful and long-lasting. There are very few divorces of mother and child. Father-child bonding, especially in the twenty-first-century model of fathering, can also begin early and be long-lasting. Bonding will become an important component of the baby's development of his own sense of self and his ability to bond with other people. There may be ups and downs in the bonding process and in the mother's exuberant love for her baby, especially if she is fatigued or depressed. The bonding ideal is reached when both parents and their baby are together early and often, because so much is happening to the rapidly developing young infant each day. Parents who adopt children can also bond but they will have some catching up to do. If the child is out of infancy, bonding may still occur but the lessons to be learned early on may not be as easy to teach. Without good bonding, children are apt to grow up to be less trusting and less happy.

Growth and Development: With knowledge of how and when the brain grows and develops, you will come to learn at what ages children can most easily learn various life lessons and at what ages they cannot. Parenting techniques that work for an infant's brain are often very different from those that work best for school-age, adolescent, or adult brains. Keep in mind that children do not all develop at the same rate or reach their developmental milestones in the same order.

At birth your baby's brain will already contain approximately 100 billion neurons, nearly enough to last him a lifetime, but only a small fraction of those billions is being put to use at birth. In his first year, his brain will be growing in size and developing more rapidly than it will at any other time in his postnatal life, and it will be rapidly absorbing and storing information. In his first two years, an infant's skull will need to grow to make room for his expanding brain. By the age of two it will have tripled in size to become 75% as large as an adult's brain. When you talk to your baby or coo to him, multitudes of brain cells will respond as they actively acquire, sort, and store information. Some of the neurons and the synapses associated with them will be activated and others will be strengthened. For the most part, these synapses and neurons will remain in place for a lifetime, whereas those synapses that have not been activated by about the age of ten will, in most cases, disappear. As an example, the ability to learn all sounds and languages is present at birth but gone for most by age ten unless the child has already put them to use.

You must seize this early opportunity, because never again will you have such a chance to make an impression on what your child comes to believe. In this period he will learn lessons that will be with him forever—lessons that will shape his personality and his character. Make sure that the lessons he is learning are healthy ones. It is easy to make the case that the adolescent years, when the child begins the process of separating from his home, are the most difficult ones for parenting, but those later years will be made much easier to manage if you do your job well in these early ones.

Helpless as infants seem to be, they are constantly learning from their environment. The "helpless" infant's capabilities continue to increase rapidly and, by nursery school age, your child should be walking, talking, and interacting at an increasingly advanced level. Parents who have been away from their young child for even short periods are often amazed to find out when they come home that in their short absence their infant has smiled, rolled over, sat up, taken his first steps, or said his first words. It almost seems that every day has a surprise event.

Nature/Nurture: In the two previous chapters we talked about the importance of knowing who your child is in terms of his inborn traits and how they will make him behave (or not behave). Some infants are highly reactive and will require a lot of soothing—soothing that will reduce the chances that they will grow up to be fearful and anxious adults. Soothing involves soft tone of voice, holding and other physical contact, patience, and a lot of love. Being overly strict can get your child to behave with the feeling that he must obey to survive, or it may turn him into a rebel. A child who is anxious or fearful will require supportive parenting to help avoid later delinquency and psychological problems. This will take time, patience, and love, but the rewards are worth it. Both situations are worth discussing with your pediatrician.

Stress and failure are not always bad things. We learn to cope by trying and adjusting if we fail. Do not protect your child completely from stress (as if that were possible). Comforting him in failure is okay but telling him you are proud of his effort to try something new is great. Not letting him face stress, an inevitable part of life, and not letting him learn to deal with it while still in your care is a mistake.

Planning for the Future: Even at this early stage in his life, your child may be thinking about what he will do when he is fully grown.

> When I asked Cameron, aged four, what she wanted to be when she grew up, she immediately told me that she would be Lady Gaga. I was impressed that she gave me such a quick response, a response suggesting that this was not the first time she had thought about her future. I also noticed how times have changed since my son, a generation earlier, had told me that he wanted to be a garbage man.

Be on the lookout, and when you see what you think may be real talent, recognize it and encourage it. Remember that Mozart was already great by the age of five. As your child's skills grow, so should his self-confidence and self-esteem. Do learn, as your child matures, what activities play to his strengths, and encourage them, especially if they are skills that will serve him well in his future life.

Fact or Fantasy?

On another occasion, four-year-old Cameron led me into our family room, in which there are stuffed animals on the wall and a number of almost life-sized animal replicas on the floor. First she asked me if the imitation moose on the floor was real. I told her no and led her slowly over to him. She followed me somewhat fearfully and, after I petted him, she hesitatingly did the same. Then she asked me about every animal in the room, trying to find out, not which ones were real, but which ones were still alive.

Cameron was of an age at which she clearly did not understand that there could be a moose that was not real. It has been known for some time that infants are unable to distinguish the real from the unreal—a valuable piece of information for parents that helps us understand them better and consequently treat them differently than we do older children. Their ability to separate the real from the unreal will develop over time. By the age of eight years this ability should be pretty much in place, but even then parental reminding may be required. By age twelve, that process should be complete.

When infants see monsters on TV, they have no reason to believe that they are not real. When they see violence in cartoons, they are unable to understand its significance but they are learning that violence can be funny, as when a bunny rabbit knocks a fox off a cliff. When he sees advertisements for fast-food products and for snacks, your child sees no reason to question whether these products are healthful or good for them. He has no comprehension of the reality that ads have been produced by people wanting to sell products or ideas. Instead, a young child feels that if he sees it or hears it, it must be true. Advertisers know that when a young child watches TV, he will not only believe what he sees but will retain the information they give him— good news for the manufacturer of the products being pushed. In a good move, the Disney Channel has announced, responding to pressure, that by the year 2015, they will no longer show commercials that advertise foods that are not nutritionally sound. Why, I wonder, are they waiting so long to implement this change?

Tots and Teasing: Because of the fact/fantasy issue, young children are not always able to tell when someone is teasing them. What may seem to you to be fun can be very hurtful to a young child. Here's an example from my life:

> *I had the privilege and pleasure of being alone with three-year-old India for a short vacation at Disney World. While there, we stayed at a motel and had most of our meals at a table outside of our room. During one of our conversations, India asked me if I was teasing her. When I said, "I guess so," she promptly told me that teasing was mean and that it hurts people. The following morning she said something that made me ask her, "Were you teasing me?" "No," she replied, "I was tricking you. Tricking is fun."*

This vignette not only illustrates India's wonderfully emerging ability to converse and to communicate, but also points out that teasing, even if it is meant in fun, can be seen very differently by someone who is not yet able to separate the real from the unreal. Some of my favorite people are four years old. It is at this age that they have matured enough to communicate well verbally, as did India in the teasing vignette. They want to learn and to have their newly found skills appreciated. They want to please and be close to those they love. It will not be long before other influences take away some of their desire to be with you. Enjoy this time and use it wisely. What follows is an example of the time when the ability to recognize fantasy is emerging in a slightly older child.

> *When I asked a boy who was celebrating his sixth birthday whether he was married, he looked at me in surprise, smiled, and said, "No."*

Over the years I have asked many children this question and have almost always gotten a response similar to that of the boy in this vignette. Why do they react this way? At age six, children are still not fully out of the fact/fantasy stage and are not always sure whether or not I am being serious, as I imply from catching their initial look. Then, when they decide that I am just kidding or think that I am, they will smile and answer. Younger children will not get the joke and, thinking that I really don't know the answer, respond very seriously, "No." Asking the same thing of a thirteen-year-old child will produce a response that implies that they wonder why I would ask such a stupid question. The lesson here for you is that for children at this developmental age, be careful what you say. As your child begins to make the reality separations, help him understand the difference. Be prepared for the once very real personages of Santa and the Easter Bunny to fade from his reality.

The Media and Media Literacy: Because of this inability to separate fact from fantasy and the potentially harmful misunderstandings that can go with this inability, I support the recommendation of the American Academy of Pediatrics (AAP) that there should be no TV viewing by children under the age of three. Even shows that may seem harmless to you may be inappropriately interpreted by your young child. As the child gets older, the media-literate parent will ask, "Do you really think that SugarPlus is the best cereal for you?" When the child responds, the mother will ask, "Why do you think that SugarPlus is good for you (or why don't you)?" A

114

child at the age of one or two years is too young to have or understand this sort of conversation.

Three hours of daily TV watching before the age of three is associated with a 30% increased chance of subsequent attention problems. Additionally, it has been shown that on average there is a 9% increase in bullying associated with every hour of daily TV watching before the age of four years. To repeat and re-emphasize: children under the age of three should watch no television, period.

Parental Role: You must learn to understand your child and the developmental changes that will occur at various ages. Your empathy, patience, and media literacy are important tools. The seeds of character development, future success, and happiness should be planted and nourished in these early years. It is your job to see that your child has regular medical checkups, is properly immunized, and is cared for when he is sick. In this book, these subjects will be mentioned only briefly. Instead, our focus will be on those areas where American adolescents and young people are currently having the most trouble—trouble that should have been prevented or dealt with early.

Chapter Summary: *In this period of very rapid brain growth, the influence of the principal caregivers is most critical. With your child having limited exposure to the media and our societal culture, he will be better able to appreciate and adopt the lessons of mother love, father love, and the other lessons you teach. From this stage on, reaching the child and changing his personality, skills, and habits will become increasingly more difficult and competitive. Use this time well, because your opportunity will never again be the same. And do not forget reality and the significance of his inability to tell the real from the unreal.*

15

The Early Years II: Learning

Chapter Goals: *To help you begin the process of teaching life skills and other important lessons.*

Nutrition: The AAP recommends that for their first six months, infants be fed only human milk and that breastfeeding be continued for the first year. For a variety of reasons, only a third of mothers breastfeed for as long as they originally intended. Success rates are increased in mothers who have had a previous baby, in babies who have been breastfed within an hour of their birth, and in babies who have received no pacifiers or supplemental feedings in the hospital. After the first year, breastfeeding may continue but is no longer nutritionally necessary. As you begin to add solid foods to your infant's diet in the second six months of life, pay attention to the advice your pediatrician gives you. With the move to table food, begin to teach her what foods are good for her and why, and which are not so good and why. Unless she has allergies or other medical reasons for avoiding certain foods, you should encourage her to eat all of the foods that you eat. For children whose inborn temperament makes them more likely to reject anything new, this may take longer to accomplish but repetition and persistence are useful tools. Your aim should be that she at least tastes all foods. Understand as you are doing this that most of us have some foods whose tastes or textures we may never really like.

Early Sex Education: On matters related to this subject, you should be the chief educator. Whether you decide to be the communicator of sex information to your child or not, do realize that she will learn all about these subjects eventually from peers, media, schools, and others. Because your approach may be the only one that puts an emphasis on values, you don't want it left out. The process of preparing your child for the years that will follow the hormonal surge of puberty should begin early in her life. In her early years, you should not be afraid to teach her the names of her body parts in accurate biologic language. A penis is a penis and a vagina is a vagina. If you decide to use cute substitute names, ask yourself if you are doing so to avoid the awkward feelings that you may feel about explaining such body parts. It's OK to talk about pregnancy and the birth process if those subjects come up, but at this age going into great detail is neither necessary nor advised. Talking about pregnancy provides an opportunity to talk about love—puppy love, first love, marital love, and God's love.

A Prime Time for Learning: At no other time, with the possible exception of her time in utero, will your child make such significant changes in her level of knowledge and her demonstration of skills.

Charlie, a friend of mine, is fond of saying, "Anything you learn by the fourth grade is with you forever."

Knowing what you now know about infant brains, you should also know that these seemingly helpless little creatures have the ability to absorb and store a great volume of information. The longer you wait to teach the lessons listed here, the more difficult your task will become. Learning is much easier when it does not have to be preceded by unlearning.

Learning Disabilities: A CDC report shows that developmental disabilities have increased in the United States over recent years. There are many types of learning difficulty but all should be addressed professionally if you want your child to succeed. One of the problems, common to all children, but of great importance in children who need extra time for test taking and/or oral questioning is that children do not like the idea of having their peers identify them as being different. This can become increasingly important later when the child goes to college and, because of embarrassment or not wanting to be seen as different from her new peers, does not take advantage of the provisions that have been made for her.

Language Development: Babies have the ability and living environment that allows them to learn language rapidly. By the age of eighteen months, most infants should pronounce at least fifty words well and know one hundred more. If your child is an early talker, you can be assured that she is of at least average intelligence. There may be reason to worry if she is not speaking by age two, but remember that neither Edison nor Einstein, both true geniuses, spoke before their second birthdays. If concerned about any phase of your child's development, speak with your pediatrician about it. The language that infants hear is quickly absorbed and stored, including the accent in which it is spoken. This innate ability to speak any dialect begins to fade at around six months, and some sounds that are not used may be lost before the child is one year of age.

Reading: Reading is an essential component of success in the world in which we live. From the beginning you should, talk, read, and/or sing to your child daily. Using TV, CDs, or DVDs to do your job will not get the same job done. The value of the live human voice is great and no amount of listening is too much at this age. Talking with her even when she is not old enough to understand you is still a good teaching tool. Her brain will be busy absorbing, sorting, and storing what her ears hear. Watching or helping your child learn to read can be fun for both of you, but learning to read before going to school is not a necessity. When your child learns to read, you should encourage her and have her read aloud to you. Be a good role model—a child who sees you voluntarily reading a lot may be more inclined to see reading as a pleasurable activity than as just something she has to do for school.

Playing: Learning to play comes in developmental stages. Early on, young children engage in what can be called open-ended play, play that has no set rules or objectives. In many ways open-ended play is the most creative, allowing children to use their imaginations with such things as LEGOS, Tinker Toys, blocks, and other building materials; dolls and doll clothing; rocking horses; and toy kitchens. The imagination of children can be amazing. As expected from their short attention spans characteristic of the early years, they may switch around from toy to toy in their periods of play. Infants are not yet prepared to play interactively with other children but they like having you in the room with them even if you are not watching. As she grows older, your child may engage in what is called parallel play, in which she will play with other children but more side by side than together. Later she will learn to play interactively with another person. As she gets older she will begin to enjoy play activities such as building a project together with someone or playing hide-and-seek or tag.

Behaviors to Be Learned: There is more to teaching behavior than just teaching your child how to be good and how to become self-disciplined. Following is a list of behaviors that must be taught.

Hygiene and Grooming: Babies are not able to wash themselves, and they don't have teeth to brush or much hair to comb. However, as they begin to mature, proper hygiene skills should be taught. Children who grow older without being put in charge of these tasks may never adequately acquire these hygiene habits. As you begin to release control of grooming tasks, supervision and monitoring should continue, but should become less and less necessary. By the end of this early period of development, your child should be well on her way to the habitual practice of washing, bathing, hair brushing, and tooth brushing. By the age of six, she should be able to dress herself and know what clothing is appropriate for different occasions and what isn't. Modesty in dressing should be a part of her lessons.

Courtesy and Manners: Like many things, television can have a good side and a bad side. It can teach healthy lessons as well as unhealthy ones. An example of how it can help to reinforce the importance of good manners:

India, then six years of age, and I were spending the day together at my house. When she spotted a Barney doll and picked it up, I asked her if she liked Barney. She replied, "Yes," and told me that Barney wasn't on TV anymore. I checked this out and found that the purple dinosaur was actually a regular on the Sprout channel (a channel I recommend for children aged six and under). The short episode we watched together began with one of the smaller dinosaurs complaining to her friends that she had not been allowed to cross the

bridge that she needed to cross to get to an important appointment.
When none of her friends could find a good answer for her, one of
them suggested that maybe if she said "please" to the bridge-tender,
she would be allowed to pass. They all chuckled but then one of them
asked Barney what he thought. Barney said that it was worth a try
and that if it worked, she might also want to say "thanks," hoping to
make her return trip easier. The dinosaur tried this technique and
it worked.

The next morning, my wife, who had not been privy to our
Barney viewing, commented that India was being very noticeably
polite. Later, when India reverted to omitting the "please," I asked
her what Barney would say and she promptly said, "please" and later
"thank you." Over the months that followed, India and I did not
forget the Barney message.

As illustrated in this vignette, programs like the long-running *Barney* (1987) have been shown to improve kindness and good manners. The Sprout Network contains many other shows that stress kindness, caring, and positive peer interaction. Although these are very good shows for younger children, the impact of their pro-social messages peaks at about age seven and then falls off rapidly, perhaps because older children find such shows "boring."

By the age of six, India was well on her way to understanding that there are no dinosaurs in this world, much less purple ones. Maybe she still retained some of her reality/fantasy way of thinking, but whether she knew or thought that Barney was real or imaginary, she had gotten and retained his message. The lesson for you is that children should be taught good manners in these early years and be expected to use them in conversation, at the table, and in other situations. This is another case where actions are most likely to become habits when they are performed early and often.

Chores: Young children can and should be taught to do chores within the limits of their abilities. At first these chores may be as simple as picking up their clothes, getting the mail from the mailbox, or taking dirty dishes to the kitchen. As she matures additional tasks should be assigned. Chores should not be things for which children are paid but instead should be used to teach them that they are part of a family in which everyone has an obligation to contribute. Once again the lesson is that the longer you wait to begin work on the important lesson of responsibility to family, the harder it will be for your child to embed it in her way of thinking.

Safety: I almost didn't include this topic because I know that most parents are aware of and do guard against the environmental risks that their children face. They know that infants have no way of knowing that stoves can burn; electrical appliances can shock; cars can run over you; lakes can be deep; and that falling down steps can break bones. It's your job to teach these things and to provide protection until such time as your child learns the importance of safety and practices it. It should go without saying that age-appropriate car restraints are a must. Later we will talk about teenagers and their somewhat natural, but still unsafe, risk-taking behavior.

Chapter Summary: *In this period of very rapid brain growth, your child will be a learning machine and it will be your job to provide input to that machine. In her next stage of development, the early school years, she will be receiving input from a lot of sources and your efforts to reach her and affect her personality, skills, and habits will become increasingly more difficult and competitive. Use this time well because your opportunity will never again be the same.*

16

Chapter Sixteen

The Early Years III: Potential Problems

Chapter Goals: *To address some of the problems of parenting a young child.*

The Most Difficult Times: In a child's first six years, there are two times that stand out as the most difficult: the new baby phase and what has been called "the terrible twos." No matter what approach you take to these problems, they will pass, but with time and skilled attention, they can both later be seen as understandable components of a child's normal development.

Adjustments: Pregnancy will change the lives of both parents, but those changes are usually small compared to the ones that follow the birth of a baby, especially a first one. Feeding, changing, bathing, and cuddling all take time and effort. Fatigue can be severe, especially for the mother who has had an especially difficult labor. If your baby is one whose nature makes him loud, very active, and poor at self-regulation, things may be even more difficult. For first-time mothers, especially those who do not have their parents or grandparents handy, inexperience can add to maternal frustration. Mothers who were ecstatic at birth will often have periods when they are less than happy with their new occupation and with their new baby. A co-parenting father who chips in and helps with the work, tells the mother he loves her, or compliments her on the job she is doing, can not only help the mother, he can also do much to encourage marital harmony.

Separation: Although Juliet told Romeo that "parting is such sweet sorrow," there is nothing sweet about some separations for some people. Two examples that we will mention here are the sleep problems related to moving an infant to his own room, and problems such as dropping a child at a daycare facility. Other important separations are when your child leaves his home on the way to an adult life and when a person loved by someone dies.

Sleeping: The sleep problems that are most common in the early years are those of establishing regularity and the ability of the child to separate from his parents at bedtime. Unfortunately for some parents, their babies are born with traits of temperament that make the establishment of a good sleep routine more difficult. This would include traits such as having a high activity level; decreased ability to develop regularity; and high intensity of response. Children with the pains of colic or illness will also present a real challenge in trying to establish a healthy sleep routine, but fortunately colic does not last for more than a few months. Even after year one, 50% of infants may still have some sleep issues requiring parental intervention.

After the age of three to four months, less soothing is usually needed as the infant gains the ability to self-regulate and can learn to fall asleep without parental support. If parents continue to soothe, the child comes to expect it. When this happens, vigorous protest may occur when exhausted parents try to quit. You may try the "checking" strategy: put your child to bed after soothing, say goodnight, and leave the room. If he continues to scream or cry, check in at short regular intervals, say every five minutes, offering soothing and reassurance in words but not using any other soothing techniques. If the child continues crying, continue to check in until he is asleep. The purpose is to help him develop his own soothing strategies. By the fourth or fifth night of this approach most infants will show significant improvement. This method of helping your baby sleep alone will not work as well if soothing was not used early on. The theory is that in the early days, the infant lacks self-regulation and the parent compensates. The management of helping a child to separate from you at daycare or school, described later in this chapter, is very similar.

Parents may often disagree on how soon a baby should be moved to his own room. The reasons for not moving him can include maternal exhaustion from labor, the time spent in baby-tending chores, and not wanting to have to go far to feed her hungry baby, especially if he has an erratic feeding schedule. In infants of all ages, there is a natural tendency for parents to go to a baby's room to check on whether he is still okay. For this latter issue, having a monitor in his room can help.

Other Necessary Separations: Variants of the infant sleep separation issue are related to a natural fear of a child who is being separated from his parents. When you do need to drop him off in daycare, or Sunday school, or with a relative, it is best that you be aware that any separation can cause feelings of abandonment. For some children this is a minor issue; for others, it is more than that. When you do return after a short while, he should begin to learn the difference between abandonment and limited, non-permanent separation. If you see much anxiety, leave him only for a very short period of time and show him that you do return. Depending on how well he does, you may begin to extend the time period that you are away. Repeatedly popping in to reassure the child that you are still around is much like the technique of repetition discussed later in the book for dealing with childhood fears and anxiety.

The normal nighttime sleeping activities of parents and their infant may keep all parties awake. This is a good reason to work for an early departure of the baby to his own room. A compromise that can sometimes satisfy the problem of the exhausted mother's need for close proximity to her nursing baby can be for the mother to express her milk during the day and have the father feed him in his crib room at night. Infants establish habits early, and the longer parents wait before moving the child to his own room, the harder it can be. At all ages, it is important to have quiet time before bed; the establishment of bedtime routine; and the setting up of a non-stimulating bedroom. A good routine might include feeding, reading, rocking, singing, and perhaps having soft background music in the room.

The problem of separation will be discussed in later chapters on the importance of a child separating from his parents and moving on to an independent adult life. Many of the issues that are addressed here must be readdressed at that later stage.

The *"Terrible Twos"*: The child, now walking and talking, is increasingly feeling ready for the world and ready to get what he wants when he wants it. Part of the reason for this behavior is that he has not yet learned how to be patient, how to share, and how to communicate very well. Sometimes this difficult period begins even earlier than the age of two; but whenever it comes, it is not a fun time for anyone. Fits of frustration and anger should be dealt with by parents whose anger does not match the level of their child's. When there is a temper tantrum, one approach is to walk away and later, when everyone has cooled down, to address the issue. Your principal weapons here should be putting to use your understanding of a couple of the factors that lead your child to a tantrum state. If you understand the reasons for a two-year-old child's behavior, your patience should improve. Realize that age two, like all the others, is a time when lessons are to be taught. Realize also that your child is now halfway to my favorite age, the "trusting fours."

The first step in dealing with the issue is to accept the fact that your child's inborn drive to survive will lead him to want what he thinks he needs when he wants it. Sharing and patience are not built-in skills. Step two is to understand that at two years of age a child is not yet fluent enough to express his thoughts and feelings in a cogent fashion. Remind yourself that he is only two.

Hone your communication skills and learn to use them in age-appropriate ways. Two techniques might help. First is a language called Parentese that I learned as a father and as a pediatrician. As I became aware that children tend to back away from men who approach them rapidly and who speak in their natural deep and somewhat loud voices, I began to speak this new language that is much like the language that women normally speak. Parentese is a slow, lowered volume, high-pitched, singsong, stretched vowel language that is less frightening and better understood by infants and toddlers. Even more useful is the use of empathy, the ability to understand another person's feelings. Empathy, described in an earlier chapter, is an important skill at any time but it is especially helpful in the early years before good language and communication (speaking and listening) skills have been acquired. An empathetic response to a tantrum requires the ability to read faces and body language. When your little boy is angry, an empathetic response that works surprisingly well begins with reading his facial expression and body language. In most cases of "terrible two" behavior, that is easy to do. The second step is to say something in patient Parentese, such as, "It looks like you're very angry," followed by something like, "I bet you're angry because you wanted the cookie I wouldn't let you have." This response will often stop a tantrum in its tracks. If your child's negative behavior and affect have been improved by your comments, you might continue with something along the lines of, "Cookies are really good, aren't they," looking for him to respond. When he does, it wouldn't hurt to cuddle him briefly and then tell him why you didn't give him the cookie and that you will give him one later for his snack (if that is your intention).

Troublesome Behaviors: Many of the problems of adolescence and beyond have their beginnings in these early years.

Sadness, fears, shyness, excessive hyperactivity, and excessive aggressive behavior may be normal at this age or they may be signs of future trouble. All are serious and should be discussed with your pediatrician, who may refer you to specialists in these areas for evaluation and management. Sadness, when unrelated to obvious causes such as grief, may be an early sign of depression. Fears, if excessive, may be signs of anxiety and phobia. Hyperactivity may signify attention deficit hyperactivity disorder (ADHD), a cause of school and learning problems. Aggression may warn of future violent and bullying behaviors. In the case of an aggressive child, you should be especially careful about what electronic games he plays and what other media activities he is exposed to.

Fears are not unusual at this age, especially with the child who has not yet learned to separate fact from fantasy. They should not be mocked or trivialized. They should be dealt with patiently and with explanations that situations that are making the child fearful are not in most cases dangerous situations. In some cases these fears may signal the later onset of clinical anxiety, a condition that is best dealt with early rather than later. Often the fears are related to the unknown or unfamiliar. Repeatedly exposing the child to places or situations that are not dangerous can help the child to overcome his fears.

The Issue of Lying: How should we deal with the fact that almost all six-year-old children will lie, sometimes hourly. As your child gets older, the lying will probably become less frequent, but this must be balanced against the fact that they will get better at it with practice and experience. By the time a child is in the eight-to-eleven-year range, most parents have only a 25% chance of knowing when their child is lying. Lying is a survival skill, a way to deflect punishment or disapproval. Thus, lying should not surprise you. One of the problems with the establishment of lying rules is that we, as adults, have a way of separating various forms of lying, ways that may not be available to or understandable to your young child. Adults often tell what they call "white lies" to protect the listener from what they really think. Another form of lying, one that is especially popular with teenagers, is lying to avoid the serious (to them) crime of ratting or snitching on someone, knowing that there can be serious peer consequences from telling the truth. Because children in these early years are not able to distinguish fact from fantasy, they may find it hard to tell the differences among these three types of lying, and not fully get your message that it is wrong to lie when you so obviously use white lies. An example of a white lie:

We have a Chihuly-like light in our living room that is hard for people to ignore. Comments we get on it range from "It's beautiful" (possibly a lie) to "That's different" (I don't approve of white lies but I don't want to come right out and hurt your feelings) and "It's not my cup of tea" (a gentle way of telling the truth, as they see it.)

There are a number of ways in which you may deal with your child's untruthfulness. You will usually have no trouble detecting a lie by a young child who is trying to avoid getting into trouble. Without calling the child a liar, your correct response might be to tell him that telling the truth is important to you. Later on you may take the approach that we all make mistakes but it is not OK to lie about them.

Cheating may be considered another form of lying and should be managed in much the same way.

Violence: Violence prevention and the management of any family bullying begin early. The first step is to follow the no TV before the age of three rule because during these early years, your child cannot separate factual violence from fictional violence. Seeing a rabbit solve his problem by throwing a wolf off a cliff is not a lesson that I want my child to learn, especially if he believes it is really happening. In this regard, before you spank your child consider the message you are sending him on problem-solving. Before you decide to buy him any electronic games, be sure that they are not ones that portray violence in any form. The CommonSenseMedia.org website is an excellent place to check out any games you may be thinking about buying.

Related to violence is the issue of safety. Wearing seatbelts is a must. At one time parents used to tell their children not to talk with strangers nor accept rides from them. Now concerns run deeper regarding child protection, and it is important that your child be in the company of a responsible adult at all times. This includes knowing the rules that will be observed at the house of any sleepover to which your child is invited. Is there a trampoline, swimming pool, or hot tub that might be tempting and potentially dangerous? In short, you cannot be too careful.

Impatience: Infants often have difficulty when they are forced to wait for something they want ("I want a cookie") or when you take too much time doing something that they are not fond of, such as standing in a long grocery line. Although his impatience may be understandable, it must be dealt with. One way to do that is to have him wait relatively short times for things and compliment him for any patience that he does show. Then slowly increase the waiting times. Sometimes, the best solution may be to leave him at home when you know the lines will be long. However he, like you, must learn eventually to deal patiently with long lines and traffic tie-ups.

Selfishness: Your young child will often be focused on himself and on his needs to the exclusion of most other people and things. It will be your job to teach him that other people have value and have rights that he must learn to respect. A

129

child may naturally want to have everything that looks attractive, even if it belongs to someone else. He must be taught that, even though his desire is quite natural, it must be controlled. Teaching him to respect the rights of others will not come in one lesson, but the teaching should begin even at this early age.

Chapter Summary: *In this chapter we talked about problem areas that you should accept as normal for this age. Knowing who your child is will help you deal with the problems that will face you and your child, such as sleep problems, the terrible twos, lying, violence, and impatience.*

17

The Latent Period I: Looking Back

Chapter Goals: *To stress the importance of this seemingly silent period of development. This chapter will deal with the importance of continuing the lessons that began in the early years: lessons that have been learned, lessons that should have been learned, and lessons that need continued teaching.*

The Latent Years: These years are called the latent period because unlike the periods preceding and following it, not much seems to be happening. Actually, much is happening. Like all of the four age periods we deal with in this section on nurturing, this period is one of transition and a lot is going on. By the time your child enters school and its more formal learning atmosphere, she should already have learned and accomplished a lot.

What Has Been Learned or Should Have Been Learned? You and your child now know each other, and in this period that bonding attachment should be strengthened. Your little baby has learned to walk and talk and has become toilet trained. With fewer reminders from you, she should be caring for her own hygienic and grooming needs and practicing the courtesy and good manners that have been taught. Although much should have been accomplished in her earlier years, lessons that were started then may still need to be reinforced and monitored until such time as they become habit. If she does not have good manners and good grammar by the end of this period, it is less likely that she ever will. Having learned good manners does not mean that she will always use them, but you will still be there to remind her when she slips. Your child's inability to separate fact from fantasy should have been fading away, and by age six should be almost gone. There are still likely to be instances, however, in which she misses the point, and until she is twelve, when you see an ad or program segment that is potentially harmful, it might be wise to pause the TV and ask her about what she has just seen and what she believes to be true.

Lessons in Process:

Communication: Communication, a skill whose teaching began in the earlier years, must be approached in this period at a much different level. The ability to be empathetic and patient is still important, but now that your child can talk effectively, the emphasis here will change. As her communication skills grow, have discussions with her in which you both share your thoughts and opinions. To be an effective parent you must have good lines of communication with your co-parent, with your child, with her school, and with the parents of her friends. You should know in what areas she needs help or encouragement and in what areas she is to be commended for her efforts.

"You can observe a lot just by watching."

—Yogi Berra

You can't learn with your mouth open. Learning involves a lot of listening and the ability to interpret visual clues such as smiles, frowns, or shrugs. For this latter reason, face-to-face communication is clearly the best. Communication by phone is not as good because you can't empathetically read the face and body language of the person with whom you are talking. If you can't observe facial expressions and body language, you may miss some distress signs. Being able to see such signs, you will be better able to say something or do something immediately to prevent any misunderstanding of what you are trying to say. When long distances separate you from the person with whom you are communicating, electronic viewing with software programs such as Skype can be a satisfactory compromise. Poorer still, in terms of ability to know how your comments are being received, in probable descending order of their potential for miscommunication, are "snail mail," email,

132

texting, and social media. In all of these latter communication modes, you not only have lost the visualization of face and body language but now you have cut off any important clues that may have been heard in voice tones. The potential for hurting feelings or having the other person completely miss your point is increased without face-to-face and voice-to-voice communication.

My office right hand, Jane, who typed all of the letters I composed, would delay sending those she thought I might want to rethink. For instance, if I wrote in anger or my letter might suggest that I was angry, she would hold it for a day. Often when I cooled down I would be sorry about the tone of what I had written and wish that I had not sent it. Jane, anticipating this, would tell me that she had not yet sent the letter. The final choice was mine, but she was smart enough to protect me when she thought I might at a later time think better of what I was about to send.

Emails, on the other hand, go out quickly and cannot be retracted. Even though communication occurs all the time, it is important that you set aside periods to have conversations with your spouse and with your child. Dinners, especially family dinners, are great times for serious communication, banter, and socializing. As your child gets older, it becomes very important to include her as an active participant in all dinner-table conversations. At first she may be reluctant to enter in. When you ask her questions that involve no more than "How did you do in school today?" or "Did your team win?" all she has to do to respond is to say little more than just "OK" or "Not OK." This is not the best way to invite her to join adult type conversations. Ask her instead "how and why" type questions that require her to think a bit and in the process learn how to express her thoughts to others. Ask her such things as how does she feel about something, did she or any of her friends do anything to help someone at school, or did she witness any generous acts or any bullying? Then wait for her to answer, listen carefully to what she says, and comment, preferably not negatively or judgmentally, if possible.

Communication opportunities will arise if you look for them in a variety of other ways, such as when you are driving, walking, biking, shopping, playing, or working together. Use these times to learn more about your child and how she thinks. Always make it clear that you love her, and as often as possible that you respect her and why. Use these together times to make your points regarding subjects of character development.

Learning: Maximization of your child's potential requires education.

Education means more than just formal schooling. Your child's brain, which reached 75% of its adult size when she was two, is now 95% fully grown. It will not be fully at adult size and capacity until somewhere in her twenties. This learning machine is still absorbing, processing, and storing information at a great rate, but not as rapidly as it once was. Much of what was previously absorbed and stored is being strengthened by repeated exposure. Many of the synapses that she had in the newborn period that have not yet been used or have been used only infrequently are being discarded. Although we all have an innate IQ when we are born, repeated stimulation will make us smarter. Your child needs to take advantage of this learning period and be encouraged to engage in intelligent conversation, reading, study, drawing, and/or playing music. Even good TV time cannot be considered equivalent learning time, because most of what we learn while watching is passive learning.

Time Management: The goal is to eventually have your child take over responsibility for her own sleep preparations, bedtimes, and getting up times. Adjustments can be made depending on how well she is able to follow the sleep rules you have set. These rules should address preparations for bed (e.g., cleaning and tooth brushing) and also allowing adequate time for reading, prayers, and perhaps singing. As your child matures, you may provide her with an alarm clock and make her the one responsible for seeing that she gets to breakfast on time. In the earlier years, scheduling of your child's time was less important than it now becomes because of the significant amount of time that must be spent in school and school-related activities. This extra time requirement on school days must not come at the expense of time for sleep, eating, conversation, exercise, and play, etc. Weekends might be a better place to put her media time, but remember that no more than one to two hours daily or seven to fourteen hours weekly are recommended.

Exercise and Play: An hour of exercise is recommended each day; this can come in many forms, but aerobic activity should be its major component. The hour need not take place all at the same time, and can include play activities such as tag, soccer, and T-ball. Play is important at all ages but, as said earlier, what we play and with whom we play will change as we age. Other play activities that are not exercise can be helpful developmentally. Games such as chess and checkers can be intellectually stimulating. All competitive games can be good for learning how to win and how to lose. We should learn not to gloat when we win—often a lesson best learned from someone who gloats when she beats you. Perhaps losing is more important than winning as a preparation for life. After a loss, try to have your child explain why she lost, what she might have done differently, and how she can do better next time. The importance of practice should be stressed and the role of chance in winning and losing should be explained.

Character Development: Continue with your efforts in this department by stressing caring, sharing, and concern for others. Your child may be old enough now to discuss current news items that raise moral issues. Teach about moral and ethical values and, if you believe as I do, the importance of having a good relationship with God.

The Road to Happiness: Happiness is best achieved when a person is doing well with their character development, when they are physically fit and healthy, and when they are achieving success in school, sports, music, or other activities they enjoy. A child should be happy when she is secure in knowing that she is loved by her parents and by her peers. Self-respect and self-esteem are good building blocks of happiness. In the chapter on happiness we described three types of happiness: happiness that can be described as an emotional state of joy; happiness that comes from being engrossed in an activity that one loves; and happiness that comes from living a meaningful life. You should talk through each of these definitions and let your child know that all are OK if done while remembering morals and ethics. Happiness that comes from leading a meaningful life is the most rewarding, with the engaged life a close second. The first type lasts the least amount of time and produces less long-lasting satisfaction than the other two.

Role Modeling: What you do, how you do it, how you talk, how you dress and care for yourself are all noticed—each is an important form of sending messages. Your child will also notice what you don't do and the times when you are not available, especially when she wants you to be. I have known more than a few children who have strongly objected to parenting techniques to which I too might have objected, who then grew up to be parents who used these same objectionable techniques. Always remember that you are teaching your child how to parent by the way you and your spouse parent. Children learn from what they observe in your behavior in addition to what you think you are teaching.

Chapter Summary: *The term "latent years" was defined, and we looked at lessons that should have been completed in the early years, plus some that are still in process, begun in the early years but requiring further teaching in these years.*

18

Chapter Eighteen

The Latent Period II: The "Tween Years"

Chapter Goals: *To address formal school entry and lessons that are new to this period, and to introduce and prepare for issues such as puberty and separation that may be emerging and will take on increasing significance in adolescence.*

School: This is the period when full-time schooling begins and in reality becomes the principal occupation of your young child. Your job is to support and encourage his schooling and his school. Become involved. Help him with his homework, but not to the extent that you do it for him. Monitor the time and content of what he is doing, or not doing. Much more on schooling will be discussed in the chapters on education.

Your Child's Other "Parents": The Media and His Peers:

Media Literacy: During this period, your child's media involvement and interests will most likely change and be broadened to include the use of computers, electronic games, and telephones. You will still need to set time allowances and content restrictions on what he watches, paying particular attention to what is being portrayed and advertised. Do monitor and restrict media content. Use your media literacy to teach him how to become media literate himself and how to watch and critically interpret what he sees, hears, and reads while engaged with the media.

Peers: In the preschool period, you, your family, and your home environment were your child's principal nurturers. During these years his world will expand to include significant nurturing relationships within the school and neighborhood. Although these external influences may not be as powerful as they will be in the teen years, they will be present and will continue to grow. Get to know the parents of his friends. Before you let him spend time in a friend's house, you will want to feel comfortable about the house rules and the parental stance on monitoring behavior and reporting bad behavior back to you.

Setting a Life Plan: If you have not already begun, now is the time to begin talking with your child about his life goals. He should already know that you want him to grow up to be a good person. Tell him that at each stage of his life. You both should be looking at careers and avocations which might be a good fit with who he is. Let him know that eventually the choice of vocation will be his but that you will continue to be with him as a guide and monitor. As the subject of career choice becomes more focused in the teenage years, you will increasingly look at the possible routes to vocational goals that are on his most likely list. In this process, think about what he must learn to achieve them and what that learning will cost.

Although inborn traits and talents may have been noticed by you earlier in your child's life, at this age they should be becoming more apparent, if you are paying attention. In thinking about his future, consider these talents and also the areas where he has little or no talent. Also factor in his likes and dislikes. When you note a talent that is truly special, consider whether it is worth emphasizing. By stressing only one talent, however, remember that he might be missing out on discovering others which he may be even better at and like more. On the other hand, trying to involve your child in too many activities, a frequent parental mistake, is not a great idea either. Helping your child to excel in anything can be a great way to have him become generally more self-confident. Any self-confidence that he gains in one area can be applied to other areas; the confident child is more likely to try things that others might tend to avoid.

Whether you are choosing an activity or your child is making the choice, ground rules should be established before he begins. For example, decide how much

138

time to put aside for practice and how to deal with the possibility that either of you, for whatever reason, wants to cancel the activity. When your son has you sign him up for an activity that he finds he neither likes nor is very good at, what will you do? You don't want him to be a quitter and you don't want him to stop before he has given the activity a chance. You also need to realize that some activities may be contributing nothing to his fitness or education. A compromise might be having a rule, made before the activity starts, that specifies the amount of time that must pass before any quitting is allowed.

A Halftime Review: At the end of the latent period, your child will have moved halfway through the years that he will spend with you before he becomes fully adult. Much like a football coach at halftime, you should look at the half that has just concluded and make plans to do even better in the second half. Much remains to be done and time passes more quickly than most of us believe it will.

Preparing for the Future:

Avoiding Potential Moral and Health Problems: Violence and sexual impropriety are two currently all too common adolescent behaviors. Although both subjects are covered in later chapters, prevention should be addressed in this age group as well. Tell your child that his brain will not become fully adult until he is in his twenties. Talk with him about the dangers of tobacco, alcohol, and drugs. Stress the need to resist the usual adolescent inclination to take risks in very dangerous areas, a tendency that is especially common in boys.

Violence Prevention Education: Violence prevention steps include careful parental monitoring of all media messages, whether they are from TV, the Internet, radio, or electronic games, in all of which violence is common. If you are watching football with your child, comment on any excessive violence you see and point out that studies indicate that such violence may not be as harmless as it seems. Continue to monitor any electronic games he plays and any shows that he watches or listens to.

Too often violence is seen as being a reasonable solution to problems that could be more effectively dealt with in safer ways. Talk about bullying, what is wrong with it and why. Ask him how he would feel if he were the child being bullied. Emphasize that bullying comes in a variety of forms and is always bad.

Sex Education: In the late years of the latent period, your child may become increasingly aware that something very different is happening to his body. If you have not yet begun your course on sex education, you should start now. As uncomfortable as you may feel about addressing the subject material involved, the facts and your interpretation of their moral implications need to be learned. Teach him about body maturation and stress that there is more to maturity than having an adult-looking body. Talk about how babies are born.

Although the issue of modesty is more important, or should I say more revealing, in girls, boys also should be briefed on the subject. If an inappropriate sexual scene appears on a TV show, chide yourself for not prescreening that show but take the opportunity to comment on what has been seen. Tell him that there are people who watch nude people on the Internet and tell him why you do not want him to do so. When sex scandals, such as the Penn State coaching disgrace, are in the news, use the time as a convenient way to comment on the subject. If you don't comment about something everybody is talking about, it is almost certain that as he gets further along in this age period, he will hear the story elsewhere, perhaps with a different twist than the one you would give it.

Life Skills and Money Management: Learning how to manage money is one of the life skills that your child will need to learn. What he learns in this period and the teenage years should, if well learned, prepare him to use money wisely and to know the importance of budgeting, saving, investing, and the avoidance of debt.

Chores: Chores that were appropriate for your younger child should be adjusted as he ages and becomes more capable, commensurate with his time and his abilities. Chores might include cleaning bathrooms and other rooms around the house, work that will relieve someone else who also has a busy schedule. He should be taught that these jobs are his way of contributing to the family and, in a sense, learning to pay for his room and board. Spell out when each chore is to be performed and inspect the job to make sure it is done to your satisfaction. Set rules for rewards and for the consequences of failure. The only excuses for not doing his chores might be illness, a tough exam schedule, his birthday, or other special occasions. Be careful that no job interferes with his sleep, study, and other necessary pursuits.

Doing chores with your child can serve two purposes: seeing the chore is done and spending time together. As an example, while he is doing his kitchen chores, you can be teaching him how to cook while at the same time bonding with him. Working together in the yard is another example of a multipurpose chore: your child will be learning how to do yard work and also bonding with the parent who is working with him.

Allowances: Chores are jobs without pay. Allowances are pay without jobs. Allowances are given in love and to help teach the lessons of money management. They are not paid for the performance of required chores but may be withheld if the chores are not done. Too many of today's youth go off to college with no idea of how to save, balance a checkbook, deal with credit card payments, or refrain from borrowing at high interest rates. Later allowances may be used to begin teaching about the subject of investing. The age at which you start giving allowances is up to you, but it is my belief that, by age six, children should be getting one. A commonly used way to decide on how much to give is to set an age-adjusted weekly amount, say twenty-five cents times their age in years. When giving an allowance or gifting, be aware that many of today's children who have been given so much and have lived in unearned luxury may have difficulty in the "real world," where they will have to work for what they get. It is not so much the amount as the opportunity an allowance gives a child to learn how to handle money. Let him know what his allowance should cover and what it need not cover, emphasizing that he should not expect you to be buying things that he is to cover on his own. If ice cream is not included among those things that you will buy, remind him when he spots an ice cream store and wants a cone that he has money. What he wants to do with the money, if it is within reason, should be up to him. Exceptions can be made for special occasions on which you will treat him. Encourage him to save so that when the time comes for bigger wants he will be prepared, but the experience of being unprepared is also a good learning lesson.

Earned Income: When there are extra jobs that need to be done, it is acceptable to reward your child with extra money for doing them—provided, of course, that he does them well and without the need for a lot of prodding. To avoid any later argument, the pay rate for doing the extra work should be agreed upon beforehand. Good lessons can be learned in a pay-for-work model.

Gifts are appropriately given as celebrations of special days, such as birthdays, graduations, and Christmas. Over-gifting is a common mistake. Parents should not compete with other parents in their social group to see who can provide the most lavish birthday party. Often children born of these parents already have more than they need, and a better gift might be to teach them that it is better to give than to receive. An option to do this might be by contributing in your child's name to charities that support families less fortunate, and explaining to him why this is a good thing. The Heifer Project, for example, provides poor families in Africa with a cow or goat that is then used by the recipients to make much-needed money. Other charities make direct contributions for clothing and/or education. Still others give you an opportunity to "adopt" needy children around the world.

Chapter Summary: *Formal schooling will begin and become your child's principal activity, one that will require you to adjust his weekly schedule. His life skills training must continue. The influence of the media and of his peers will be growing and especially important in the areas of violence and sex. Setting of life goals increases in importance, and as signs of puberty begin to appear, preparations should begin.*

19

Adolescence I: Puberty

Chapter Goals: *We will address the hormonal surge of puberty and three related issues: growth, fearlessness, and sexual maturation. A number of the subjects covered here are addressed more fully in later chapters devoted exclusively to them, but they are included here also because of their relevance.*

Puberty, the process by which the body physically becomes adult has, over time, commenced at younger and younger ages. In girls a stimulus for earlier pubertal onset may be linked to obesity due the fact that estrogen is stored in fat. A recent study placed the age of pubertal onset in boys between the ages of nine and ten compared with an average of over eleven just ten years earlier. Among the reasons given for the earlier onset of puberty are that today's children grow up with the advantages of antibiotics, vaccines, adequate food supply (sometimes more than adequate), vitamin and mineral supplements, surer water supply, and absence of lead paint—all things that were either not present generations ago or only partially present. These same changes probably account for the fact that today's generation of children are on average taller than their parents. At the same time, the gap between the time of puberty and the time of successful marriage has widened. Full physical maturation does not occur until the early twenties. Emotional and intellectual maturation may arrive much later, if ever. How then to have your child postpone the biologic endpoint that was put there for reproduction and species survival?

The Growth Surge: With the exception of the time in utero and the early infancy years, the teen years are the most active of all the physical growth years. That growth can be divided into two categories: the healthy and expected normal body maturation growth and the unhealthy, obesity-related growth. This period of very rapid growth comes matched with periods of great hunger. Feed the hunger with adequate nutritious food but beware of overfeeding. Sugar and sugar-filled soft drinks may taste great but any satisfaction that they bring will be short-lived and will do little to slow your child's quest for hunger abatement. Teenagers tend to be restless, active, and great snackers. Understand this and place only nutritious snacks such as fruit in plain sight. Remember that there are dangers inherent in frequent trips to fast-food establishments.

Another important component of weight control is exercise. This item is often in very short supply in the schedule of teens. Physical education programs in schools have largely disappeared and, with the universality of air-conditioned homes, the idea of playing outside in the heat can be less than appealing.

Fearlessness and Risk: Adolescents, especially adolescent boys, are by nature risk-takers. For teenagers impulse control is not usually a strong asset. Much of teenage learning is based on trial and error methods—methods that do not work for highway speed, addictive substances, and inappropriate sex. The stakes are too high to tempt the possibility of serious consequences. Even when your child does know of possible serious consequences, her temperament may let her believe that the known risk does not apply to her. Too many teens don't understand what addiction really means, and led by their natural teenage curiosity, peer pressure, and/or media messages, they may be tempted to try tobacco, alcohol, and other drugs. Often, in seeking to belong, teenagers include dangerous choices as part of their normal but dangerous trial and error methods.

Unintended Injuries and Death: The good news is that in recent years the number of teenage highway fatalities has been dropping. The bad news is that motor vehicle accidents are still the leading cause of death in this age range. Deaths are most common when passengers are in the car, when it is dark, and when the driver is in the first year of being licensed to drive. Other factors are alcohol and other drug use,

144

distractions, not using seatbelts, and, of course, reckless driving of the style so well demonstrated in many exciting movie chases. Investigations have shown that 47% of those fatally killed in teenage crashes did not have a seatbelt on. The incidence of accidents caused by distracted driving, although less often fatal, is rising. In regard to the causes of distracted driving, all of which are more common in younger age groups, drivers admit that on some occasions while driving they have eaten or have imbibed (86%), placed phone calls (81%), texted (37%), read maps (36%), combed or styled their hair (20%), applied makeup (13%), or surfed the Internet (13%).

All accidents are potentially preventable. Your job from early on is to teach prevention and to monitor compliance with the rules that you set. By the age of six your child should be able to buckle her seatbelt without being told to do so, but teenagers too often "forget" this lesson. After that there should be consequences of failing to act safely, with a prearranged understanding of what those penalties will be.

Experimentation with Tobacco, Alcohol, and Other Addictive Drugs: Just a few words here on this subject, which is covered much more fully in later chapters devoted to the subject of addiction. Although called legally adult for most things at age eighteen, American teens, despite the appearance of being physically and sexually mature, are still operating with immature brains. Because of this, the way a teenager responds to these substances, which are never without risk, is more likely to lead to addiction than when they are introduced later in life. Nicotine addiction, related to the major causes of death in Americans today, most often begins in adolescence, perhaps because teens are natural risk-takers. Whatever the reason, the power of addiction to grab hold of future behavior is not anticipated or well understood. The legal drinking age is not the same as the safe drinking age, especially for boys whose brains mature later than those of the average girl. If your child is to become a responsible drinker, try to convince her to wait until at least age twenty-five, when her brain is more certain to be fully mature.

Bullying: Bullying, a serious issue at any time, is often more serious for teenagers. At this age, when teens very much want and need to be have peer friends and be a part of peer groups, being bullied can be especially painful. Cyber-bullying, a newer form of violence, has become all too common. Being bullied is never fun, but being bullied on your Facebook page, a site that is read by many of your child's peers and may become a part of her permanent record, may be the worst form. Not only do others read the page, but many of them think the attacks are funny, a phenomenon that I cannot understand and one you should discuss with your child. Your job is to prevent her from being a bully herself and to help her avoid and deal with any bullying directed at her. The better and more open your relationship is with your child, the more likely she will be to report any bullying to you, whether it is directed at her or on someone else's social network page. (For more on bullying, see the chapter Bullying and Other Violence.)

Media: Long before your child reaches her teenage years, you and she should become media literate and understand that because media types and media messages are constantly changing, your media literacy education must keep up.

Sex Education and the Sexual Urges of Puberty: When the powerful and natural hormonal changes of puberty arise, many if not most children are not well prepared for them. It is your job to not only prepare your child but to make yourself available for the questions that are almost certain to arise. Brushing them off because you are uncomfortable with the subject is a serious mistake. If questions arise at inconvenient times, tell her that her question is too important to answer at the moment but that you will sit down with her shortly to discuss it. You want your child to know that even though her other "parents"—her peers and the media—will provide her information on these subjects, you will be there as her in-house expert. If you choose to exclude yourself from this important subject, rest assured that she will receive instruction from others. Know that she will hear about the subjects of safe sex, contraception, and abortion whether you like it or not, from her peers, TV, radio, the Internet, magazines, newspapers, or in sex education classes at school. You must set behavioral rules and define the consequences that will follow different types and severity of rule violations. By the time of the earlier years of adolescence, you should have already established a sex talk relationship. Even more difficult for you may be asking her when she thinks it is OK to have sex or about what her peers are doing. As your teen matures, talks should address topics such as date rape and its relation to peer pressure, and should emphasize values and life goals; yours and hopefully hers.

Your discussions on sex will increase in complexity as your child matures. The age-old "birds and the bees" talks won't be adequate except at a very early age. It has been suggested that if you feel especially uncomfortable with the conversations you will need to have, you may try raising the most difficult issues while you are driving and don't have to make eye contact. When you want to have serious conversations with your family about almost any subject, you should enforce no cell phoning, no texting, no video watching, and no electronic game playing during the talk. Many of the problems in the area of sexual impropriety, a major issue with today's youth, might have been prevented if their parents had done a better job of educating and protecting. Not all of the information your child receives from others will be correct, nor will it all or even any of it be morally based. Only you, and perhaps your church, mosque, or temple, will reliably impart the value and moral side of sex. The goal of a loving, intimate, moral marriage may be sidetracked by so-called safe sex in adolescence. Although she will learn what safe sex is, she should learn that the best sex is morally based. The more your child knows about the subject, especially the value-related part, the more prepared she will be for the decisions she will have to make.

Dating: Even though this may not be an easy subject for you and your teenager to deal with, properly managed, dating can provide a good tool for introducing her to adult sexuality. Because this is a chapter that assumes your child is a girl, it references dating rules for girls—but boys also should have dating rules, and both boys and girls should understand the reason for these rules for themselves and others. Before she begins to date, you should let her know your views on the *Five W issues: when, who, why, where, and what.* Rather than waiting to bring up a whole set of new guidelines and rules when your child says she has been asked out on a date, the W rules should already be in place with the reasons for them understood. The first W refers to the age at which you will allow your child (girl or boy) to begin to date. Don't wait until she tells you she has a date to tell her that she is too young. It is your choice, but I would push this date back as long as I could and no sooner than the age of fifteen for double-dating, and even later for single dating. Not only are there unsafe sex issues but a study has shown that alcohol use and delinquent behavior is more likely at early dating ages. Exceptions might be for well-supervised school functions. Your decision on the dating age could come from what those in your parent peer group have decided.

The second W, who she will be dating, is important because you will be more comfortable about the date if you know who it is that she is proposing to date. Before the time comes for her first date, ask your child what kind of boy she would like to date and why. When she finishes her remarks on this important subject, you should comment and tell her how you feel about the subject and why. Then ask her how well this guy who wants to date her fits her description of a good date and why she thinks so. Let her know that character is in your opinion the most important quality that she should look for. There should be no close second. Factors in your decision-making process might include: do you know the boy; does he fit her ideal as she has expressed it to you; and who are his peers? The age difference between your daughter and the boy she wants to date should be another important part of your decision, and in no cases would I recommend that you let her date a guy who is more than two or three years older than she is. In regard to age differences, girls usually enter adolescence at an earlier age than boys, and with her sexual maturation will come ogles and date requests from boys who are older. To minimize any ogling, have your daughter dress modestly at all times. If either of the parents of the boy she wants to date is a member of your parent peer group, you should be in a much more comfortable position.

If not in your peer group, it is important for you to talk with the boy's parents and size them up on the dating questions you have. If you are unable to gain comfort after conversation, beware. Depending on how well you know the date and how you feel about him, your response may go all the way from yes to no, with in-between possibilities related to single dating vs. double dating; where the date will be; how long the date will be; and will an adult be with them. As with all of these dating issues, it is always best for you and your co-partner to discuss them ahead of time and agree on how you will respond to her requests to date.

The third W why refers to the fact that, understandably, you should ask her to tell you why she thinks she needs to go on this date. Is it for a prom or other school function, or something else? The fourth W question is about where the date will be. If the date is planned to be at a parent's house, you will need to know if a parent is going to be home and if the parent has a set of rules that you agree with and that are routinely enforced. Will there be any drinking allowed? If not, how will the adult in charge be sure that no drinking occurs and that no one who has been drinking attends? If it's not at a home you approve of but instead is for a movie or something else, you will have to talk with your daughter about your concern that she might be tempted to go somewhere more dangerous, knowing that it will be hard for you to monitor where she is. Some parents use tracking devices for the purpose of monitoring their child's whereabouts, but such devices are not fail-safes. Even so, if your child believes that the device is doing its job well, it can be used as a prevention tool. Not only will she be more careful about where she goes but she can tell her date why she dare not go. In deciding on whether to say yes or no to her request, follow your gut reaction and how you feel about the fifth W factor: what does your gut tell you after having put the first four W factors together? If you will feel comfortable that she believes that teenage sex is verboten, as are all traps that can lead to forced sex, you can be more trusting. If she has been a girl who has obeyed the rules and talks and acts like she understands them, you can be more trusting. And finally, it is important to remember that dating rules should also apply to boys.

Exceptions to Your Dating Rules: There will probably be times when your dating rules can be broken. Sometimes rule-breaking can be allowed for special situations such as the school prom. When your daughter asks to have her curfew time extended for one hour on the prom night, it is certainly OK to grant her request on a one-time basis providing that her recent behavior has been satisfactory and there has been no previous serious violation of the rule she now wants waived. When rules are otherwise broken, you may tell her that you are upset by her lateness, but take time to let any anger you feel subside before you have your serious discussion of the issue with her. How late is too late? Is it five minutes or thirty minutes? She should already know what her punishment will be because that decision was made and shared with her before her departure and, preferably, was a part of a much earlier agreed-upon plan for rules and rule-breaking. For breaking the lateness rule, you might decide to tell her that on her next approved date, you will expect her to be home one hour earlier.

Don't wait until you suspect trouble or know that you have problems to set and explain the Five W dating rules. It is best to let your child know ahead of time what your policy is and what your reasons for it are.

Chapter Summary: *You must, for the sake of your child, be much more involved in her life than is typical of most of today's parents. It will take a lot of thought, time, and effort to get your job done, but in the end, it will be well worth it. Learn who your child is and use this knowledge to direct the route of your parenting. Pay special attention to the importance of peer acceptance to your child and of the role that the media can play in her life. If you haven't already done it, form or join a parent peer group. Prepare her for future decisions she must make. Finally and perhaps most importantly, let her know that you love her and value her.*

20

Adolescence II: The Teenage Tunnel Years

Chapter Goals: *In this chapter, my aim is to help you understand the tunnel years and to help you prepare and successfully guide your child through the process of separating from you and becoming a focused, character-driven adult. In my optometrist's office, I saw a poster that summed up what many believe to be the feelings of many teenagers.*

TEENAGERS
Tired of Being Hassled By Your Stupid Parents?
ACT Now
Move Out
Get a Job
Pay Your Own Bills
While You Still Know
EVERYTHING

Separation and the Tunnel Years: The term "tunnel years" is used to describe the all too common phenomenon in which adolescent children seem to live in a different world than that of their parents. For parents, it is often very distressing that their teenage child seems to be separating from them. Indeed, this is what he is doing and whether you like it or not, it is what he should be doing. Too often teenagers seem to be more interested in being a part of their teen culture and following its drumbeat than being with their parents in the relationship that you have previously loved. They speak a different language, and each generation seems to adopt a different style of music and dress. In this tunnel period, too many parents feel left out of their child's lives and don't know what to do other than perhaps wait patiently and hope that in time he will emerge from the tunnel as a fully grown, responsible adult.

Parental approaches to the inevitable separation issue fall into three groups: under-protection, overprotection, and sensible protection. In today's society, the style that seems the most common and the one that, in my view, is a major contributor to the problems this book addresses, is early release, under-protective parenting. These parents will justify their position by saying something to the effect that children need to make their own decisions and that their parents' job is to let them do so—"accept the fact that they are in a tunnel and leave them alone until they emerge." A second group, the overprotective parents, discussed at more length in the next chapter, do guide their child through his teens but do not fully prepare him for the separation process. What I call the sensibly protective parents are the ones who realize the strength of their child's love for them and his need for them. These parents will continue to guide him through these potentially stormy and life-changing years with firmness and support, releasing him slowly based on his demonstrated ability to make proper decisions.

All animals learn early that they must grow up and eventually care for themselves, as birds must learn to jump from their nests. Your child knows, perhaps biologically, that he must eventually grow up and take care of himself, but he also should know that you, his parents, love him and want to help him. Despite what he may seem to imply by his behavior and his argumentative style, he wants you and needs your wise and respected counsel. He does not want to be treated as if he is in a tunnel even though, on the surface, it may seem that the wisdom of his peers and media seem to be much more valued than does the wisdom of his "out-of-date" and "alien" parents. Remember that on shows aimed at teenagers, the media often portray parents as out of touch. Children who have been raised lovingly and well will greatly value their parents' opinions. In these tunnel years, try to understand the importance of your child's need to separate and become an independent adult. Understand your child's dilemma: he wants and needs his peers but he also wants and needs his parents.

Arguments: Arguments with your child are not fun, but accept the reality that for many teenagers they are a preferred method of learning and for settling disagreements. Failure to understand this and to respond appropriately may drive your child further into the teenage tunnel and diminish your ability to influence him. Many adolescents, according to their parents, seem to be a cross between skilled courtroom attorneys and world-class debaters. Teenagers, for reasons not entirely clear to me, seem to prefer arguments, perhaps because they like excitement. Perhaps this is because his peers all argue, and to be involved with them he must adopt their style. The natural tendency of adults, when confronted by an arguing teen, is to tell him to calm down and make his point in a quieter fashion. It is OK to tell him that disagreements can be quietly talked through and brought to mutually acceptable conclusions, but you should be aware that your overly vigorous suggestions that he calm down may cause him to pull away, consult with others instead, and make key decisions on his own. Parents are advised to accept the reality of teenage arguing and learn how to listen patiently and respond quietly in the discussion style and tone you wish your child would use.

Rule one is to listen carefully to what your child is saying and take time to consider the point(s) he is trying to make. It has been said that "the secret to communicating is listening." When he is finished with his rant, try to restate his conclusions in civil fashion and ask him if you have gotten his point. This will let him know that you are interested in what he has to say. When his comments are reasonable, tell him so, but depending on what his conclusions are you may also tell him that even though what he says is reasonable the conclusions you have reached are different. Tell him what your opinion is and give him your reasons for it.

Rule number two is that you consider the points that he has made and ask yourself if some form of compromise is possible, knowing that with compromise there can be learning and increased trust. Unfortunately, such careful handling of arguments will often result in more of them, but you may hope that they will eventually be at a lower volume. View any increase in the number of arguments as a good sign, a sign that your child is willing to discuss topics with you that he may previously not have known how to address. And reassure yourself that eventually he will emerge from the teenage tunnel. In your use of a calm discussion style rather than a heated argumentative style, you will be teaching him how adults are supposed to communicate without angering him by telling him so.

Anger: Anger is different than argument. Loud shouting can be part of normal teen response, but when there is a hint of anger, it is time for you to say "cool it" and then continue the argument or discussion when things cool down. Anger that is excessive, depression, and especially suicidal thoughts can be signs of more serious problems—problems that require professional evaluation.

Preparing for the Future: Help your child set goals for his future and help him acquire the tools that he will need to achieve them.

"Man is a goal-seeking animal. His life has meaning only if he is reaching out and striving for his goals."

—Aristotle

When I talk with teenagers, I address their future goals and planning with the following question and most commonly receive some variation of the following:

I ask, "What do you want to do after you finish high school?" By far the most frequent response is surprise by the teenager at the question, followed by something like, "I guess I want to go to college." I then ask, "Why do you want to go college?" The teen most often replies with some variation of "Because my parents want me to."

From this response I have learned that his parents have not spent much time helping him prepare for his future. They apparently are from the school of thought that says you should let your child make all his own important decisions, if and when he decides to make them, with no guidance from you.

Children often search for goals but, not knowing exactly how to begin, are vague in their thinking about what comes next. The whole business of life after school is an important topic that you should be discussing regularly. However, when you do this you must be careful not to force your career goals upon your child. The answers that I have liked best in the many times I have asked the first part of this question were quickly given, suggesting that for these children, this subject was not a new one. Responses such as "I want to be a veterinarian" I grade highly, not only because it shows that some thought has already been given to the subject but because it also implies a sense of caring. Let me say that this sort of answer almost always comes from girls. Why, I do not know. I do know that getting into veterinary school may be tougher than getting into medical school, but the fact that this teenager already has a direction picked will put her well ahead of her peers in achieving her goals, even though time and circumstances may well change her goals. Some, who are focused on graduation as their principal goal, have no clue as to what comes after that.

"If you don't know where you are going, you might end up somewhere else."
—Yogi Berra

Career Choice: Health, fitness, and character are components of future career choice, but in this chapter we will focus on direction, learning, sleep, and life skills. Shoot high, but be willing to adjust as you and your child learn more about his skills, what he likes, and about what opportunities are available that would suit him best. Early on you should begin discussions on the subject of future vocations with your child. As you think about the subject, measure your thoughts against what you are learning about his abilities and talents, and his likes and dislikes. As the choices narrow, it's not a bad idea to be looking around at future educational institutions and planning a high school curriculum that fits with his tentative career choice. It's not wrong to consider your own interest and talent in music and to encourage your child in that direction, or in sports based on your own talents, but beware of overdoing this. Stay conscious of the fact that your child may neither like what you like nor be good at it. The vignette below, even though involving a teacher and not a parent, is my personal life example of how I was set on a career path as a teenager.

When I was a high school junior, Marvin Goldberg, my science teacher, asked me what I wanted to do when I finished school. At

155

that time, I had no clue. I asked him what he thought I might do and he told me that because I was good in math and science, careers in engineering or medicine might seem attractive. He then commented that, at that time, engineers were not in short supply. In doing this, this great teacher addressed three key points: my abilities, my wishes, and the need for such training in the current world of work. From that point on I was aimed at a future in medicine..

Marvin Goldberg was not a school guidance counselor by training but he was certainly that and more in my life. Speaking of school guidance counselors, they may be good people to help direct your child, but in today's economic crunch, they are often in short supply and most often occupied with children who have disciplinary issues. Mr. Goldberg did the job that my parents had not done, or perhaps I would not have listened to them as closely as I listened to him. In any case I decided what I wanted to do.

At the time of our life-directing conversation and for years after, I thought little about how he separated out the fields of engineering and medicine based on the chances of finding employment in those areas. Now, hearing about the fact that approximately 50% of the current crop of law school and Ph.D. graduates are having trouble finding work in their chosen field, I understand his remarks much better. Also in the news is the fact that one-third of businesses are having trouble finding skilled workers, often workers with no college background. Before you send your child off to a degree that is not very certain to find him work, consider that maybe there is another path that fits his skills and likes, and that will not leave your pocketbook drained of tuition funds and/or your son faced with the repayment of large college loans. Is it a failure to pursue a vocational career such as being a mechanic or take on a craft that he loves and is good at instead of going to college? It is definitely something to think about. Because of this, I now ask young people not just what are they planning to do when they finish school but what they know about the future opportunities in that job.

My points are that it is your job to help your child find a life direction, and to do that you must consider not just his skills and talents but also the openings that will be available or unavailable when he is prepared to enter the work force. There are many who would like to be astronauts, but few are chosen.

156

Preparation Tools:

Learning: Carefully monitor your child's efforts to learn at school. If the school says that there should be ten minutes of homework time allotted for every grade level, then make sure that your high school senior is averaging two hours of homework each school night. Do not accept the excuse that his homework was done at school unless you know that the school does provide adequate study hall time. Praise your child for all of the effort he puts in—much preferable for his continued learning than focusing your praise on the good grades he receives. In our rural-agricultural past, non-school learning came for boys by watching and working on their father's farm, and for girls in their mother's household. Practicing the skills they were learning with parental supervision led to the earlier adoption of skills and less of the belated career searching so common today. Today's busy schedules often do not allow time to study and practice. A joke in the *Wall Street Journal* goes, "When the tourist asked, 'How do you get to Carnegie Hall?' the local told him, 'Practice, practice, practice.'" Remember also the saying "Practice makes perfect"—perhaps a bit of an exaggeration, but still well said.

Sleeping: At no time in life is sleep more important than it is in adolescence. In talking with teens about a number of issues that concern them, I have learned to ask how much sleep they are getting. Knowing that only 30% get the required nine hours nightly, I am quick to point out that sleep deficit is responsible for many of the learning and behavior problems that are so common in today's youth. Teenagers have different biologic times for sleep than younger children do, related to the fact that their sleep hormone (melatonin) is released later in the day than it was when they were younger. This means that they will naturally get to sleep later and consequently need to stay in bed later. A problem with this is the early start times for school, especially for teens, in most areas.

Life Skills Training: As mentioned in a previous chapter, life skills training is an important parental responsibility. See any such school courses as supplements to and reinforcements of the lessons you must teach. You should begin this discussion in the early years and continue it until your child has gained the proficiency needed to become a successful adult. By the time your child leaves you, he should have good social (dining, social interaction, sexual awareness) skills; good communication/ conversation skills; good academic (study and money management) skills; good vocational (work, job-seeking, and time management) skills; and good self-management (eating, dressing, hygiene, safety, and healthcare) skills.

Paying Jobs: In a previous chapter, we looked at the subject of chores and allowances and concluded that chores should be done as part of a child's contribution to his family and allowances are given as the start of teaching money management. Here we comment on jobs at home for which you pay your child and jobs for outside employers.

Working for others is a common weekend and summer activity for teenagers. Whatever path you choose regarding your child's chores and pay, your rules should be clear, well-defined ahead of time, and enforced. I have no problem with this during the summer provided that the place where the child works is an appropriate place for young people to be, and the parent knows what sort of people the work supervisors are. Working during school time is a different matter. Any hours of extra work at home, or at a job away from home, must be considered in relation to their daily and weekly time schedules. It is hard for me to believe that there will ever be adequate time on a teenager's weekday schedules on school days for any extra work. On weekends there may be, but before your child takes on any added time responsibilities discuss with him what is on his schedule that he is going to give up. At this time, 71% of children are now paid for doing weekend and summer work, and they are paid better than the 24% who were paid for similar work in the 1980s.

Chapter Summary: *In these tunnel years, your job is to try to understand life from your child's point of view, accept the fact that he must eventually separate from you, and prepare you both for that separation. Work on helping develop the life skills and career direction that he will need.*

21

Almost Adult: Ages 18–24

Chapter Goals: *To address the need to finish your job of preparing your child for her life as an adult. When you send her off to work or college, your job is not quite over.*

Chapter Outline: We will begin with a review of where your child should be at the end of her high school years, look at two principal tasks that are probably not yet completed, and finish with the subject of parental failure to release.

Life skills training should by now have been almost completely accomplished. She should now have good manners, speak well grammatically, be practicing good hygienic technique, and be dressing and grooming herself modestly and well. She should be eating nutritiously and staying physically fit. She should be practicing good study habits, have healthy sleep patterns, and she should not be smoking or using any illicit drugs. She should be a good girl—one who cares, shares, and lives as a moral, ethical person of character. In my own strong personal opinion, she should be regularly attending religious services. If she has committed all of these things to habit, you may pat yourself on the back, but do not think that your parenting job is quite finished.

Although your almost adult may be moving on to college or to a distant job location, you will still need to monitor her behavior and be her guide, but not so obtrusively that she turns you off. Now your role is more as a counselor than as a den mother. In two areas especially, she will most likely need your continued help: the achievement of career success and the selection of a good life mate.

Career Choice: In the last chapter we stressed the point that too many children enter adult life with no idea of where they are headed, relying on chance alone to lead them to successful vocations and avocations. A recent survey showed that fully 40% of students had learned nothing academically during their first two years at college. The reasons given for this sad phenomenon are multiple. One of them is that the majority of students have no real idea why they are in college other than that their parents wanted them to go. Another is that a great number of their newfound peers encourage them to drink, and then drink more. Although drinking is illegal for most college students, many colleges do not believe that it is their role to help uphold the law. I was told by a professor at a school in the D.C. area that he had been advised to not test students on Mondays or Tuesdays because of hangover issues from weekend partying. When there is intoxication, the incidence of sexual activity rises.

In the last chapter I talked about asking high school students what they wanted to do after they finished college (if they did finish) and receiving answers that showed they had put little if any thought into selection of a future career. Even if they have chosen a career, the majority of respondents to my question seem to know nothing about what they must do to achieve any career goals they may have set. These young people are drifting and wasting the money that has been spent on their tuitions. Their parents have not done a good job of helping them with the difficult but essential life choices that should already have been at least tentatively made. The word "tentatively" is very important in this context.

Although I have based this chapter on young people aged eighteen to twenty-five, scientists are calling the age from eighteen to twenty-nine the "age of emerging adulthood" and pointing out that brain maturation, with its pruning away of unused synapses and strengthening of those that remain, may continue until the later age. The implication is that, although planning for career and spousal choices are important, there is likely to be a lot more going on. And with this implication, the job of active parenting is not quite over, especially at a time when increasing numbers of post–high school children are living at home.

When I was in college, my father told me that, in his experience, people who were not settled on a career choice and actively pursuing that choice by age thirty would not be successful. He further said that by age forty, they should have reached some level of success in their chosen career. Over the years, I have seen the truth of this statement too many times in friends with great talents who at age thirty were still not embarked on a clear career path. Despite their talents, they were never able to get fully back on track. Fortunately for me, I was, thanks to excellent guidance from my high school chemistry teacher, on the path to being a physician, and although I did make a detour or two in my twenties, I was back on track well before I was thirty. As a parent, it is your job to help your child and push her to make important life decisions. This process should have begun much earlier than the completion of high school, but when it hasn't been, it is critical that you push your child to get her on track. Even If she seems properly focused, it is still important that you stay involved and provide continued support and guidance. She still needs your parenting.

Choice of a Life Mate: Although they are still a part of many world cultures, gone in this country are the days of parent-arranged marriages. But just because they are gone does not mean that you should have no role in your child's spousal choice. You should assign yourself a big role and you should have begun your job much before college age. Your modeling of a good marital relationship is as important as any other teaching aid. Not only will you be doing a service for your child but also for the grandchildren that will follow.

Being the question-asker that I am (some would say the snoop that I am), I have developed the habit of asking young people what they are looking for in a spouse. By far the most common responses I get are along the lines of saying they are looking for someone who is fun to be with, is good looking, has a good future, and likes the things that they do. None of these are bad attributes in a person, but there's a better answer.

When I asked Becky, a young friend of mine, what she was looking for in a spouse, she immediately replied, **"Character."**

Character is the answer that I was looking for but so rarely receive from young people. Talk to your child about this answer and why you think it is the best one.

161

Then ask her three follow-up questions: "What do you mean by character?"; "What kind of a person would your person of character be looking for as a life mate?" and finally, "Are you living the life that would make your man of character want you?" Listen carefully to the definition that she gives you and comment on it. In a time of high divorce rates, do you think that if this quality had been addressed sooner, the chances of marriage success would have been increased? You won't, in our society, be the one picking a spouse for your child, but having done this Q & A drill with reminders along the way, such as asking her when she is dating if her date is a person of character, you have positioned her well for making a wise choice of mate. As follow-up, I was fortunate enough to have been invited to Becky's wedding and to know her, now the mother of three young children, as a wonderful example of how good a marriage and family can be. The chances that Becky and John will ever divorce are, in my mind, nil. The earlier you can get your child to agree that Becky had it right, the sooner you can begin to relax.

Separating: Although separation is to be desired and encouraged, there are a number of potential problems that should be recognized and addressed. Being unprepared for issues of sex, drinking/drugs, and social immaturity can all lead to long-term or permanent problems. In his book *I Am Charlotte Simmons*, Thomas Wolfe tells the tale of a college girl, with what seemed to be excellent character training, who fell prey to temptations that she was not adequately prepared for in a world without parents. For more than a few freshmen, their college careers are essentially over by the end of their first semester. If there are any doubts about your child's readiness or fears that she may find the whole experience overwhelming, consider your options. To make the complete transition safely, beginning at a local community college or university may make great sense. For more on sex and drugs, read the chapters devoted to those subjects.

Releasing: Although your children will always be your children, it is your job to make sure that they become responsible adults and that you let them do so. Your hope is that they will be fully independent but will, at the same time, still want to be a member in good standing of your now extended family. A failure to adequately release comes in several forms that can each cause its own set of problems. A recent Pew Research Center study showed that 20% of young people ages twenty-five to thirty-four are currently living with their parents or in other multigenerational arrangements—the most since the 1950s. Current economic factors obviously play a role in these numbers, but so do failures in separation/release training and execution.

Factors in Non-Release: The failure of parents to pay adequate attention to the lessons that needed to be taught in earlier years is a key factor. These include those mentioned earlier in this chapter plus life skills training, work experience, caring, sharing, and much more. In addition, three other parenting problems stand out:

Helicopter Parenting: Parents who are called helicopter parents can be very overprotective of their children, especially in regard to school activities. The term may have come from the mouth of a child interviewed by the great Israeli psychologist Haim Ginott, who said, "Mother hovers over me like a helicopter." In using this well-meaning method of parenting, helicopter parents are showing an unwillingness to have their child assume responsibility for their own behavior, an essential part of fully growing up and separating. Even knowing that your child may fail or perform less than her best at times, you must let her do so. Your role when she fails will be to make comments and suggestions, and in some situations take disciplinary action. Focus more on how much effort she exerted or did not exert on the project than what grade she achieved. You should not wait until she is taking her SAT tests or is in college to let her learn the lessons of success, and the ability to learn from underachievement and failure. Helicopter parenting is at the ground floor of a multistory building made by parents who let what they believe to be love get in the way of releasing their child.

Mother-in-Law-Itis, a Form of Helicopter Parenting: When your child does form a serious relationship, especially a marital one, be careful that in your zeal to have her marry the best you do not turn off her potential mate with your intrusive behavior. In such a situation, unless you can give your daughter a pretty good reason for your intrusiveness, do not be surprised if she also will turn you off. In the early stages of dating, it may be OK to remind her of the type of mate she said she wanted and ask her again if this guy, in her opinion, fits that description. Always remember that even though you would like a perfect mate for your child, no one is perfect. Once she is married, it will be your job to be a supporter and not a critic.

Enabling Behavior: Parents should be aware of the dangers of and avoid another kind of so-called "love" that can be very counterproductive. Enabling occurs when a parent intercedes when their child has gotten into trouble. Rather than letting logical consequences occur and act as teaching guides, the enabling parent habitually steps in to help the child avoid those consequences. What follows are three different levels of enabling from an early stage to a much more extreme final story.

Example 1: Making excuses for a child who has not turned in a school assignment or who has been late to or skipped school is enabling. Either of these behaviors has a logical punishment, a punishment that the school should apply. Covering for your child will not teach her that there are consequences for misbehavior. Instead, you should tell her how you feel about what she has done and why. You should also tell her that even though you love her, or perhaps because you love her, you will not intervene. If you have done nothing to punish her for the infraction and have taken away the school's ability to do so, you are in fact encouraging the behavior. If not properly dealt with, it will almost certainly continue and escalate.

Example 2: Another example is hiring the "best lawyer" you can find to defend your child from a drunken driving charge when indeed she was intoxicated and driving. This is not good parenting and tells your child that whatever she does, legal or otherwise, you will be there to defend her. This is not love—it is enabling. We have all read cases of drivers with more than one previous DWI offense killing others in a highway crash. Mothers Against Drunk Driving (MADD) was started by a mother who was understandably furious about a situation in which a drunk driver, who had been released without adequate penalty, killed her child. In her opinion and mine, this death could have been prevented if the judge had properly punished an earlier offense instead of just putting the driver on probation. In almost all first-time DUI cases when no serious damage has been done, judges will be lenient, perhaps sentencing the driver to a drunken driving school. It would be much better to sentence the child to an evaluation by an expert in chemical dependency and use that information before final sentencing. A significant number of those who drive drunk have serious drinking problems and, if not dealt with adequately, will drive that way again. When mentioned previously, I put quote marks around the words best lawyer, because I believe the family did not hire the best lawyer for their child. A better lawyer is one who has more understanding of the issues and makes a plea to the judge that she put any punishment on hold until an assessment has been done of the child's behavior, especially her drinking and/or drugging behavior. Then, if the evaluation showed the child needed treatment, the good lawyer would bargain for a reduced sentence or for probation if the child satisfactorily completed treatment and follow-up. Parents who enable a child to escape the consequences of a DUI who later hits and kills someone are, in my opinion, as guilty as the child who drove the car.

Example 3:

Mrs. B. came to visit me to ask about her daughter, who had moved back home after losing her job and all of her money. This was not a new issue. The mother knew that her daughter had been using drugs for a number of years and had earlier dropped out of school because of her usage but, and it's a big but, the mother had never punished her, nor had she directed her to get the help she obviously needed. I suggested that if she did take her daughter in, she should insist that she be evaluated and placed in a treatment program by a competent evaluator. The mother needed to let her daughter know the consequences of further drug use and enforce those consequences. When I next saw this mother ten years later, she told me that her daughter had returned home again. She had never gone for evaluation or treatment.

This true story of an enabling and obviously co-dependent mother may seem extreme, but it makes its point. What this mother thought of as love was enabling. Rather than helping her daughter, her "love" was destroying her, and the clock was ticking.

Chapter Summary: *Continue with the guidance you have been giving on a number of subjects, focusing particularly on issues of life skills and on arming your child to be able to embark on the road to choosing her correct career and spouse. However, do not make the mistake of failing to release her.*

The Traps of Adolescence:
How Are We Doing and How Can We Do Better?

With health, fitness, and character development as our prime goals, let's take a look at how we are doing and what we can do to protect our children from the many traps that have been laid out.

The subjects addressed in this section are subjects in which our society is generally failing.

There is a heavy load here of my personal viewpoints. In some cases, especially in the chapter on sex, I have left many parenting choices up to the reader, but you should be able to tell by now how I would feel about many of them. Where you fit on the questions of strong parenting as opposed to "let her do what she wants" parenting is up to you, but know that whatever her inborn nature, with the latter style, you put your child at increased risk.

22

Chapter Twenty-Two

Unhealthy Eating

Chapter Goals: *In this chapter we will talk about the current obesity epidemic and other problems related to bad eating habits. In the next chapter we will address good eating habits—proper nutrition. A later chapter will address the related issue of exercise.*

The Obesity Epidemic: Many experts have predicted that we are raising the first generation of American children who will not live as long as their parents, a prediction based principally on the alarming increase in the rates of childhood obesity. It is estimated currently that 17% of children aged two to nineteen are obese, a rate that has tripled over the last twenty years and is almost five times what it was four decades ago. If we broaden our area of concern to include children who are classified as overweight, more than one-third of children and adolescents are either overweight or obese. None of these statistics should be surprising because 33.8% of American adults are also obese. The CDC predicts that by the year 2030, that number will rise to 42%. In this country, obesity has become a sign of the times. Have you heard the expression "fat city"? Shouldn't we call ourselves a fat country living in a world that is becoming increasingly fat?

Obesity Defined and Measured: Obesity is defined as having a greater excess of body fat than the amount found in those who are classified as overweight. Most commonly this is determined using the BMI (body mass index), a number calculated from measurements of a person's height and weight. To calculate a BMI, take a person's weight in kilograms and divide it by their height in meters squared.

For children, it is much easier to go to the website BMI Percentile Calculator for Child and Teen: http://apps.nccd.cdc.gov/dnpabmi/.

People's weights have been grouped into four categories based on their BMIs: A BMI of less than 19 is underweight, BMIs from 19-25 are normal (healthy), from 25-30 overweight, and over 30 obese. The American Academy of Pediatrics (AAP) recommends that a child's BMI should be calculated regularly beginning at age two. The resulting figure should be given to the parents, explained, and accompanied with nutritional advice. A small percentage of people who have normal BMIs actually have excess body fat when measured by tools called calipers. On the other hand, very muscular individuals may have elevated BMIs and not have excess fat.

Consequences of Obesity: Based on an estimated 300,000 obesity-related deaths annually, obesity has been called the second leading cause of preventable death in the United States, and the rates of serious health consequences are rising. A CDC study published in 2013 reports that relative to normal weight, all grades of obesity were associated with significantly higher all-cause mortality. The most important of these consequences are diabetes, hypertension (high blood pressure), and elevated cholesterol levels, each of which can lead to heart disease and stroke. Obesity itself may cause more weight gain. Currently there are tens of thousands of teens with weight-related type 2 diabetes, a disorder that was once called adult-onset diabetes. Not only are these children getting the disease earlier, but the oral medications that are used for older patients are often not nearly as effective when used by younger people. Being obese is also associated with certain types of cancer, sleep apnea, arthritis, inability to concentrate, fatigue, and social and psychological problems such as stigmatization, poor self-esteem, anxiety, and depression. In middle age, those who are obese may develop cognitive decline over 20% more rapidly than those whose weight is in the normal range. Medical costs for the obese child are currently 30% more than the medical costs for his non-obese counterparts. Overweight people are often unwilling or less able to engage in sporting activities and other forms of exercise that could help reduce their obesity. Being teased, discriminated against, or otherwise socially embarrassed because of their excess weight can and frequently does lead to snacking and food gorging. There is nothing good about being overweight.

Fat Cells: The adolescent years and those preceding them are the principal times when the body lays down new fat cells. Once formed, these cells will be there for life (barring later liposuction or surgical removal). When a person older than the adolescent gains weight, he does it not so much by laying down new fat cells but by accumulating fat in the fat cells that are already present. Dieting can reduce the size of these fat cells, but they do not go away and they remain "hungry." If your child can escape this adolescent mass accumulation of fat cells, he will find it easier to stay slim for the remainder of his life.

Causes of Obesity: Although there is no doubt that genetic factors can be related to obesity, they cannot account for the current epidemic rise in this problem. Children from low-income families are at increased risk, as are those who come from single-parent homes. In the relatively recent past, there have been many changes in what we eat, where we eat, why we eat, and how we eat, and these changes have played a major role in the obesity epidemic. Fast food is eaten by the average American teen twice each week. Many families with jam-packed schedules prefer fast foods because they take less time to prepare than cooking and dishwashing at home. The fast-food restaurants know that foods high in fat, sugar, and salt sell very well. When and if you are at a restaurant, fast food or otherwise, take a moment to look over the menu with your child and discuss the benefits and drawbacks of the various menu options. This job is easier to do when restaurants, either voluntarily or by mandate, provide information on calories, fat, sugar, salt, and other ingredients.

Media: Advertisers spend a lot of money trying (successfully, I might add) to sell fattening and otherwise unhealthful foods. Sugarcoated cereals and high-calorie soft drinks are pushed. The average teenager currently gets 13% of his calories from soft drinks. On television programs for younger children, 83% of all advertisements are for fast foods or snacks. This number drops in adolescent programming but is still an unacceptably high 25%. On an average Saturday morning, there is one food commercial every five minutes and healthful foods are advertised only 3% of the time. Advertisements of fast-food restaurants are also in the game with their messages of delicious but fattening meals. To further entice the young, toys and things such as "happy meals" are regularly advertised. In the United Kingdom, a thirty-year longitudinal study showed that for each additional hour of TV regularly watched by five-year-old children, there was a 7% increase in the incidence of obesity. What is presented here is just a small sample of what is known about food and media, but by now you should have gotten the message: the media and obesity are cousins.

But more than just ads link media time to obesity. Even if there were no food ads on television, there is the all too common couch potato syndrome in which it is very easy to sit on a comfortable couch in an air-conditioned room, getting no exercise and at the same time snacking, without paying much attention to what and how much is being consumed. Less enjoyable essentials, such as chores, study, and exercise, are cut back or eliminated by practiced couch potatoes.

School lunch programs also contribute to the obesity problem. Not only do their menus favor high-calorie, high-fat foods, but students are often limited in the amount of time allowed for them to eat. Consequently they have to eat and drink rapidly, paying little attention to how much or what they are consuming. Sending your child to school with a lunch you have packed can help, but do not be surprised if you learn that he has used what you gave him to trade for a fat-laden goody. School vending machine owners know what sells best and therefore offer high-calorie, high-sugar snacks and drinks.

Anorexia Nervosa and Bulimia Nervosa: Anorexia is a disease in which there is an obsession with weight. Target weights set by the anorexic teen are far below what is normal for their age. Their goals are reached by starving themselves and/or by over-exercising. A person with the disease bulimia has the same desire to be underweight as the anorexic person but deals with his problem by induced vomiting and/or taking laxatives. Binge eating can be seen in both but is a much more characteristic of bulimia. Over-exercising is more common in anorexia but can be seen in both. Both of these eating disorders can cause serious medical and psychological problems and both are potentially fatal. The highest incidence of these problems is in the nineteen to twenty-four age range, but recently both are being diagnosed increasingly in younger children. It is estimated that as many as 20% of young people have or have at one time had one of these disorders. Genetic factors can be contributory, as can psychological factors such as feelings of low self-worth, obsessive compulsive disorder, and perfectionism, but the overwhelming cause of the great increase of eating disorders is sociocultural.

Because it has become very fashionable, as portrayed in media images, for women to be very slim, it should not be surprising that females with these disorders greatly outnumber males. Today's average fashion model is five foot nine to six feet tall and weighs between 110 and 118 pounds, compared to the average young female who is five foot four and weighs 142 pounds. To make things worse, already slim/skinny models or actresses are often made even slimmer using electronic photographic reducing tools.

Recognition of these disorders in their early stages is often difficult, especially for those with bulimia, who often stay in the normal weight range until late in the course of their disease. If your child is losing weight or changing his eating and exercising patterns, think of anorexia and bulimia. When either anorexia or bulimia is recognized or seriously suspected, referral should be made to physicians who are experts in the field of eating disorders.

Atherosclerosis and Other Nutritionally Related Problems: For good reason, high blood pressure and high cholesterol levels have been called silent killers, because the person with them has no sense that there is any problem until lab work is done and blood pressure monitored.

Cholesterol: "'Bad cholesterol," technically called LDL (low-density lipoprotein) cholesterol, is a component of total cholesterol measurement. It is LDL that lays down deposits called plaque, which accumulate over time within the walls of arteries. These deposits can reduce or block blood flow and are the major cause of heart disease and stroke, the first and third leading causes of death in this country. Higher levels of "good cholesterol" (high-density lipoprotein or HDL) can help to offset the effects of the LDL process on plaque formation. Both LDL and HDL levels can be improved with proper diet and exercise. In a diet aimed at LDL reduction, you should reduce the ingestion of saturated fats, found principally in meats and full-fat dairy products, and minimize or avoid altogether the consumption of trans fats, which are often found in margarines, cookies, and cakes. Helpful in the diet are things like oatmeal and other sources of fiber; fish and the omega-3 oils that many of them contain; almonds and walnuts; olive oil; and foods with plant sterols and stanols.

The AAP currently recommends testing for cholesterol levels in children between the ages of nine and eleven years, and again in late adolescence. Children with a family history of high cholesterol levels or heart disease and those with no reliable family history should be tested as early as two years of age. Even if a good diet and exercise do not seem to help with cholesterol and high blood pressure levels, both should be continued for your child's lifetime (and yours). With these caveats, medications may be required for management of high levels and may be started as early as ten years of age. Medications such as statins can be very helpful, but they can have side effects, and usually are not prescribed until after a trial on a cholesterol-healthful diet and adequate exercise.

The good news is that the CDC reported an 11% decline in cholesterol levels in the age range from six to nineteen years, comparing the years 1988 to those from 2007 to 2010. Suggested reasons are a drop in trans fat consumption and a drop in smoking and secondhand smoking.

Salt: High salt intake can cause an increase in blood pressure in a significant number of people. Because it is often difficult to tell who these susceptible people are, it is recommended that we all keep our salt intake low. Like obesity and high cholesterol, blood pressure abnormalities may be genetic.

Sugar: Because sugar has no real nutritional value and because it may displace healthy nutritional choices, sugar-containing food and drink should be used with caution or avoided altogether.

Chapter Summary: *An obesity epidemic is threatening the lives of many American children. Because of poor nutritional practices, the silent killers, high blood pressure and high cholesterol levels, are also an increasing problem.*

23

Eating for Health

Chapter Goals: *To lay out a healthful and nutritionally balanced plan that will tell you what to eat, when to eat, where to eat, and how to eat.*

A Few Suggestions:

Healthful Eating and Development of a Food Plan: If at any time you suspect that your child is overweight, confirm with your pediatrician your suspicion, and then re-examine your meal plan with her. Beware of telling your child that she is fat. Not only is this approach not likely to help, but it might inspire a response that leads to self-consciousness, or worse, anorexia or bulimia. Instead, every child should be told that we all need to develop healthful eating and exercise habits. Show her by your role-modeling what those are.

Infant Feeding: As we commented earlier, infants should be exclusively breastfed for six months and continued on breastfeeding for an additional six months, during which solid foods are introduced to the diet. Currently only 20-30% of infants are breastfed as suggested in these AAP guidelines.

What We Should Eat: Develop a plan that addresses the issues of obesity, atherosclerosis, and healthy nutritional balance. Before you set up your food plan, you should learn what proper nutrition is. Pay attention to what your pediatrician tells you and study the United States Department of Agriculture (USDA) dietary guidelines. For people who are genetically predisposed to obesity, high cholesterol, or high blood pressure, these guidelines are especially important, but all of us should eat in a way that best serves our good health objective.

The USDA recommends that when we eat, half of our plate should be green (i.e., vegetable or salad). Despite this recommendation, only three out of ten high school seniors report eating green vegetables nearly every day. USDA dietary recommendations also include limiting consumption of sugar sweetened beverages; switching to low-fat or non-fat dairy products; eating a diet rich in calcium; eating a high-fiber diet; and eating five servings of fruit and vegetables each day.

Armed with the knowledge of what to eat and what not to eat, and how much to eat, you should develop your daily—or better yet weekly—meal plan. In the beginning this may seem like a lot of extra work, but once a system is instituted and regularly followed, you should end up spending less time shopping and preparing meals on the fly, the way a majority of people now do. If you are a shopper who looks for bargains, then it makes sense to design your weekly plan on the day when the shopping specials appear in your newspaper.

Always remember that your job is to prepare your child for life after she departs from your direct control. With this in mind, you should be teaching her about nutrition and eating style so that she becomes comfortable making healthy choices and building what she has learned into her own style and habits. Do not wait until she is ready to move out of your house to begin teaching her these nutritional lessons and having her commit them to habit.

Food Supplements: The American Academy of Pediatrics recommends that all breastfed infants receive Vitamin D supplementation. For infants on formula or milk fortified with Vitamins A and D, a quart of milk will supply the daily needs. Other foods can also contribute. Iron as supplementation is not needed for exclusively breastfed infants for six months. For other infants and older children, 32 ounces of formula with iron or A&D milk can supply that need and can be supplemented or partially replaced with other foods. Check with your pediatrician about possible fluoride and calcium supplementation.

How Often Should We Eat? I recommend that you plan six meals a day defined as breakfast, lunch, and dinner with a healthful snack such as fruit between each meal. The shortening of times between eating can prevent overeating. When mealtimes are far apart your child may become so ravenously hungry that she makes sneak attacks on the snack cabinet and shovels down food at mealtime. On the other hand, allowing her to eat anytime she spots a food that looks appealing will result in excess weight gain.

Eating Rules: Snack rules should cover snack content and availability. Foods and beverages with high sugar content can quickly bring satisfaction, but any sense of being filled that follows tends to last for much shorter periods of time than do the periods of satiety which follow the eating of healthier foods. Sugar has a tendency to produce what is called sugar craving and its cousin, sugar addiction. Easily visible "treats" such as cookies are often too tempting (even for me) and should not be placed on easily seen countertops or, better yet, not purchased. A good idea is to always have a filled fruit bowl on your counter. Another good idea is to dedicate the middle and most visible shelves of your refrigerator to fruits and vegetables.

Clean Plate Club: Should you require that your child finish her meal before she can get down from the table? If you think so, ask yourself why. Isn't obesity a major problem in this country? Do not tell your child, as was told me when I was a child, that we need to finish our plates and think of the starving children in Sudan or other such places. Studies suggest that more than half of American families are members of what could be called a Clean Plate Club. Most club directors (i.e., parents) do not realize that such clubs may lead to significant overeating. A useful educational technique is to have your child examine her plate carefully before she begins the meal and to tell you what she sees. After you have done this, ask her to decide which food on the plate she is least likely to finish and why. This drill can help her to see that on each plate there are foods with different degrees of importance and content, and to learn early when to say enough is enough. Too often, in our overly busy lives, we shovel down everything that is in front of us, leave the table, and move on. Said another way, there is nothing wrong with not finishing everything on your plate, especially in these days of obesity. Parents should control what foods are eaten and when, but the child should, within reason, control how much she eats. Always be aware that growth spurts and growth slowdowns are a part of normal development and with them comes appetite change. If you've ever watched a teenage boy at the table, you will get this message.

Taste Everything? What do you do when a child refuses a food? Two-year-olds, having experienced the tastes and textures of a limited number of foods, may approach a new taste or texture with caution or complete rejection. Many toddlers need to try a food five to ten times before they actually accept and enjoy it. Expect this but do encourage diversity. If you have identified your child's temperament and placed her as one of the 15% who can be designated as "slow to warm up" or having the tendency to withdraw from new stimuli, you will especially need to use a slow and understanding approach to deal with this personality trait. Ask her to at least taste each food and then regularly present it until she gets through the newness of it all. It is true, however, that there will be certain foods that she may never like. If you know there is a food allergy, you should plan her meals accordingly.

How About Second Helpings? Why do we so naturally think that the amount of food that we serve up to others is the correct amount for them? Accept the fact that there are many reasons why a child's appetite (and yours) may vary from day to day and in different periods of life. At times, especially during the growth spurts of adolescence, your child can and should put away a lot of food. Vigorous exercise, which should be encouraged, can also increase hunger. When a pattern of under-eating develops, do think about possible illness or eating disorder, but do not push her to eat. At times when your child has eaten slowly and finished what was on her plate, it is probably OK to serve seconds. When you decide to do so, you should ask her what she wants and how much she wants, but on both of these subjects the final decision should be yours. Remember that children do have growth spurts and times when their growth is limited.

Dessert? Desserts are often used as bribes to get a child to finish everything that is on her plate. To me this is just another way of saying you must consume more calories before you can get more calories. There is nothing wrong with having dessert at a meal, but it should not be seen as a necessity. Additionally, when it is supplied, it should be nutritionally sound and fit with your overall feeding plan. Fruit can be a great dessert.

How About Buffet Style? The problem with buffet-style serving is it turns over the control of what and how much goes on each plate to your child. For your young child, you should serve each plate. Because your child must eventually learn to eat buffet style at school and other places, teach her at home how to fill her plate, observing how much she takes and how much she eats of it. When she is done, make your comments. When she does not finish the plate that she has filled for herself, do not make her continue eating but do comment on the waste. The use of smaller plates is psychologically helpful. Reserve your bigger plates for salads, the reverse of what is usually done. Another psychological tip is that if the food is red, as in spaghetti with tomato sauce, a white plate will make it more obvious that she is filling her plate, whereas if it is macaroni and cheese, a red plate might help her limit intake.

Where to Eat: Meals and snacks at home should be consumed at a designated eating spot or spots. Food should not be eaten in front of the television set or while working on the computer. When you eat in either of these places, your attention is likely to be distracted from what you are eating and how much you are eating.

Eat Slowly: Slow eating is nutritionally and socially beneficial. Part of the nutritional plus is that if you slow down, decide what you are eating before each bite, and decide whether you really need to finish everything that has been laid out for you, you may eat less. An additional benefit of slow eating is that, over the course of the resulting longer meal, the food that you first ate may be kicking in while you are still at the table and giving you a sense of being filled. With quickly eaten meals, you often finish still hungry and fill your plate with a second helping or begin the search for something else. One way to slow down eating is to insist that the eating utensils be laid down after each bite and not picked up until the food in one's mouth is completely chewed and swallowed. As parents, you should remember that you are being watched. You are her principal role models, and if you are eating too rapidly, why should she obey you when you tell her to slow down? While eating with your child, spend time on manners instruction, emphasizing proper utensil handling, keeping the mouth closed during chewing, not talking with food in her mouth, and leaving the table only when you say so.

"All great change begins at the dinner table."
                                        —Ronald Reagan

Dining: Dining time should be a social time when we eat with someone else and focus on conversation and communication. In most of today's busy families, mealtime is often just a time to eat and run. Family meals should be regularly scheduled, preferably daily. At times it may be just you and your child or you and your co-parent who are eating, as on date nights, but dining times with all family members present are important, should be regularly scheduled, and should have a mandatory attendance policy.

Conversation while dining does not mean that the meal should consist of the adults talking only to other adults with the children held to listener roles. Children should be encouraged to talk, and when they do speak, they must be listened to. When included in interesting (to her) table conversation and when you listen when she talks, she will be considerably less likely to want to leave the table. If children are not used to being engaged in table conversation, there may be periods of long silence until they become more comfortable in their roles as full-fledged dining partners. As we have said before, there should be no TV, texting, or phone calls while dining.

Special Occasions Dining: It will be difficult if not impossible to follow your daily meal planning at times like birthdays, Thanksgiving, and Christmas, but even here some of your everyday style and menu planning can be followed without ruining the joy of the celebrations.

Chapter Summary: *The importance of what we eat, when we eat, and where we eat cannot be overstated. Hopefully what you have learned here will encourage you to feed your child in a nutritious way, preparing her for her later role as a food manager for her family.*

24

Education I: Update

Chapter Goals: *To make you aware of the problems with education today and provide approaches that might help your child avoid them.*

"Education is the best provision for old age."

—Aristotle

Learning should be a lifelong process. The brain is at work from the time before we are born until the time we die. It will be influenced by sights, sounds, smells, tastes, and touches. Each of these sensory inputs will be absorbed, compared with what has already been stored, and stored more "permanently." Learning is much more than what we learn in school. In fact, many of life's most important lessons should be learned in the preschool years.

Current Status: Compared to other countries and to previous generations in this country, we are underperforming. The National Academies, the country's leading advisory group on education, reported that in 2009 the U.S. ranked twenty-seventh of the twenty-nine wealthiest countries in both science and math. We used to think we should be number one. Along with this, they reported that there is a direct correlation between these numbers and reports that nearly one-third of American manufacturing companies have trouble finding skilled workers. Our gross national product (GNP) is falling behind those of countries that are scoring better. By a number of measures, our children are not doing very well in school or college. SAT scores in 2010 were at their lowest level in forty years. The No Child Left Behind program has revealed great deficiencies in school learning. Not only are our children falling behind in academic learning, they are falling behind in moral and ethical learning, as can be seen in the current high rates of teenage sexual misconduct, violence, binge drinking, drug use, and foul language.

There is more than ample evidence that the amount of time spent in school and in study has not kept up with the models used in other countries. Not only that, it has decreased. U.S. Secretary of Education Duncan has said that he "believes our school day is too short, our week is too short, and our year is too short." More than a century ago, his governmental counterpart said, "Today's child must attend school 11.1 years to receive as much instruction quantitatively as a boy received fifty years ago in eight years." This downward slope continues.

The Early Years: At no time in a person's life is his brain as active as it is in the early years—twice as active at three years of age as it will be in adulthood. What can be learned in these years may not be as easily learned at another age, or perhaps not be learned at all. Not only is his brain very active, but his environment is not nearly as cluttered with media and peer influences as it will be in the years that follow. In these early years, your child will be immersed in his family and home environment and little else. This is a prime time for immersion learning. Use it wisely.

Language: Babies have the ability to learn language better than anyone else. The language they hear is quickly absorbed and stored, including the accent in which it is spoken. They also easily learn syntax (the organization of words in a sentence). More than one language can be learned at this age, with the accent and sense of syntax that goes with each of them. Learning to speak a new language after the age of ten becomes increasingly difficult. Even then, when it is learned at a later age, the accent of the older learner will in most cases be easily recognized as different from that of the child who has learned the language in his early years. For example, a Japanese student who learns English after the first few years of his life often cannot correctly pronounce the English sounds for the letters R and L.

Immersion classes in schools or immersion schools can provide an excellent language learning environment, but because the immersion does not occur as early in life, when there is little distraction, and because the immersion is not as deep nor as long as it is for an infant, the acquisition of syntax and sounds may be much more difficult. The information regarding immersion classes and schools is interesting, but you the parent should know that language is best taught early, and that means talking, singing, and reading to your child on a daily basis. Those children who do not have parents who help them learn to speak proficiently will start their academic lives with a built-in lag. Children who do not learn proper syntax and grammar at an early age will find it much harder to acquire later. For many people, including a distressingly high number of teachers, proper grammatical usage seems a thing of the past. Like most learning, it is easier if you get it right the first time, rather than having to unlearn the incorrect before learning the correct.

Emotional Attachment: The prime time for the development of emotional bonding skills is between birth and eighteen months of age. At these times of parental or caretaker bonding, your infant's brain will be learning from you how to be empathetic, happy, hopeful, and sad, and blending this information with the information that constitutes his genetically acquired temperament.

School: When your child reaches school age, your job in his learning process is not over. As he grows older, you will have choices about who should teach him and where. Later in the chapter we will mention his other two "parents," the media and his peers, and the roles that they can play, both good and bad.

Nanny Care, Daycare, and Preschool: If you place your child in the care of a nanny, a daycare, or a preschool, know that he will be greatly influenced in these very formative years by what he sees, hears, and feels. Choose your place wisely.

Head Start: This federally funded program, based on an understanding of the importance of early stimulation and learning, was started to provide care and education to preschool-age children from homes where poverty or unhealthy environments were issues. Many of these children were not provided with the lessons that should have been taught in their earlier years.

Public School: Because not all children develop at the same rate, some will be more prepared for the lessons of first grade than others who are the same age. Development of different intellectual skills, for example math, does not develop at the same age in all children. Further complicating the matter is that a child's nature is the principal determinant of when and if he will develop various skills. Eventually the slower developer should catch up in ability, but he may never completely overcome the learning deficit acquired with his slower start in the early grades. A third factor is that girls, on average, develop their academic skills sooner than boys. The message here is to delay entry into school as long as you legally can in hopes that your child will be the one who excels. Better to have him be the oldest child in the class than the youngest. In addition to intellectual maturity, social maturity is another factor to consider. By this I mean that even for the very bright child, the idea of skipping a grade may be academically OK but the child may be less skilled socially than his older classmates.

In considering when to enroll your child in school, at least three factors should be considered: chronological age, developmental age, and gender. We are all different, but as a generalization, a girl who is born in January will be more ready for learning than a boy born in the same month, and she will be eleven months more mature than a girl born in December. As schools began to move the cutoff date for school entry earlier and earlier in the year, the child born after the cutoff date became a beneficiary. The child with a December birthday no longer was the youngest in the class but instead would be only three months chronologically behind the September child who was now the oldest in his class. Where given the option, some parents have wisely tried to hold their child back a year to allow catch-up time. School administrators, understanding that children are maturing rapidly in the early school years, have wisely moved the cutoff date for acceptance into kindergarten later and later, making the cutoff dates earlier in the year (e.g., September rather than December). In school districts that start a new class every six months, the chronologic, developmental, and social maturity differences of children is minimized, but these schools are not very common. Homeschooling is another approach that may be especially useful for children whose development, both intellectual and social, would put them at a disadvantage in their early years.

Once enrolled, school becomes your child's main job, the one where he will focus much of his efforts and a considerable amount of his time. Your job will be to help him as much as you can. Many children have some degree of anxiety about their first school experience. This anxiety of being in a new "home" with many strange children and a teacher he does not know should subside fairly quickly. If the anxiety is more than a little or persists, talk with your pediatrician and also with the school about the possibility of you sitting in the back of the class for a few days until he becomes more comfortable. Understand that as big a day as this first day may be for you, it's a much bigger one for him. It is not uncommon for children to later feel this same anxiety when they change schools, either because of a family move or graduation to a new level.

You should get to know your child's teachers and should monitor his grades, his grades relative to his classmates, his homework assignments, his homework compliance, and his progress. In addition, you should know of any behavior problems such as hyperactivity, bullying, or talking out of turn in class. Early success is important. Problems with learning can show up early and must not be minimized. Doing well in the early grades will provide a good foundation for moving up. Aptitudes will be revealed and may begin to play a part in the reassessments you will be doing on his potential life direction. Doing poorly may lead to a dislike of school and a disinterest in study. Early school failure or mediocrity, defined as performing below one's ability, are not good and should be a focus of parental attention. Inability to grasp academically or to behave appropriately can be warning signs that suggest a need for an early evaluation for learning ability and/or attention deficit disorder. Among other things, a child who does poorly in school is more apt to become the class clown or bully. Your child should be regularly questioned about his school day—about the academics, the play, and the social times. Your interest will let him know how important the whole experience is. Ask about his friends and how and on what basis he rates them.

Schools have come to believe that the development of a child's self-esteem is of paramount importance in the learning process. This belief has led to an avalanche of stars on charts, certificates, award ceremonies, and trophies, but with little evidence of academic gain. Now the whole concept of making the promotion of self-esteem paramount is being seriously questioned. In the area where I live and across the country, teachers are tempering their praise and "pushing children to work through mistakes, and to take on more challenging assignments." Unlike praise for performance that has led some heavily praised students to choose easy courses or to drop out rather than get mediocre grades, teens should see teachers' valid and gentle criticism of their efforts as praise suggesting that they can do better with their abilities. The once popular concept that intelligence is locked in from birth has not only been questioned by experts, but it is now believed that children who are taught that they can grow their intellect are more motivated to learn.

25

Education II:
Additional Educational Options and College

Chapter Goals: *In the previous chapter we pointed out that Americans are not doing well educationally compared to other countries and compared to what we used to do. We will continue here with the discussion of schooling options and then take a look at college.*

> *"To educate a man in mind and not in morals is to educate a menace to society."*
> —Teddy Roosevelt

Other Educational Options: For a variety of reasons, many parents are choosing educational options other than public schools for their children. Perhaps most prominent among their reasons is that, as already mentioned, the educational record of many public schools, as measured in a number of ways, is not always stellar. Among the exceptions are certain magnet schools and schools in affluent areas where teacher pay rates are high enough to attract the best teachers. Some parents choose not to send their children to public schools because they do not like what the parents believe are immoral or politically biased messages being taught by many teachers. In many public and some private schools, foul and sexually inappropriate language has become the norm. For some, unmonitored bullying may be a factor. Despite widespread parental interest in the following options, the great majority of states do not provide funding for them. Among the options:

Open Enrollment: Parents are allowed to choose any public school in the state for their child to attend provided the school has room for them.

School Voucher Programs: Where this system is in place, low-income parents are allowed to use public money to attend private schools. Studies in New York showed that African American children were 24% more likely to attend college if they attended a private school.

Charter Schools: Where parents, usually low-income parents, have a choice of where to send their children to school, charter schools have become very popular. Each state and school district may have different rules that apply to charter schools. In return for this public funding, which is usually less per student than the amount that goes to public school students, charter schools are held accountable for producing predetermined measurable educational results. Run as nonprofit organizations, they may accept donations. Although privately owned and managed, charter schools must not charge tuition and must be nonprofit. Other than these limitations, they are allowed to choose their own teachers, teaching method, and curriculum. Sometimes called "schools of choice," parents make the decision as to whether they want their children to attend but should be aware of the fact that many charter schools are oversubscribed and admission may involve a lottery process. A great advantage of these schools is that because they do involve parental choice, they are more apt to have active parent involvement in their children's educational process.

Parochial Schools: The principal reason parents will choose parochial schools is for the moral, ethical, God-loving messages that they deliver. Classes are mostly made up of children from similar religious backgrounds. Church, temple, and mosque weekend classes can be an important component of becoming a person of character, and attendance should be encouraged.

Private School: This is an attractive option for many but for most is much too expensive to even consider. Besides the financial hurdle in the most expensive schools, there is the question of tough admission standards. A major advantage is that many of these schools, even those with lower teacher pay scales than public schools, have the ability to pick top teachers and keep class sizes small. For the most part, the children in these classes tend to be very motivated, and motivation is catching. Many of these schools are also church-based.

Homeschooling: Homeschooling is becoming increasingly common. According to the National Home Education Research Institute, the number of children who are being homeschooled has doubled in the last ten years. Additionally, their SAT scores were higher and their socialization was better than other high school students. Parents who commit to homeschooling must weigh the time commitment that the parent-teacher must make. Both homeschooling parents can still have outside jobs and homeschool, but negotiating that option without one of them working well into the evening is difficult. Many have criticized homeschools because the teachers are often untrained as teachers and because they do not often have a good grasp of all the subjects that are available in public schools. Another criticism is that these children are being deprived of the opportunity to socialize with their peers. To the latter comment, one homeschooling mother said to me that although she knows there is a need for socialization skills, the skills that she wants her child to develop do not include foul language, inappropriate sexual references, or blasphemy. The emergence of homeschooling groups, some of which may be at least partially publicly funded under charter school umbrellas, has provided parents with teaching materials and with weekly group sessions where children mingle and are taught subjects in which their parents are not skilled.

This socialization concern has been largely solved by participation in neighborhood activities, attendance at church or temple, and in programs such as scouting where healthy peers may be more easily found. Despite criticism from public school teachers, homeschool students are performing generally very well on standardized testing and in colleges. An additional advantage of homeschooling is that the homeschooled child's schedule can be adjusted so that she gets an adequate amount of sleep, not having to wake up early to catch a school bus. The child can also benefit when the time usually allotted to transportation to and from school is allotted to additional classroom time.

Single-Gender Schools: With the rise of the Women's Movement in the 1950s, there was a largely successful push to integrate single-gender schools and colleges. That pendulum may now be swinging back in the direction of single-gender education. In 2008, the U.S. Department of Education showed some single-gender schools had less sexual harassment, fewer distractions from lesson focus, and fewer behavior problems. Additionally, it found there were more leadership opportunities, more sense of community among staff and students, improved self-esteem, improved student achievement, and more opportunity for social and moral guidance. Expect more on the subject of single-gender education in the years ahead.

College: College graduates do better in the job market than do their non-collegiate peers, but are they really learning significantly more? Many begin college poorly prepared and many do not perform well while there. According to the Council for Aid to Education, 40% of students entering college cannot read, write, or do math at collegiate levels; as college students, 45% show no significant learning improvement in their first two years, and 36% show none after four years. Currently, only 57% of college students will graduate in less than six years. We are not doing well.

When you send your child off to college, she will be out from under your wing and from the supervision, guidance, and encouragement that you have been giving her for years. Is she really mature enough to leave for a new world where there will be little if any adult guidance available? With the arrival of puberty coming earlier and earlier and the arrival of maturity coming later in life than not so many years ago, these can be risky times for children. By the time your child graduates from high school, her academic issues should have been sorted out but her social development may not have been. For this reason more and more families are holding back the departure of children who are younger than their classmates for six months or a year to allow them time to catch up. This off-school time can be spent on a volunteer or paid job or at a local community college.

Because eighteen-year-old students are legally adult, many college administrators and faculty do not believe it right for them to inform parents of behavior problems or of substandard academic performance. This deprives the non-mature but legally adult student of support from you or from the college authorities. Additionally, college officials for years have said that it is their job to teach but not their job to act as parents. Two major psychiatric disorders, schizophrenia and bipolar disorder, both requiring expert evaluation and therapy, often do not become apparent until college age, when loving parents are no longer closely available.

One of the problems, as we stressed earlier, is that many students have no future thoughts about their after-college plans. I put this comment here to remind you that parents have a responsibility to help their child develop a plan for her future. Educators Arum and Roksa write that among today's students, "Drifting through college without a clear sense of purpose is readily apparent." These researchers also note that the increasingly popular college study groups are not as good for learning as is an equal amount of time spent studying alone. Students who spend time in fraternities and sororities tend to show less academic gain. "Liberal arts majors show significantly higher gains in critical thinking, complex reasoning, and writing skills over time than students in other fields of study."

Your child may be legally an adult, but she is still dependent on your support, financial and otherwise. Academic failure or underachievement can be career threatening. You should set standards, discussed with your child ahead of time, on how long you will continue to support failure or underachievement. To be informed of potential academic issues, you should require that your child, on threat of withholding tuition and other college funds, keep you informed of her academic progress and grades. Some colleges allow students to sign a release to send reports home. As I advise this, I worry that some may interpret this as feeling that I believe "helicopter parenting" is acceptable. It is not. By the time you send your child off to college, she should be well along in her expected and necessary separation process. Nevertheless, she may not be fully ready and she may need, but not always ask for, your help. You must stay actively involved until such time as your child is able to show mature behavior in regard to her college and life activities.

The Influence of Peers: Belonging to a peer group, especially if the group has high academic potential and motivation, can be very helpful. As much as possible, help your child find a peer group that she might be interested in and that fits her abilities and wishes. This could be a religious group, a club or a team of some sort, or a neighborhood group that has developed over time. Especially in the teen years, the importance of fitting in with peers can be ranked very high. Teens want to belong. Although things are getting better, there are still those hardworking, excellent students and "nerds" who are left out of important school peer groups and seemingly looked down on. This situation is often worse in inner-city schools, where the drive to excel at schoolwork is considered by many to be of no value.

The Influence of Media: To repeat, time spent with the media can be a huge issue. TV watching by children less than three years of age can result in delayed language development. The average American child in grades three through twelve will daily spend 3.5 hours daily watching television and/or DVDs; 45 minutes with video games; one hour of non-school related work on a computer; and 1½ hours with radio, CDs, tapes, and/or MP3 players. That is a lot of time—time that could be better spent engaged in more important activities. As previously noted, school performance goes down when there is a TV in the bedroom.

Internet Teaching: The Internet has become an important learning tool, and other media types can also be used for learning purposes. Unfortunately, not all of what is taught is true, nor is it all beneficial. Media-literate children, with your help, should learn to differentiate between the two.

Many predict that in the future media will become an increasingly common and valuable educational tool. A growing number of schools are already using the Internet to assist in their teaching efforts. Lessons such as those taught by the Khan Academy on its Internet site seem to be excellent for learning and liked by those who use them, but the results are still not in on how well the education that they provide compares with more traditional classroom teaching. I predict the use of Internet teaching will greatly increase in the years to come.

Chapter Summary: *Education should begin early and remain an essential ingredient for all of our lives. The many important lessons that can be taught or absorbed from a healthy learning environment will remain with a child for life. Parental guidance is important through the high school years and beyond.*

26

Chapter Twenty-Six

Exercise and Fitness

Chapter Goals: *To teach the importance of proper exercise and why you should teach your child to become a habitual exerciser.*

Why Exercise? Regular exercise is essential for best health at all ages and can be fun at the same time. Exercise helps control weight, blood pressure, and cholesterol levels. Additionally, it results in improved flexibility and healthy bones, muscles, and joints. Children who exercise often feel less stressed and better about themselves than those who don't. Besides the fact that exercise-promoting sports and games are fun, they help the exercising child sleep better at night, be better able to handle physical and mental challenges, and learn more easily in school.

Play is important, not only because it can provide exercise but because it can contribute to cognitive, physical, social, and emotional wellbeing. Play can and should be fun. The older style of child-driven, made-up play games has unfortunately been almost entirely replaced by adult-structured play.

How Much Exercise? The CDC recommends in its Physical Activity Guidelines for Americans that all children and adolescents get at least sixty minutes of exercise daily and that the majority of that time be in exercise of the aerobic type. The sixty minutes of exercise recommended each day does not all have to be at the same time. As a matter of fact, exercise periods can be used to break up long periods when your child would otherwise be sedentary. The National Association for Sport and

191

Physical Education (NASPE) offers expanded activity guidelines for infants, toddlers and preschoolers that directly address the sedentary issue, and recommends that infants and young children should not be inactive for prolonged periods of time—no more than one hour unless they are sleeping. Likewise, school-age children should not be inactive for long periods, even if that means they should regularly get up from their sedentary time and walk around for a while. Some experts are now recommending that continuous sedentary time should be no more than thirty minutes.

Exercise guidelines are not just for children but also guidelines for adults. Do not ignore the latter, because like your child, you also need an adequate amount of exercise for its health benefits. It will be much easier to push your child to learn and obey the guidelines for his age group if you follow those that have been developed for a person of your age. The "do as I say, not as I do" approach is not the way to be an effective parent. An excellent way to role model is to exercise by walking, hiking, running, swimming, and playing vigorous games with your child. In addition to the physical benefits you both receive, this time can be a great time to communicate and bond with each other. There are many ways you can exercise together if you think about it. How about parking your car a block or two from school and walking with your child to get there? How about walking up stairs rather than taking elevators?

A century ago, most children spent a great deal of their time outdoors, either working on the farm or playing. With increasing urbanization, farm work and the exercise related to it have decreased, as has outside play. Currently, almost one in four American children does not participate in any free time physical activity. With the arrival of air conditioning, the temptation to stay indoors, especially in the hot summertime, became a major factor in the decline in outdoor play and the exercise that came with it. When given a choice between playing soccer outside and getting all hot and sweaty, or staying inside in the air conditioning playing soccer with your Wii device, the latter is much more attractive. Although there are aerobic games you can play with programs such as Wii, most are barely aerobic or not aerobic at all.

Schools and Daycare Centers: Only 8% of elementary schools have daily physical education (PE) classes, and less than a quarter of high school students participate in PE activities. Despite the obvious benefits of exercise, the typical American youth has no regular exercise program, nor does he spend the amounts of time and energy that are recommended for physical fitness. Instead he has given in to the magnetic pull of media activities. Three-quarters of preschool children are currently enrolled in daycare centers. While there, they are not receiving recommended amounts of physical activity but instead spend the great majority of their hours in sedentary activities. Because of worry about possible accidents, the play equipment that is advised by many licensing boards has become so safe that it is not only less physically challenging but also, for many children, less exciting than it used to be. Despite legal concerns, I expect that the main reason for no exercise is that it is so much easier for the daycare provider to sit your child in front of a television rather than taking him out to play.

Media and Public Service Announcements: If children between the ages of two and seven watched TV for twenty-four hours each day, they would be exposed to 1.25 hours of exercise-promoting messages in the whole year. For those aged eight to twelve, the total would only be 1.15 annual hours, and for thirteen to seventeen-year-old adolescents, 0.25 hours. Providing so few minutes to teenagers on the value of exercise is disgraceful but, when you think about it, why would the producers and advertisers of children's shows want to air messages that say, "Get away from this program, and go outside and play"?

What Types of Exercise? The sixty minutes of exercise recommended each day should be divided into three types: aerobic, muscle strengthening, and bone strengthening.

Aerobic exercises, examples of which are stair climbing, brisk walking, running, biking, and swimming, should take up the majority of the required hour each day. In addition to the muscles, the lungs and heart will get a good workout with aerobic activity; your child will be strengthening his heart and promoting a greater blood and oxygen flow throughout his body. Brisk exercises such as running produce more aerobic gain per minute than do moderate exercises, such as moderately paced walking.

Muscle strengthening exercises, also called body building, include such things as pushups and barbell presses. They should be included at least three times weekly in his exercise hour. Weightlifting exercises that are suitable for older children and adolescents may not be recommended for young children, but they can be replaced by gymnastics, time on the jungle gym, or tree climbing.

Bone strengthening exercises, also called flexibility exercises, include such things as skipping rope and gymnastics, and should be part of every child's exercise time at least three times each week.

Some activities will provide more than one of these types of exercise. For example, active basketball practice can not only meet the requirements for vigorous aerobic exercise but also for those of bone strengthening. Gymnastics training can provide all three types of exercise.

Chapter Summary: *To maximize the fitness of your child in an age in which lack of physical fitness is increasingly evident, it is important that your own exercise practices are healthful ones and that you teach them to him and monitor his compliance. While you are doing these things, maximize the opportunities you have to communicate with him and to teach him good communication techniques.*

27

Teenage Sexuality

Chapter Goals: *To address the problems related to premature sexual activity, the underlying risk factors, and what you as a parent can do to help your child stay out of trouble. Properly taught sex education, an important part of behavior modification, is discussed in the next chapter.*

Potential Problems:

Premature Sexual Activity and Unwanted Sex: Forty-six percent of high school seniors have had sexual intercourse and 14% have had four or more partners. Of these, 60% said that their first sexual intercourse was something that they wished they hadn't done. Feelings of being pressured to have sex were reported by 29% of teens. The younger they were, the more likely this was to be the case. Of the 72% of eighth and ninth graders who date (a shockingly high number), 24% reported that they had done something sexual that they didn't really want to do.

"Date-Rape": Ten percent of girls who had sex before the age of twenty claimed that their first sexually active experience was not voluntary. Worse still, one in four girls and one in six boys surveyed had been sexually abused by the age of eighteen, and 10% of female students reported being physically hurt by a boyfriend in the past year. Date rape is facilitated when alcohol or drugs are used by either the victim or the abuser. This is especially true when a "date-rape drug" is put into the victim's drink for the purpose of lowering resistance and also to diminish their ability to remember what happened. Consequences for the victims of sexual abuse are real and can include poor school performance, anger, eating disorders, depression, and school dropout. These symptoms are not unlike those of a child who has been severely bullied.

Pregnancy Risk and Protection: In the year 2010, over 350,000 American teenagers between the ages of fifteen and nineteen became pregnant. Although these rates are much too high, the good news is that they were down 40% from what the rates were in 1999. We do not yet know how much of this lowering was due to sex education, safe-sex practices, abortion, higher rates of abstinence, or a combination of all four. I suspect that all these factors are involved

Disease Risk and Protection: One in four teenage girls has had a sexually transmitted infection (STI). STIs (formerly called venereal diseases) have always been a serious health issue but have greatly increased in importance since the recognition of HIV/AIDS in the 1980s. Gonorrhea, one of the most common STIs, was at one time easily treated with antibiotics, but recently more and more cases have become drug-resistant. Another STI, the one caused by the human papillomavirus (HPV) is a forerunner of most cases of cervical cancer and can also cause vulvar and vaginal cancers and is related to an increasing incidence of head and neck cancers. Even though most all of these complications of HPV infection are in females, it is currently recommended that both boys and girls be vaccinated against HPV.

Risk Factors:

Puberty: The normal hormonal surge of adolescence leads to sexual desire. As you have just read, this powerful drive too often leads to inappropriate sex, unwanted pregnancy, and sexually transmitted infection. Your job as a parent who wishes your child to grow up to be healthy and to advance into adult life as a person of character has been made increasingly difficult by many factors—biologic, developmental, and cultural. Biologically, American children are entering puberty at younger ages–as much as two years earlier than they previously were. In a condition called precocious puberty, some children develop sexually even earlier. At the same time they are becoming fully responsible adults at later ages. What this means is that your child will be subject to the risks of adolescent immaturity compounded by biologic urges for a much longer period than in times not so long ago. To make matters worse, cultural changes, many of them closely related to media presentations, are delivering different messages than the healthy moral ones that you should favor. The currently popular use of "sexting" has not helped and should be a topic for parent-child discussion.

Girls on average reach puberty at an earlier chronological and emotional age than do boys. Because of this girls are in their immaturity at an increased risk of unwanted activities. It should go without saying that the potential consequences of sexual activity such as unplanned pregnancy and HPV infection are greater in girls than they are in boys. Boys too must be protected from the possible negative consequences of inappropriate sex and be knowledgeable about the consequences of inappropriate sex not just for themselves but for their partners. Too often, boys are pressured by peers to sexually "score" without any consideration of the harm they may be doing to the girl or to themselves. And worse, scores are kept, counted, shared, and bragged about. This is a form of bullying, a subject that is discussed more completely in the chapter on violence but in this case you should make it clear that you want no child of yours to be bullied, be a bully, or be a bystander who does not respond appropriately. Appropriate response would be for your child to tell the bully what he thinks of their actions and why he wants them to stop. At the very least, the bully should not continue to be a member of his peer group unless they are willing to listen to and heed what your child says

Immodesty:

The origin of modest behavior: *Many years ago a couple walked into a garden with no clothes on, did something that they should not have done, and left the garden fully clothed and ashamed of their nudity. They had become modest.*

Modesty is indeed the best policy. There is no secret about what Victoria is selling in her "fashion" stores: she is selling sexy, and she says so. Her styles have

197

become increasingly popular with younger and younger teens. Currently popular fashion styles for women include many outfits designed to emphasize deep cleavage, navels, and skin. Advertisers, knowing that sex sells, use models in suggestive clothing 30% of the time, only partially clad 13% of the time, or nude in 6% to do their selling for them. Fortunately, public protest was able to halt the Abercrombie and Fitch plan to sell padded bras to preteens, a move that would have made little girls into what some writers called "prostatots." Too often mothers would have bought these outfits so that their daughters could be dressed in the fashion the mother herself liked to wear. I found it interesting that on recent travels to Asian countries, I saw no teenage girls—or, for that matter, adult women—who looked sexy. I did see many who looked beautiful.

When a girl dresses sexy, she sends a message. What message do you want your daughter to send? Could this sexy looking appearance be the reason that some girls become sex targets, even if that is not their intent? To combat the problem of immodesty, schools around the country have begun what are called Prom Police programs. Photos of dresses that are considered appropriate prom attire and photos of dresses seen as inappropriate are posted on bulletin boards around the school in the weeks preceding a prom. At prom time, any person who shows up immodestly dressed is turned away.

Your Job:

Role Modeling: Live, behave, dress, and talk the way that you want your child to live, behave, dress, and talk.

Peers: Some peers groups can be risky and others helpful. Teenagers, perhaps more than those in any other age group, want to fit in and to be popular and accepted by their peers. To accomplish these wishes, they are more apt to do what their peers are doing or what they think their peers are doing. A good defense against inappropriate sexual activity is helping your child choose the right group of peers, a group that is sexually responsible. A group that is formed of children who have been taught the same moral lessons can be protective. Moral teaching and moral beliefs do help. Attendance at church, mosque, or temple is good place to start. Of sexually inexperienced girls, 38% have said that their reason for not having sex was that it was against their religion or morals. The rate for boys was 31%. Studies show that when your child believes that her peer group members are sexually active, the pressure for her to have sex is increased. Teens tend to believe that more of their friends are sexually active than really are. Those who believe that their peers are sexually active, even if they are not, are two and a half times more likely to have sex than are those who believe that their peers are not sexually active.

Dating Issues: Rules that are explained and that have known and enforced consequences can be effective prevention tools. In the earlier chapter on adolescence, I talked about the five W rules of healthy dating: when, who, why, where, and what.

Know where your child is at all times as best you can. If your child gets out of school at 3 p.m. and you don't get home from work until 6 p.m., who is responsible for making certain that she is safe during those hours? Where is she when she goes out with friends? Are there adults around who are in charge? Because we no longer have the luxury of having chaperones with our dating adolescents, we should learn as much as we can about where they are going, why, and with whom. Because over half of all teen sexual abuse occurs in residences, you should talk with the parents of your child's friend or date and make sure that they are home and attentive.

It is a parent's job to stress and define proper sexual behavior; to monitor media that suggests casual sex is not only appropriate but to be sought; to help their children avoid situations in which they are left unprotected; and to make sure that the child's appearance does not suggest a degree of maturity or readiness that they may not have.

As previously said many times, you should be media literate. Teenagers whose parents control their child's TV-viewing habits are less likely to be sexually active. An analysis of the 279 most popular songs of 2005 showed that 37% had sexual references and, in a significant number of these, women were degraded. Unfortunately, not many parents can understand the dialect used in rap or hip hop music even if they listen to it with their child. In such cases, ask your child what the lyrics say and what they mean to her.

Even with the protections of a good, God-loving belief system, modest dress, good peer group, no drinking or drugging, and safe dating practices, in this society unwanted sex or date rape can be a real risk. Talk over this possibility with your co-parent and develop a prevention plan. Do the same with your parent peer if they are receptive to the idea. You and your co-parent should discuss with your child the possibilities of date rape and other date violence, both physical and emotional, and give guidelines for being watchful and escaping when there are signs that trouble may be coming.

When you hear of unwanted sexual advances to your child or another, you have a responsibility to report. Calling an involved parent is a good start, but you should do so knowing that many parents may angrily deny that their child was involved. Reports of violence to police should be considered, but be careful. Not all police will respond the way that you want them to, and reports to them may incite more violence from the abuser. Cautiously discuss the possibility of you reporting such behavior with your child ahead of time, acknowledging to her that you are aware that children do not like being "rats." You do not want your child to avoid telling you of such incidents for fear you will, in their opinion, overreact. You should also be aware that abused people too often feel that something they did was the cause of the abuse and are made by the abuser to feel guilty about it. Stress how strongly you feel about this subject so that your child is not surprised when you take action, if action is required. Beware of leaving her with a feeling that she might become the brunt of peer anger if she is the one who tells you and you take action.

Preparing for the Future: Help your teenager understand options for the future that are more attractive than early pregnancy and parenthood. The chances that your child will delay sex, pregnancy, and parenthood are significantly increased if her future appears bright. This means helping her set meaningful goals for the future, talking to her about what it takes to make future plans come true, and helping her reach those goals. Tell her, for example, that if she wants to be a teacher, she will need to stay in school in order to earn various degrees and pass certain exams. It also means teaching her to use her free time in a constructive way, such as setting aside time to complete homework assignments. Explain how becoming pregnant or causing pregnancy in someone you should care about can derail the best of plans. Childcare duties and expenses can make it almost impossible for a single mother to afford college.

Studies by the CDC show that only 50% of teen mothers receive high school diplomas by age twenty-two vs. 90% of those with no children. For most teen mothers any hope of pursuing the careers they wanted is over. Within the first year of becoming teen mothers, half are on welfare. For those girls who have not given birth during adolescence, the chances of poverty drop 15-25%. Sons of teenage mothers have a 13% greater chance of ending up in prison than their comparably aged peers. Add to this the fact that teen fathers are rarely in the parenting picture, further compromising the life of the teen mother and her child.

Chapter Summary: *We have begun the discussion on adolescent sexuality, a discussion that will continue in the next chapter. Topics covered here were the ever earlier onset of puberty, the potential problems of adolescent sexual activity, the risk factors, and your job as a mission driven parent.*

28

Chapter Twenty-Eight

Sex Education

Chapter Goals: *To help you educate your child in appropriate sexual behavior. To protect him you should set, explain, and enforce rules to guide and protect him in the course of his path from puberty into adult life, marriage, parenting, and beyond.*

Primary Sex Education: Should the principal sex educator of your child be the media, his peers, the culture in which he lives, his school, or should it be you? As much as you may find the subject of sex an awkward one to discuss with your child, you should be his chief sex educator. The school may do a good job of correctly presenting the facts, but the material they present may be principally based on the achievement of "safe sex." Only you and perhaps your church, mosque, or temple is likely to teach the subject of best sex, a morally based marital intimacy. Even if they sometimes or often don't appear to appreciate or be interested in what you have to say, all children need a lot of communication, guidance, and information about these issues. You, whose judgment your child values, must learn the facts and present them to him and respond as fully as he wishes whenever he asks a relevant question.

Early in your relationship, you and your co-parent should begin discussions on this subject, making decisions on how and when you will begin and what you will say. Understandably, for many the whole idea of talking with their child about sex, especially about controversial sexually related topics, makes them uncomfortable. But the stakes are too high to do a minimal job in this very important and potentially very dangerous area. Begin with role-modeling. Show your child by your dress, your comments, and your behavior the lessons that you will later tell him. The traditional plan, of giving him a harmless children's book on sex and later the proverbial "birds and bees" or stork talks, will not get the job done. If that is all you do, you will be in effect turning your child over to the "wisdom" of the media and his peers. Discomfort or not, you really don't have a choice. When a question or a crisis arises, you should be the one he turns to.

Questions will arise early and you should be ready for them, although your messages to a three-year-old child will be much less complete and vivid than the ones you will give to your thirteen-year-old. Reassuring research clearly shows that talking with your children about sex does not encourage them to become sexually active. In fact, evidence is accumulating, such as the falling teenage birth rates reported in the last chapter, that sex education can be effective in producing the desired results. When your three-year-old child asks where babies come from, you can at the age of three let it go with a simple "from Mommy's tummy," but later, when the questions are asked about how the baby gets there, you should be prepared to answer truthfully and fully. When your child asks you a question, clarify what he wants—he may only want a short answer and not a lot of detail. You should talk about the different types of love that include God's love, comments on puppy love, brotherly love, mother love, father love, marital love, and lust.

You and your co-parent should agree that you both want to be "askable" parents, readily available and reliable sources for your information-seeking child, whether boy or girl. Share with your child that you may not have all the answers but together you will work on getting them. Your discussions with him should be interactive so that you have a chance to learn how he feels about a variety of related topics, and which he thinks are the most important drivers of his behavior at the time of your conversation. You should give your child ample opportunity to say what's on his mind and consider carefully what he says before responding. There will most likely be instances when, even though what he says differs from your message, his ideas may make some sense to you. When you are able in good conscience to change your position to more closely match his, you will be teaching him that you do listen to and respect what he feels and says.

In addition to answering questions when your child asks them, you should be parents who regularly address the subject of dating and beyond depending on what you believe might be going on in his life at the time. If you can't think how best to start the discussion, consider using situations shown on television or in movies as conversation starters. Before you tell your child what you think, ask him what he thinks about what has just been viewed or heard. Comment on his comments and then tell him candidly what you think and why you take the position that you do. Media mentions of abstinence and protection are rare, but when they are seen or heard they do offer good opportunities to talk.

Entering the stormy adolescent period, your child values your wisdom and guidance above that of all others. If you continue to act as the parents he has come to know and love, you will retain your number-one position even though at times, especially when his peers are present, it may seem otherwise.

Media Education: Unfortunately, the great majority of sex education delivered by the media does not have a healthy message. Messages that our children too often take away from the mainstream media are that immodest dress is in style (as it indeed seems to be), that casual sex is common (as it seems to be), and that sex has no serious consequences (not true). Over 75% of primetime TV shows contain sexual content, often as many as eight to ten times an hour, and only 14% of sexual incidents mention any risk or responsibility.

"Television and other media have arguably become the leading source of sex education in the United States today."
—Victor Strasburger, M.D., pediatric media expert
and bestselling author

Advertisers provide the majority of the funding for TV, radio, and Internet shows. It should come as no surprise that, in return for their expenditures, advertisers want to sell products or deliver messages. Often the products and messages they wish to sell are not in the best interests of children's health and are not in accord with your parental beliefs about attitudes, values, and behavior.

Sex Education: Even assuming that you would prefer that your child remain abstinent until married, the subjects of birth control, vaccines, and mechanical protection against sexually transmitted infections (STIs) should be discussed. You can be sure that if you don't discuss the options, he will learn about them elsewhere, and what he learns may not be factual or morally based. Also understand that if you do not address the issues, his belief that you are completely open may suffer. In your talk, tell him about abortion, birth control, contraception, disease-preventing condoms, and "morning after" pills (three over-the-counter varieties are now available to anyone over the age of seventeen). What information you give him about these topics should be current and accurate. For reliable information consult with your health care provider and/or medical experts such as those found on web pages from the National Institutes of Health (NIH), the Mayo Clinic, and Johns Hopkins. To help you in thinking through the topics of sex education, the website National Campaign to Prevent Teen and Unwanted Pregnancy and their Ten Tips for Parents may help. Many inexpensive books and videos are available to help with any detailed information you might need. You should make your position known on the moral side of all information you present and remind him that the best protection is still abstinence.

Pornography: In his book *Sex and Man at Yale*, Nathan Harden describes current Yale-type sex education. During what is called Sex Week there were school sponsored "in-classroom screening of hardcore pornography and the giving of permission for sex-toy manufacturers and porn production companies to market their products to students." More recently, Sex Week is being replicated at Harvard, Brown, Duke, Northwestern, the University of Illinois, and the University of Wisconsin. How will you feel about sending your child to one of these schools, academically excellent though they may be?

Homosexuality: In our society, gay and lesbian relationships have become relatively commonplace; have become a common part of media shows; and have gained the attention of all of us. The subjects of gay bullying and gay marriage are in the news frequently. No matter how you feel about the subject, your child is entitled to your opinion about it and to your reasons for it. If you believe that homosexuality is wrong, what will you say and do if you become one of the growing number of parents who do not approve of homosexuality but whose child nevertheless chooses it a his way of life? The vignette that follows addresses three related issues.

When the adult child of a good friend of mine told his mother that he was gay, the mother's response came in two parts. First she told her son that she believed that homosexuality was wrong and almost in the same breath commended him for having the courage to tell her. Then she told him that, even though she did not agree with his decision, she wanted him to know that he was still her son and she would still always love him and want to be a part of his life.

What would you say? This mother has told her child that she does not agree with his decision. She should have previously told him how she feels about the subject and why she feels the way she does. Recognizing the desire of most young people of not wanting to be different, she has commented on his courage in making his feelings public at least to her. And because he is still her child, she has reminded him of this and that he will always be a child who has her love.

Personal Questions: You might call this section the "really tough questions" section. Once you begin the serious discussions that are recommended, you must be prepared for a time when your child may ask you about your own past history. You and your co-parent should have discussed ahead of time the issue of how much of your own premarital experience you wish to reveal to your child. If you decide to tell all and the "all" contains information on behavior that you regret, is admitting that you made mistakes a part of what you want to say?

Your prearranged agreement could be to answer the question in one of two ways. Lying is not one of them. You can either tell him that it is not a topic open for discussion or tell him the truth about your past. If it was behavior that you regret, tell him why you think it was wrong. What if your life was an example of the kind of behavior that you would recommend for your child and your co-parent's was not? Does your co-partner want to say that the subject of personal teenage behavior is off limits or does he or she want to tell the full truth? The slogan here is "Be Prepared." Maybe your partner does not agree with you on this topic or a number of sex-related topics and how they should be presented. How do you resolve your differences, or do you accept them as legitimate differences and let your child know what each of your positions is and why? A problem with this latter approach may be that in most of the subjects that you discuss in regard to sex, you would like to leave your child with one message, not two.

Chapter Summary: *This chapter has focused on the subject of sex education and its importance. The question of what you will discuss in your sex education course goes all the way from talking about the importance of belonging to the right peer group to the significance of modesty; dating dos and don'ts; an explanation of the differences between love and lust; lessons on methods to avoid unwanted sex; and the subject of pornography. For a variety of reasons, you should be your child's chief sex educators. Both you and your co-parent should have discussed your roles in this arena and made sex information a part of regular and open discussions with your child. As embarrassing as it may be for you, no sexually related topic should be excluded.*

29

Bullying and Other Violence

Chapter Goal: *To help you protect your child from being the victim, perpetrator, or accomplice of harmful and violent activities. In this chapter, we will look at homicide, suicide, and bullying. Accidents and sexually related violence are covered elsewhere. At the conclusion of the chapter are some of my thoughts on the massacre of elementary school children at the Sandy Hook School in Newtown, Connecticut, and how it might have been prevented.*

Suicide: The many causes of suicide range from the suicide of terrorists; the self-immolation of martyrs, such as those in Tibet who are protesting Chinese oppression; to group suicides; to suicides of military personnel with post-traumatic stress disorder; to the suicides of people suffering from severe depression. By far the most common precursor of suicide is clinical depression. Symptoms of this treatable disease may include frequent sadness and crying, boredom and low energy, low self-esteem, difficulty with relationships, frequent complaints of physical illness such as headaches and stomachaches, and most seriously, thoughts or expressions of suicide or other self-destructive behavior. A number of these symptoms may occur occasionally in most of us, but in clinical depression the symptoms are more severe and more persistent. Children who are stressed, who experience loss, or who have attentional, learning, conduct, or anxiety disorders are at a higher risk for depression, as are those children with a family history of depression. About 11 percent of adolescents have a depressive disorder by age 18. Girls are more likely than boys to experience depression. The risk for depression increases as a child gets older. Major depressive disorder is the leading cause of disability among Americans age 15 to 44. When depressed or anxious, youths may turn to alcohol or drugs, hoping to self-medicate their symptoms. Although intoxication can relieve symptoms, when the drug wears off, the condition is often worse than it was when the chemical solution was tried. The good news is that, with professional help that may include medication and psychosocial therapy, depressive disease can be successfully treated.

Homicide: Violent crime rates are highest in the twelve to twenty-four-year age range. In 2007 an average of sixteen young people between the ages of ten and twenty-four were murdered each day, with 84% of the killings being done with a firearm. Over 50% of homicides and suicides are gun-related. Among youths aged twelve to nineteen, 18% admit to having carried a weapon to school within the last month. Even when unloaded or securely locked up, firearms in the home increase the risk of death. For African Americans, murder accounts for 45% of all teenage deaths.

Media and Violence: Extensive research has associated exposure to media violence with aggression, violent behavior, and bullying. Although many studies have shown that the mere presence of guns can increase aggression, a recent study in the journal *Pediatrics* showed that gun violence in films has more than tripled since 1985 in those movies rated PG-13. Children aged fourteen to sixteen who watch more than three hours of TV each day are roughly five times more likely to commit violent acts than the average child of their age. Although a few studies have shown that in some cases media can have prosocial value, many more studies than could be reported make the point that media exposure to violence can be harmful. A large study in eight different countries showed that heavy television viewing was associated with bullying. Practicing your parental media literacy techniques can be very helpful in the prevention of violent activity. Use the V-chip that is present on all new TV sets to limit what your child can watch. When you are watching TV with your child and see acts of violence, pause the program and ask your child such questions as, "Would you solve this problem this way?" and whether she says yes or no, ask her why. Ask her what would happen to her if she did use violence to solve real-life problems. When she becomes able to think more critically, you will have to hit the pause button less and less frequently.

Television: As far back as 1992, it was shown that by the time the average American child reaches the age of eighteen, she will have viewed an estimated 200,000 acts of television violence. Since 1992 the numbers have increased. It has been anticipated that we can expect 14,000 primetime murders this year. Of the 10,000 hours of broadcast television shows evaluated in another study, 61% showed interpersonal violence, much of it in an entertaining or glamorized manner. The highest proportion of violence was found in children's shows where, as pointed out earlier, fact and fantasy are hard to separate. The great majority of the animated feature films produced in the United States between 1937 and 1999 portrayed violence. Since then the amount of violence with the intent to injure has been increasing.

Video Games: On the basis of violence, the Entertainment Software Ratings Board (ESRB) has rated 90% of video games as inappropriate for children ten years of age or less. Despite this, children in grades four through eight will, if given the option, preferentially choose violent video games. The ESRB found that 70% of children in grades four through twelve reported playing M-rated (mature) games. In many of these games, the goal is to kill a variety of enemies in a variety of ways. Scenes of nudity, sex, and sexism (prejudice or discrimination based on gender, especially aimed at women), criminal behavior, and racism are often found and are all part of the "fun." One game, Grand Theft Auto, awards extra points for killing women and another maximizes points if you first have sex with a prostitute. Remember that these are games children play.

Music: Rap music is notorious for its violence-related lyrics and for its aggressive sexual content. More than 80% of violence portrayed in contemporary music videos is perpetrated by attractive protagonists against a disproportionate number of women and blacks. Rap music is also notorious for being difficult for parents to understand.

Sporting Violence: In 2011, there were more than 350 players in the National Football League (NFL) who weighed more than 300 pounds. The increased impact potential of being hit by one of these giants can increase the risk of lifelong orthopedic and brain injury. The extra weight these men carry has the same potential risk as obesity. The more we learn about the adolescent brain, the more we know that the effects of head injury in teenagers can be much worse than in those with more mature brains, even when the injury seems less violent. This raises the question, "Should you allow your child to play violent sports?"

Bullying: Bullying may be defined as intentional repeated attacks that may be physical (hitting, punching), verbal (name calling, teasing), or psychological/relational (intimidation, ridicule, social exclusion) and that involve a power imbalance Aggressive one-on-one verbal behavior is not uncommon among teens but it is not considered bullying unless it is repetitive. That does not mean that such behavior should be ignored. Dan Olweus, a pioneer in the field of bullying said, "If it's mean, intervene."

Bullies are not all the same. Emily Bazelon, a key source of material for this section, separates bullies into five groups. The first is what might be called a "thug in training." If not stopped most of these thugs will continue their bullying and in later years face a 60% conviction rate. A second type Bazelon calls "clueless and perhaps autistic thugs" are looking for the attention and admiration of their peers but fail to realize how unpopular their behavior makes them. Some bullies are also victims of bullying and these are the ones most likely to consider suicide. A fourth type is the child who seems to be popular and powerful, who tries to dominate by force. The fifth type is the social media bully. Girls tend to bully girls while boys will bully both boys and girls. Some but not all bullies have psychological issues such as depression and anxiety. All bullies need to be helped, as do their victims.

Group Bullying: One-on-one bullying is still around, but as portrayed in the documentary film *Bully*, there may be a much more common bullying worry. In the movie, "traditional" one-on-one bullying is presented, but much more frightening are the scenes of large groups of children picking on a target or multiple targets. The targets in the film included a boy who was an introvert and not very socially skilled, another who had an appearance that the bullies found funny, and another who was a lesbian. In the movie, the first of these victims committed suicide. The second learned to live with the bullying because he knew of nothing else to do after the school authorities effectively blew him and his parents off. In one scene, in which everyone on the bus should have known that they were being filmed, we saw this boy being hit on the head, punched, and choked by numerous fellow riders. The seemingly likeable gay girl, believing she could make a difference, did not give up on that option until later in the movie. When she realized that the change she hoped for was not going to happen, she told her family that she wanted to move to a more cosmopolitan area. Persecution directed at people who are of different religion, color, or nationality is not new to our world. Now add to that list what are called LGBTs (lesbian, gay, bisexual, and transgender) children, who are currently a common bullying target.

Peer Protection: Your child's friends can be major determinants of her behavior. Get to know these friends and their parents. Children who have good friends in their company or who are members of teams, music groups, or social clubs are less likely to be teased or otherwise bullied. Encourage your child and her peers to talk with and befriend others who may seem isolated, as the girl in the following vignette did.

An attractive and popular high school junior in our neighborhood, knowing that the brother of her sister's best friend seemed anxious about the thought of riding the bus on his first day of high school, sat next to him on the bus and, by befriending him, helped him become comfortable and accepted by his new peer group.

Remember that one in four American children grow up in homes where drinking or drugging is a problem and many of these children would welcome attention and inclusion in the lives of children who have non-troubled parents.

Parental Role in Violence Prevention: Be a good role model and teach your child how to peacefully solve problems. As much as possible, avoid angry displays in front of her, and punish her only in ways that do not involve venting any anger you might feel in screaming, violent, or belittling behavior. Knowing that drinking and drug use are more common in bullies, watch your own drinking behavior and do not use illicit drugs.

High levels of negative mood, high activity levels, and inflexibility are genetic traits that make children more likely to be aggressive and bullying. If your child fits this pattern of traits, you should be especially vigilant. Sleep disturbances have also been mentioned as causal factors. Respond firmly to any suggestion of inappropriate behavior in your child. In families with more than one child, the almost inevitable pecking order battles between siblings can be used as anti-bullying teaching devices. In addition to anything that you do to break up such behavior, ask the one who is picking on her sibling questions such as, "How would you feel if someone did that to you?" or "How do you think your little sister likes that?" Expect answers and make comments on their answers. They should be told that there are proper ways to get what they want and wrong ways. Make aggression, violence, and bullying regular topics for discussion. Ask your child, "How are things going at school and on your electronic devices?"; "Does anyone you know get picked on or bullied?"; and "Does anyone think that you are a bully?" If your daughter does see any bullying, how does she respond?

Your Child the Victim: When your child does feel that she is being bullied, empathize with her and reassure her that you are on her side and will try to help her solve her problem. The importance of your understanding and support can make all the difference. Work with her to keep her safe.

Tell your child that she should ask for help whenever a bullying situation is not quickly resolved. Bullies should be reported but, because of the fear of embarrassment, or not wanting to become known as a "squealer," it is not always easy for a child to do this. By making bullying a part of your regular discussions, you will make it easier for her to report aggressive and bullying incidents to you and to understand why you must sometimes involve others, such as school officials and the police. But be aware that when bullies are reported, one of their urges may be to retaliate. Walk your child through the reporting process and why you are doing what you are doing.

Your Child the Accomplice: We live in a society where many have become desensitized to violence, perhaps in large part because of what is learned in their media time. Many if not most teens in the bully's audience, think that the bully is funny, especially when the bullying is on the Internet. Rather than responding negatively as they should, they encourage the bully by their non-response. You do not want your child to be a non-responder.

School Response: In the movie *Bully*, schools were not particularly helpful, nor did they see the problem as more than a normal part of adolescence. Hopefully your school does not feel this way. On the brighter side, a growing number of school districts have signed on to bullying education and managements programs that are proving very successful. Such programs as Rachel's Children, the Olweus Bullying Prevention Program, or the Federal HHS Stopbully.gov program can provide useful assistance. In schools that already have student assistance programs (SAPs), bullying programs can be added.

Cyber-Bullying: To the list of bullying types that have been around for a long time we can now add a fifth type that Bazelon calls the "Facebook thug." This type of bully is more often a girl and often one who is nastier online than she is in person, especially if she has the protection of online anonymity. The risk of cyber-bullying is increased because the bully may do her damage anonymously.

Social Media Literacy: You and your co-parent must decide at what age your child should be allowed to have her own phone and at what age you will allow her to use her phone for texting. Just because your child has access to computers does not mean that she should be allowed to have her own social media accounts.

Facebook and Twitter are not the only media sites that can be problems. If your child has access to a computer, an iPhone, or an iPad type device, it may be very hard to keep her off. Currently the average American teenage girl sends/receives 60 text messages per day. About 15% of children under the age of eleven have their own mobile phones. Despite the fact that Facebook insists that their users be at least 13 years old, there are seven and one half million users less than that age.

Safe new apps allowing children to communicate are becoming more and more plentiful and easier and easier to access. One of these, KidzVuz, is a site to be recommended. It allows children to create and upload videos and engage in conversations. Unlike other video-sharing sites, KidzVuz is designed specifically for the under-thirteen set. The site engages children, encourages creative thinking, and even provides the tools to learn about video creation. Plus, it is fully monitored by a panel of parents and is fully compliant with the Children's Online Privacy Protection Act (COPPA). Let's face it: Younger and younger children are increasingly media savvy and, whatever we say, there is no question that most will be involved. Knowing this, do what you can to make social media literacy for your child a must so that she may achieve the goal you have set for her: growing up to be a good person—a moral, ethical, empathetic person of character.

Whatever you decide to do, your child will eventually be on her own. You will have to do your teaching before she leaves home. Before you decide to allow Facebook or other social media, explain what your concerns are and make a number of key points. Let her know that: it is safest if she keeps her audience small and doesn't let it contain a lot of friends of friends about which she knows nothing; she has the privilege of excluding anyone at any time she wants from her network; you may unplug her from her computer and social media at any time you have real concern about what it is you are seeing. Let her know that at the beginning you will be a friend on her site, monitor what goes on, and discuss what you are seeing with her. Inform her that may be problems if she lets too many people know her passwords to the site. When she decides she wants to de-friend you, ask her why. Is there some sort of secret that she does not want to share with you? If and when you decide to let her have her account privately, as most parents do, there are still ways that you can protect her. The COPPA was written to give parents control over what information websites can collect from children. How well this works remains to be seen.

Media Ratings: Media rating systems across the different media can vary greatly. Content that is seen as age appropriate for a twelve-year-old child in a movie by the Motion Picture Association of American (MPA) may be seen as "mature" by the video game raters. The ratings systems should be consistent, but until they are, you need to know what the various system designations mean for each type of media your child will use. But even then, because of the known risks of media use, you need to check out the various elements yourself. As I mentioned in the chapter on media, I would strongly recommend that you check out Commonsensemedia. org, but the final decision on what is watched should be yours. The Commonsense website, in addition to rating shows and games, comments on a number of factors such as positive role models, sex, and violence. On the site you will find a number of commentaries that can be helpful, educational, and positive. But even for good shows, don't forget your rules about how much total media time should be allowed. And don't forget that electronic devices, including telephones, should not be allowed in children's bedrooms nor at the dinner table.

Power Parenting: To change the world, the best plan is to work from the bottom up. As the parent movement did in the late 1970s, focusing national attention on the growing teenage drug problem, so should parents unite to do the same regarding this and other issues. Consider reaching beyond the limits of your own family boundaries. A good place to start your outreach is with your friends and the members of any parent peer groups to which you belong. In your discussions with other parents, the topics of aggression, violence, and bullying should be raised. If you become aware of any aggressive behavior that is occurring in your school or neighborhood, it should be addressed with your peers. Include drugging and drinking in your conversations. How do the other parents think such incidents should be handled in regard to making reports to the school, the police, or to the parents of the aggressor or the victim? Whether they agree with you or not, ask them why they feel as they do.

School boards and sheriffs are elected by the people. If they are not properly addressing aggressive acts, they should be contacted. If you can get a group of parents, the more the better, to accompany you to meetings with them, you can hope to convince them to respond properly. You may want to get your local newspapers involved.

Thoughts on the Connecticut School Massacre: The horror of a mass killing of elementary school children in Newtown, Connecticut, for no apparent reason, and the widely publicized movie theater slaughter in July at a movie in Aurora,

Colorado, cannot help but make us wonder what has gone wrong in our society and what might we do to prevent more of the same. Although these killers had known histories of problem behavior, as did the killers in Tucson and at the University of West Virginia, their problems were not adequately recognized or addressed by those who knew of them. Adam Lanza, the sixteen-year-old Connecticut killer, had a long history of social withdrawal from his peers and others. If this had been recognized and treated, the outcome might have been very different. The great majority of children with mental health issues are not violent, but there needs to be increased understanding of the importance of providing appropriate screening and support for all children. At a time when it seems so obvious that these children need help long before there are violent episodes, expensive gun control measures and police protection are advocated, but at the same time government funds for programs such as Student Assistance Programs to help children identified as having problems by teachers and others have largely evaporated.

The link between substance abuse, mental disorders, and violent crime is not often mentioned. Studies have shown that although violent crime may be only slightly increased in people with mental illness, one large study on schizophrenia has shown that in people who were also substance abusers, the incidence of violence was more than three times higher.

Also important is that the perpetrators of such crimes were often rejected by their peers as early as the first grade.

Chapter Summary: *The incidence of aggression and violent behavior in our society is much too high. Parents can and should play a key role in the protection of their children from the sometimes very disastrous results of such behaviors. We should teach our children the Golden Rule and the great commandment to love your neighbor. Suicide is a major killer and one that should be suspected and headed off with professional help before it occurs.*

30

Addiction I: Tobacco and Alcohol

Chapter Goals: *To stress the risks involved in trying any of the addicting substances even once. In this chapter we will focus on tobacco and alcohol. In the next we will address illicit drugs, but because the use of all these substances is often so intertwined, alcohol and to a lesser extent tobacco will also be included in the next chapter. The roles of parents, peers, and the media will be addressed, as will the failure of community protective systems.*

Addiction-Related Definitions: The National Institute on Drug Abuse (NIDA) defines any illicit use of a substance as drug abuse; this includes the nonmedical use of prescription drugs. Addiction is defined as a chronic, relapsing disease characterized by compulsive drug-seeking behavior—this despite the known harmful consequences of intoxication, such as motor vehicle accidents, and the not so well know neurochemical and molecular changes that occur in the brain, especially the immature brain. Although there are some substances that are always illegal, there are others such as tobacco and alcohol that are only illegal beneath the ages of eighteen and twenty-one, respectively. In this book we will use the term illicit to apply only to drugs that are illegal at any age.

Risk Factors: Risk factors for the early use of alcohol and other drugs are abundant. Perhaps at the top of this list is the fact that adolescents are by nature curious people and natural experimenters who seem to underestimate risk, especially when they are challenged or dared by their peers. Having peers who smoke, drink, or use illicit drugs makes abstinence more difficult, and the brains of teens work differently than the brains of adults. Impulsivity is increased and the negative effects of drugs on intelligence and working memory are greater in teens than they are in adults. The deleterious effects of all of these substances are worse on the still immature teenage brain—a brain that will not fully mature until your child is somewhere in his twenties. His gray matter is growing rapidly, as are new synapses, the gaps where nerve cells (neurons) connect. Other risk factors for use can be poor self-image, poor school performance, family dysfunction, physical abuse, and parental separation and divorce. On the protective side, studies have shown that children whose parents attend church or temple are less likely to drink than are those whose parents do not.

Parental Role: The importance of parental role-modeling cannot be minimized. Perhaps more than any other factor, children observe and learn from parental drinking patterns or lack of them. If you smoke now, stop. Allow no smoking in your house by anyone. Talk to your child about smoking and addiction, and caution him not to try even one cigarette and not to hang around with boys who do smoke. Do not let him attend indoor activities where there will be any smoking. Address the issue of addiction with your child, who, in the society in which we now live, will be tempted many times to try substances that adults use legally. Points you should make about why there is a legal age limit for tobacco and alcohol use include an explanation of the fact that because the adolescent brain is still immature, there is an increased risk of addiction, and that brain scans have shown that heavy drinking can lead to decreased cognitive function, memory, and attention.

My Personal Addiction:

My personal addiction story fortunately involved only tobacco. When I was a college freshman, one of my classmates was handing out "free" little boxes, each of which contained four cigarettes. Although my parents both smoked, I had never tried even one. Back in my room, curiosity led me to light up, just to see how one tasted. From that moment on I was hooked, and before long was consuming two or more packs each day. It was not until some years later, while I was in medical school, watching an autopsy of a very ugly, cancer-ridden, blackened lung that I finally quit.

Tobacco:

"Quitting smoking is easy. I've done it hundreds of times."
—Mark Twain

Nicotine is a very addictive substance, and seven of ten people who have tried three or more cigarettes in their lifetime can tell stories similar to mine. When a young person, especially a young girl, senses that she is getting fat, there is a natural temptation to use cigarettes hoping to control her appetite. Her thinking seems to be that as her weight comes under control (assuming that it ever does), she will quit. Not understanding the strong addiction potential of nicotine and the deadly effects of other tobacco ingredients on the progression of lung cancer, chronic obstructive pulmonary disease (COPD), heart attacks, and stroke, she has made a bad and potentially irreversible mistake.

Cigarette smoking is the leading cause of preventable death in the United States. On average, smokers will die fourteen years earlier than nonsmokers, and about a third of them will eventually die from tobacco-related illness. Each year there are more than 400,000 American tobacco-related deaths in this country; 50,000 of those are on the basis of secondhand smoke inhalation. Somewhere it has been forgotten that, for very good reason, smoking is illegal before the age of eighteen.

Tobacco and the Media: Tobacco companies spend more than 15 billion dollars annually to entice youngsters to smoke. Analysis of fifty-one different studies showed that exposure to tobacco marketing and advertising more than doubled the risk that a teenager would smoke. In ads or in shows and music, smokers are depicted as independent, healthy, youthful, and adventurous. Movie scenes that glamorize and normalize smoking peaked in 2005, after which they have significantly decreased, but are still present in over half of all PG-13 movies. Knowing that 40% of eighth grade students do not believe that smoking a pack a day is a health risk, it should not be surprising that each day 3,000 teenagers will begin to smoke. Other studies showed that 44% of all smoking in children and adolescents was linked to seeing smoking in movies. On MTV, 25% of music videos show tobacco use, usually by the lead performer. On the good side, some public service spots do deliver prevention messages.

Alcohol: More than 100,000 Americans die each year from alcohol-related illness. Drinking has become a part of our culture, and only 29% of American adults report that they do not drink. Accidents, homicide, and suicide, all of which can be related to alcohol consumption, are the three leading causes of death in adolescents fifteen to nineteen years of age.

"Candy is dandy but liquor is quicker."

—Ogden Nash

Drinking plays a significant role in risky adolescent sexual behavior, including unwanted, unintended, and unprotected sexual activity, and sex with multiple partners. Such behavior increases the incidence of unplanned pregnancy and sexually transmitted infections (STIs). Teenagers who report that at least half of their friends are sexually active are thirty-one times more likely to drink, five times more likely to use cigarettes, and twenty-two times more likely to smoke marijuana. Adolescence is a period of exposure to many new stimuli and an age in which many decisions must be made—decisions that should be made with a sober brain and with parental guidance.

Alcohol and Media: Nearly $6 billion is spent annually on alcohol ads targeted at the young, who on average view one to two thousand alcohol ads each year. On TV there is one drinking scene every twenty-three minutes, and alcohol appears in 98% of movies and in 27% of popular songs. More than one-third of drinking scenes are humorous; the negative consequences of drinking are shown in only 23%. All of the top fifteen teen-oriented shows and sports programs show alcohol ads. Compared to magazines aimed at adults, teen magazines contain 48% more advertising for beer, 20% more advertising for hard liquor, and 90% more advertising of sweet alcoholic drinks. A number of longitudinal studies show that watching more movies with drinking in them is strongly predictive of drinking onset and binge drinking in adolescents. Although there are public service ads warning of various dangers of drinking, there are four hundred pro-drinking messages for every one of these helpful ones.

Parental Role: If you are a drinker, explain to your child that in moderation some people find alcohol to be an enjoyable social activity. Also point out that approximately one in ten who uses alcohol become addicted (i.e. alcoholic). Your child should know that if there is a family history of alcohol problems, he is at increased risk. In this country, one of four children grows up in a home where there is parental alcohol or drug abuse. These children are affected in a variety of ways, but the one that seems most common is that they tend to feel alone, believing that they are the only children with substance-abusing parents. Many somehow feel that they are to blame for their parents' problems. Although I know of no parents who believe it is a good idea to teach their child how to smoke socially, I am aware of others who do believe that you can teach responsible drinking by inviting your young child to join you when you have a drink. This may seem like a good idea to these parents, but two large, well-controlled, around-the-world studies have shown that children so trained are more, not less, likely to become binge drinkers and to develop other alcohol-related problems.

A neighbor, knowing how I feel about underage drinking, proudly told me that at his daughter's high school graduation party, he had allowed no alcohol or drugs and had taken the car keys from everyone who attended. He was aware of the fact that any follow-up problems, such as highway accidents, would be his responsibility. Great so far, I thought. Then I asked him about alcohol and he said that there would be no booze, but if any of the kids brought wine or beer (perhaps believing that they are non-alcoholic), that would be OK. Not so great. At the conclusion of the party, he returned all the keys without any real effort to see if the drivers were capable of safe driving.

The best way to ensure that young people are highway safe is to allow no alcohol for those who are underage. Barring this, my neighbor should have bought or borrowed a breath-testing device and used it before returning anyone's car keys. Smelling breath and observing balance are easy tests, but in these days breath testing, as described in the next chapter, should be considered.

Too many adults either do not know or seem to forget that alcohol is illegal for anyone under the age of twenty-one, and for good reason. When summoned to a noisy teenage party, police rarely if ever write citations for drinking. Most high schools and colleges, well aware of the drinking that goes on at school games and school social events, have no policy to prevent it or to deal with it. The efforts of a recent Dartmouth College president to change all this are to be lauded. In his effort he has been joined by an increasing but still disappointingly small number of other colleges. Another positive sign is that a number of colleges are now offering programs by creating what are called recovery communities for recovering students; these offer on-campus clubhouses, recreational opportunities, academic support, and recovery courses.

Chapter Summary: *The use of tobacco and alcohol by our children is a major social, health, and character problem. We must take steps as parents and citizens to stop this waste.*

31

Addiction II: Illicit Drugs

Chapter Goals: *As in the previous chapter, this chapter aims to stress the risks involved in trying any of the addicting substances even once. The role of parents, peers, community, and the media, all of which can present positive or negative influences, will be addressed, with a focus on prevention, early detection, and intervention.*

In today's way of thinking, there are many forms of addiction, including addiction to food or certain foods, gambling, sex, and much more. Here we will focus on addiction to illicit substances, but many of the suggestions for prevention presented here will apply equally well to the other addictions.

History of Illicit Drug Use: Drug use is not a new phenomenon, but in the past the principal drugs of abuse were mainly opiates, and drug use was more or less confined to use by individuals who were in socioeconomic or emotional stress. All that changed in the mid-1960s with the explosion in the rates of marijuana and other drug use by young people who were not socioeconomically or emotionally distressed. By the late '70s marijuana use by younger and younger teenagers was growing in popularity, and "head shops," where drug paraphernalia could be purchased, were common in shopping malls. For the most part, parents and professionals saw this as a "normal phase of adolescence." At the same time there were other parents who were greatly distressed by what was happening and began coming together at meetings such as the PRIDE conference and in a growing parent movement aimed at protecting their children from drug use. Nancy Reagan became a key player in this movement and in the "Just Say No" campaigns that she spearheaded. As more and more Americans listed teen drug use as a major concern, public policy dramatically changed. Teenage marijuana use rates fell for a number of years but began to rise again in the 1990s, though never back to the levels seen earlier. The problem is far from over, but in recent years the use of marijuana and tobacco use have fallen and are leveling off. We are not doing as well with binge drinking and the use of other drugs.

It wasn't just marijuana that was a problem in the 1980s. Cocaine, also thought by many professionals to be relatively harmless, became increasingly used, especially when it was formulated into "crack," a popular inner-city drug. A multitude of other addicting drugs such as ecstasy and methamphetamine became popular.

Today's teens were not alive in the "Just Say No" days and are not familiar with some of the drugs that are part of our history. Perhaps the current rise in the use of the drug ecstasy, which had almost disappeared, may be blamed on the fact that today's teens had never heard of the drug and its side effects. To further confuse the matter, a number of synthetic drugs with names like Spice, Dragonfly, and "bath salts" are so new that they have not yet been made illegal in most areas. Each of the addicting drugs is different in its potential to addict and in its dangerous side effects. Cocaine and nicotine remain high on the potential to addict list, with marijuana at the low end and the others somewhere in between. Not only is cocaine dangerous for the user but, like alcohol and tobacco, can be dangerous to the fetus. The cannabis in marijuana is neither as addicting nor as quickly addicting as the nicotine in cigarettes, but it is now almost twice as strong as it was thirty years ago. According to NIDA Director Nora Volkow, "The increases in marijuana potency are of concern since they increase the likelihood of acute toxicity, including mental impairment. Particularly worrisome is the possibility that the more potent marijuana might be more effective at triggering changes in the brain that can lead to addiction."

A major new and growing drug problem is the problem of misuse and addiction related to the use of prescription opiate painkillers, such as Oxycontin, once thought to have low addiction potential. In the five years from 2004 to 2009, the estimated

226

number of emergency department visits for the misuse or abuse of pharmaceuticals nearly doubled and now numbers over one million annually.

Crime: Drugs and drug dealing have more than filled our jails. In 2002 over two-thirds of inmates in local jails were dependent on or abusing alcohol and/or drugs prior to their arrest. A serious consequence of all of these incarcerations is that many children are growing up without an active, available, or involved father.

Media Role in Illicit Drug Use: Seeing R-rated movies is associated with a six-fold increase in marijuana use, a 30% increase in smoking, and a 46% increase in drinking. As many as eighty-four drug references per day may appear in the popular songs heard by teens. The average viewer of MTV will see one incident of illicit drug use every forty minutes. Having a television set in the bedroom is associated with a greater use of illegal substances. On the positive side, a significant number of movies do portray a character refusing to use drugs.

The Downhill Slide of Addiction:

In a visit to a methadone clinic in Manhattan, I was introduced to an attractive and personable young woman who was then a student at a local college. She told me that when she was thirteen years old, a "friend" suggested or dared her to try just one dose of heroin. She did, and from that moment on, her life was never the same. According to her, for the first time ever she felt good. She became immediately addicted and lived for the heroin high. At the time of my visit, she was at the clinic to get the methadone that she needed to live a "normal" drug-free life.

The escalation of drug use to addiction occurs for most people in stages but, as described in this vignette or in the story of my own personal tobacco addiction in the last chapter, the slide can hit bottom almost instantaneously. A preadolescent or teenager who drinks or smokes is sixty-five times more likely to use marijuana than one who abstains. Marijuana use often begins when a child, at a party or other peer-age function, is prompted or dared to try "just one joint to see how good it will make her feel." The first inhalation is often not a great experience, especially for the inexperienced smoker, and not enough may be inhaled to produce a buzz. At this stage, your daughter should plan her escape from this peer group and find one where there is no tempting illegal activity such as drinking or smoking. If she does continue to hang with her pot-smoking peer group, further trials are almost certain—trials leading her into the early stage of drug use: Stage One, "learning the mood swing."

The teenage years can be some of life's most stressful. In one of these stressful times, perhaps when school is not going well or a parent is on her case, the child may reason that marijuana might help her relax. She lights up and feels better (for a while) and may be entering Stage Two, a stage called "seeking the mood swing." Believing that she has been wrongly informed by those who told her drugs were dangerous, she may believe that she has found a safe and effective way to deal with stress. In this stage, the child is apt to find her old straight friends boring and be more attracted to a drug-using group. The trap has been set and the temptation to use drugs more and more often can lead her into Stage Three, called the stage of "preoccupation with the mood swing." In this stage she will actively seek out drugging and drinking friends and begin to experiment with additional mood-swing drugs. According to NIDA statistics, the child who smokes marijuana is one hundred times more likely to use cocaine compared with her abstaining peers. The "using drugs to feel normal stage" (Stage Four) begins when the user realizes that she has to take her drug daily just to get moving. The path to addiction is a slippery road. Although not all drug users become hooked, a significant number will, especially when the drug is cocaine.

Knowing that I was involved with an adolescent drug treatment program, a psychiatrist whose office was next to mine asked if he could visit the program and perhaps help with patient evaluations. The program directors were excited about this idea and said he could absolutely attend. He arrived for his first visit and was asked to evaluate a newly arrived patient. When he said no, he could not do that, they were shocked. He then explained that because all psychoactive drugs can change a person's personality and be associated with depression and aggression, a period of drug-free time must elapse before he could do a meaningful evaluation. He suggested that he would evaluate the child only after he had been drug free for thirty days. With that policy in place, it was surprising how many "psychiatrically disturbed" teens were well on their way to being back on track by the time of his evaluation.

Testing for Addictive Substance Use: In this world, testing for drugs makes great sense. There are at least two ways of going about this. Before doing any testing and long before any problem arises, you should discuss with your teenager when and why you might test and what you will do if a positive test occurs. Be prepared for the "don't you trust me" defense. Your eventual goal is to be able to trust your child, but in the adolescent world in which she lives, with its many temptations, trust is something that must be earned, and often re-earned. Provided you and your co-parent are on the same page, a good place to start might be to tell her before any suspicion has arisen that you plan to do routine, unannounced testing at least once a year. Your hope would be that the certainty of being tested may be helpful in having her avoid the temptation to break abstinence and provide her with a good excuse to say no when someone dares her to experiment. Talk to her about your prevention idea, hoping that she will see the random testing threat as a protective device and not as a personal slap. You may also decide to test when she gives you indications that there may be something going on that she doesn't want you to know about. Tell her your concerns and test her. After an incident of known use, your whole approach should change, and periodic unannounced drug testing should become routine.

Nicotine may be detected by blood testing, but that test is rarely used by parents because of the relative ease with which tobacco smoke can be smelled on breath and clothing. For alcohol, there are a number of single-use saliva tests, as well as more reliable breath-testing devices, that can be purchased for less than $200 and shared with other parents or with schools. Check the web for instruments and prices. Testing for other, but not all, drugs can be easily done with saliva and urine home testing kits. Because these home tests can be good but are not always completely accurate, it is often wise to have a specimen rechecked by a certified laboratory, especially if your child denies a positive result. So that she knows not to employ this denial ruse, let her know that the consequences of a failed test that she denies will lead to your use of the more expensive laboratory procedure. If that is positive, her punishment will be more severe than for just failing a home test. Hair testing has the advantage of tracing use over longer periods of time than do the other methods, but it does not do well at separating recent use from use in the previous months. When testing, be aware of common deceptions, the most common of which are substituting someone else's urine for hers or diluting her specimen with water from the bathroom. To prevent the latter, turn off the water to the sink and place a bluing agent in the commode and its tank.

Community Approach to the Prevention of Illegal Tobacco, Alcohol, and Drug Use: In this era of budget deficits, schools have, for the most part, dropped drug education and Student Assistance Programs. The latter were helpful in providing counseling to students with problems, whether self-referred or teacher-referred. At a time when violence caused by young people previously known to have behavior problems is increasingly in the news, the decision to drop these programs seems especially unwise. Another major problem is that our laws on alcohol and to an extent tobacco are not routinely enforced by parents, schools, or by the police. Law enforcement should be a tool of primary prevention.

When police are told of a function where it is suspected that there is alcohol use, they should come armed with the same breath-testing apparatus that they use on the highway for the DUI infractions they do enforce. Citations should be issued to offenders and it should be remembered that any use at this age is illegal. Schools should do the same.

Since the 1980s, there has been an Illinois program called Treatment Alternatives to Street Crime (TASC) that addresses these problems by setting up TASC courts, in which judges trained in abuse and addiction hear drug cases. Before deciding on a course of action, these judges frequently will ask for an alcohol-drug assessment by a qualified counselor. In many cases, the judge will place a jail sentence on hold if the convicted person can satisfactorily attend and complete a treatment program as recommended by a qualified assessor. In some cases probation with periodic unannounced drug testing may be substituted for prison, especially for younger convicts. An additional incentive to stay clean may be provided by the judge who mandates that the criminal record be erased if their child stays clean. The TASC program has been able to not only reduce the prison population but also to increase the number of available fathers. Unfortunately, in the current state of financial distress, state funding for the program is drying up.

In areas without a TASC program, there should be special courts for juveniles, where there is an emphasis on evaluation and mandatory treatment when indicated. The idea here is not primarily to punish children but to stop their illegal use of alcohol and other drugs, and by acting this way, to deter others. Punishments might begin with after-school detention, escalate on further offense to monitored community service such as mowing the school lawn, with further escalation of the times and conditions of community service with repeat offenses. With repeat offenses or sooner, competent evaluation and recommendations should be mandated and enforced. Finally, as a last resort before incarceration, there could be restriction from certain activities, such as attendance or participation in sporting and other school functions.

After adequate notification of a new community "no teen drinking policy" in local newspapers, radio, and television shows, and at a variety of community functions, offenders such as the father in the vignette in the last chapter, who allowed underage drinking on his property, should be punished. It seems obvious that these enforcement approaches should lead to a great diminution in underage use and abuse. As a citizen, you should try to enlist others to help you reach enough force to bring about change at the most local of levels, whether that is just your peer group, your neighborhood, your school, or your precinct.

On the positive side, there are communities, such as the one in Winchester, Virginia, that have for years sponsored community-wide drug and alcohol-free New Year's First Night Celebrations. Other communities and organizations could do the same.

"Never doubt that a small group of thoughtful committed citizens can change the world; indeed, it's the only thing that ever has."
—Margaret Mead

Some years ago, Keith Shuchard and her husband returned home one night to find their house littered with alcohol bottles and marijuana butts. The next morning Keith had a serious talk with her daughter and insisted that she be given the names of everyone who had attended the party and their home phone numbers. The list did not come easily, but when compiled, Keith called each of the numbers on the list and asked the parents to join her for a meeting at her house. Of those who did attend and hear what she had to say, there were some who vehemently denied that their child would be so involved. The others, however, joined in to put together a plan that would include many of the rules that we have spoken of in this book. Her book, *Parents, Peers and Pot*, became a national sensation, and before long parent groups were springing up all around the country and finally reaching the White House and Congress.

Chapter Summary: *The use of addictive drugs by our children is a major social, health, and character problem. We must take steps as parents and citizens to stop this waste.*

Acknowledgments

As I began this project, I little realized how much there was to know about the great variety of subjects that I wanted to cover in this book. Without the help of friends and experts and the information gained from many books, newspapers, and from excellent websites, I would have failed.

Actually, I would never have started the book if it had not been so recommended by the group of experts who came to my house to help me think through the many stories regarding teenage problems that were regularly being presented in the news media. The experts in this group were Tom Babor, Ph.D., Chair, Community Medicine & Public Health, University of Connecticut Medical Center; Buddy Gleaton, Ed. D., Professor of Education Emeritus, Georgia State University; Doug Hall, President, PRIDE Surveys; Ralph Hingson, Sc.D., Director, Division of Epidemiology and Prevention Research, NIAAA (National Institute of Alcohol Abuse and Alcoholism); Henry Lozano, Director, Los Angeles Teen Challenge and Urban Ministries; Fena Macdonald, mother of three young children; Roger Meyer, M.D., Professor of Psychiatry, Penn State Hershey Medical Center; and Peggy Sapp, President and CEO of Informed Families—The Florida Family Partnership.

I have already mentioned the important contributions of Joe Garfunkel, M.D., for years the editor of the *Journal of Pediatrics*, who acted as my copy editor and more, much more. Others who deserve my thanks are Hoover Adger, Professor of Pediatrics at Johns Hopkins Medical School, for pediatric backup; Roger Meyer, M.D., for encouragement and support; nephew Don Neely and his wonderful wife Jen, parents of two young girls, who read portions of this book and made excellent and very useful comments on what they read;

Buddy Gleaton, who wrote the section on peer parenting; and Connie Lierman, MSN, CPNP, who read this book in its almost final form and made very useful comments and suggestions from her viewpoint as a woman, a mother, and an active pediatric nurse practitioner working in an inner-city clinic. Also helpful were Elizabeth DuPont Spencer, LCSW-C, her father Robert L. DuPont, M.D., and her sister, Caroline M. DuPont, M.D., who helped in my writing; Peter DiBenedittis, whose website directed me to Vic Strasburger, M.D., who helped me become more media literate; nephew-in-law Pat Walsh, who helped me find a publisher and strengthened the book's message; Stephanie Abbott, who helped me understand how to write a book and how to present it; Sis Wenger, Executive Director of NACoA, for her support and guidance; and daughter Jane Smith, who read portions of the book and made valuable comments. Early help came from Nancy Schneider.

The book could not have been written if my loving wife Bobbie had not been willing to put up with the loss that occurred when I was so heavily focused on preparation and writing at the expense of time that should have been devoted to her. I also give thanks to the thousands of children and families from whom I have learned from over the years. And finally, my faith in the Lord my God and the belief that He put me here for a purpose have guided and propelled me.

Most helpful of the books that I read was Strasburger, Wilson, and Jordan's *Children, Adolescents, and the MEDIA*, which did a great job of increasing my media literacy. Also very helpful were Weissbourd's *The Parents We Mean to Be*, which helped me keep my focus on the importance of character; Medina's *Brain Rules for BABY*, which taught me so much about early development and learning; Pruett and Pruett's *Partnership Parenting*, which did such a

234

good job of explaining the importance of co-parenting; Rothbart's *Becoming Who We Are—Temperament and Personality in Development,* which brought me up to date on the science and significance of inborn nature; and Bronson and Merryman's *Nurture Shock,* which led me to many other useful sources. I must confess that I may have quoted liberally from all of these, often without attribution, as I got caught up in the stream of excellent flowing thoughts that were being fed into my brain.

I also read and learned from Steven Shelov et al's *Caring for Your Baby and Young Child—Birth to Age 5*; Margaret Anderson's *Raising a Family Is a Treasure*; Amy Chua's *Battle Hymn of the Tiger Mother*; Kenneth Ginsburg's *Building Resilience in Children and Teens*; and McHale and Grolnick's *Retrospect in the Psychological Study of Families.*

The websites I used most frequently were those of the American Academy of Pediatrics (AAP), the National Institutes of Health (NIH), the Centers for Disease Control and Prevention (CDC), the Johns Hopkins School of Medicine, and the Mayo Clinic. Newspapers and magazines have led me to numerous relevant studies.

As recent first ladies of our country have taken aim at specific important targets, the material I have studied has taken aim at specific important components of the whole process, such as resiliency, co-parenting, media, and purpose. None, in my opinion, takes direct aim at the need for parents to become the principal agents of change.

References

Chapter 1 - Morality and Building Character

Noonan, P. America's crisis of character. *Wall Street Journal,* April 21, 2012.

Church attendance and drug use. Pride Surveys. Report: National Summary Statistics for 2009-10. http://www.pridesurveys.com/customercenter/us09ns.pdf

Chapter 2 - Happiness and Success

Seligman, Martin E. P. (2002). *Authentic happiness: Using the new positive psychology to realize your potential for lasting fulfillment.* New York: Free Press.

Gottlieb, L. (2011, July/August). How to land your kid in therapy. *The Atlantic Magazine.* http://www.theatlantic.com/magazine/print/2011/07/how-to-land-your-kid-in-therapy/8555/

Chapter 3 - Communicating

National Center for Substance Abuse at Columbia University. (2011). The importance of family dinners VII. http://www.casacolumbia.org/templates/publications_reports.aspx

Chapter 5 - Co-Parenting and Other Parenting Models

Pruett, K., & Pruett, M. K. (2011). *Partnership parenting: How men and women parent differently—Why it helps our kids and can strengthen your marriage.* DaCapo Press.

Konigsberg, R. D. (2011, August 8). Chore wars. *Time.*

McHale, J., Kazali, C., et al. (2004). The transition to co-parenthood: Parents' pre-birth expectation and early co-parental adjustment at three months post-partum. *Development and Psychopathology, 16,* 711-733.

Gottman, J. & Gottman, J.S. (2007). *And baby makes three.* Crown Publishing.

Levine, J. A., & Pittinsky, T. L. (1998). *Working fathers: New strategies for balancing work and family.* Harcourt Brace.

Huffman, F. G., Kanikirieddy, S., & Patel, M. (2010, July 7). Parenting: A contributing factor to childhood obesity. International Journal Environmental Research and Public Health, *7*: 2800-2810. http://www.ncbi.nlm.nih.gov/pmc/articles/PMC2922726/

CDC. (2010). Unmarried childbearing. http://www.cdc.gov/nchs/fastats/unmarry.htm

Ventura, S.J. (2009, May). Changing patterns of non marital childbearing in the United States. Division of Vital Statistics. National Center for Health Statistics.

Cost of Raising a Child Calculator. Center for Nutrition Policy and Promotion, US Department of Agriculture, http://www.cnpp.usda.gov/calculatorintro.htm

Chapter 6 - Arguments, Disagreements, Disharmony, and Divorce

McHale, J., Kazali, C., et al. (2004). The transition to co-parenthood: Parents' pre-birth expectation and early co-parental adjustment at three months post-partum. *Development and Psychopathology, 16*, 711-733. [PubMed]

Medina, J. (2010). *Brain rules of baby*. Pear Press. www.brainrules.net

National Center on Sleep Disorders Research. National Heart, Lung, and Blood Institute. NIH. (2012). Sleep, sleep disorders, and biological rhythms.

Romans 8:19

US Census Bureau. Department of Commerce. The 2012 Statistical Abstract. Incidence of Divorce. http://www.census.gov/compendia/statab/2012edition.html

Fagan, P. F. (1995, March). The real root causes of violent crime: The breakdown of marriage, family, and community. Heritage Foundation. http://www.heritage.org/research/reports/1995/03/bg1026nbsp-the-real-root-causes-of-violent-crime

Chapter 7 - Your Child's Other "Parents": The Media

Roberts, D. F., Foehr, U. G., & Rideout, V. (2005). Generation M: Media in the lives of 8-18-year-olds. Henry J. Kaiser Family Foundation. Menlo Park, CA. (6.5 hours daily TV @ 18)

Rideout, V. J., Vandewater, E. A., & Wartella, E. A. (2003). Zero to six: Electronic media in the lives of infants, toddlers and preschoolers. Henry J Kaiser Family Foundation. Menlo Park, CA.

DeBenedittis, P. Media literacy, critical thinking, self-esteem. (½ million hours TV ads)

AAP website. (2012). http://www.aap.org/healthtopics/mediause.cfm

Strasburger, V. C., Wilson, B. J., & Jordan, A. B. (2009). *Children, adolescents, and the media*. Thousand Oaks: Sage Publications.

Fisch, S., & Bernstein, L. (2001). Formative research revealed: Methodological and process issues in formative research. In S. Fisch & S. Truglio (Eds), *"G" is for growing* (pp 39-60). Mahwah, NJ: Lawrence Erlbaum. (Sesame Street)

Wright, J., St. Peters, M., & Huston, A. (1990). Family television use and its relation to children's cognitive skills and social behavior. In J. Bryant (Ed), *Television and the American family* (pp 227-251). Hillsdale, NJ: Lawrence Erlbaum.

Mares, M., Mares, L., & Woodward, E. (2001). Prosocial effects on children's social interactions. In D. G. Singer and J. L. Singer (Eds), *Handbook of children and the media* (pp 183-203). Thousand Oaks: Sage Publications.

Mares, M., Mares, L., & Woodward, E. (2005). Positive effects of television on children's social interactions: A meta-analysis. *Media Psychology, 7*, 301-322.

Parent Television Council, www.ParentsTV.org. (2009). Common sense media. Is technology networking changing childhood? A national poll. San Francisco, CA: Common Sense Media. Available at: www.commonsensemedia.org/sites/default/files/CSM_teen_social_media_080609_FINAL.pdf. Accessed July 16, 2010.

Hinduja, S., & Patchin, J. (2007). Offline consequences of online victimization: School violence and delinquency. *Journal of School Violence, 6*(3): 89-112.

Ito, M., Horst, H., Bittani, M., et al. (2008). Living and learning with new media: Summary of findings from the digital youth project. Chicago, IL: John D. and Catherine T. MacArthur Foundation Reports on Digital Media and Learning. http://digitalyouth.ischool.berkeley.edu/files/report/digitalyouth-TwoPageSummary.pdf. Accessed July 16, 2010.

O'Keefe, G. S., et al. American Academy of Pediatrics. (2011, April). Council on communications and media. *Pediatrics, 127*(4), 800-804.

Patchin, J. W. (2010). Bullying, cyberbullying, and suicide. *Arch Suicide Res., 14*(3): 206-221. CrossRefMedlineWeb of Science

National Campaign to Prevent Teen and Unplanned Pregnancy. (2008). Sex and tech: Results of a survey of teens and young adults. Washington, D.C. www.thenationalcampaign.org/SEXTECH/PDF/SexTech_Summary.pdf. Accessed July 16, 2010.

Microsoft. Online safety and privacy. http://www.microsoft.com/security/online-privacy/social-networking.aspx

American Academy of Pediatrics. Mediamatters@aap.org

Roberts, D. F., Foehr, U. G., & Rideout, V. (2005). Generation M: Media in the lives of 8-18-year-olds. Henry J Kaiser Foundation. Menlo Park, CA.

DeBenedettis, P. (2012). Media values and the American way. Part III. http://medialiteracy.net/

CleanInternet.com

Getnetwise. http://kids.getnetwise.org

PicBlock. http://www.download.com/PicBlock/3000-2017_4-10425744. html?tag=tab_pub&cdlPid=10857284

eHow tech. http://www.ehow.com/search. html?s=Computer+Parental+Controls&skin=tech&t=all&rs=1

Chapter 8 - The Importance of Peers

Gleaton, T. (2012, personal interview). Emeritus Professor at Georgia State University, founder of PRIDE (Parent Resources in Drug Education), and owner of Pride Surveys. (Peers)

Chapter 9 - Sleep and Time Management

CDC. Media Advisory. (2012). Insufficient sleep among high school students associated with a variety of health-risk behaviors. http://www.cdc.gov/media/releases/2011/a0926_insufficient_sleep.html

CDC. (2011). http://www.cdc.gov/Features/Sleep/

American Sleep Apnea Association. (2012). Sleep apnea in children. http://www.sleepapnea.org/diagnosis-and-treatment/childrens-sleep-apnea.html

KidsHealth from Nemours. Sleep apnea. http://kidshealth.org/parent/general/sleep/apnea.html

CDC. (2012). Sleep and sleep disorders. http://www.cdc.gov/Features/Sleep/

Rechtschaffen, A. (1998). Current perspectives on the function of sleep. *Perspectives in Biological Medicine, 41*, 359-390.

National Center on Sleep Disorders Research, National Heart Lung, and Blood Institute, NIH. (2012). Sleep disorders and biological rhythms.

Medicine Plus. NIH. Sleep disorders. http://www.ninds.nih.gov/disorders/brain_
basics/understanding_sleep.htm#dreaming

Walker, M. P., & Stickgold, R. (2008). Sleep, memory & plasticity. *Annual Review of
Psychology* (Vol. 57, no. 5) (pp. 350-358).

Wahlstrom, K. (2009). School start time study, as reported in Bronson, P., Merryman, A.
Nurture shock. New York, NY: Twelve, The Hatchett Group.

Pack, A.I., Pack, A.M., & Rodgman, et al. (1965). Characteristics of crashes attributed
to the driver having fallen asleep. *Accident Analysis and Prevention, 27,* 769-75.

CDC. http://www.cdc.gov/Features/Sleep

NIH. http://science.education.nih.gov/supplements/nih3/sleep/guide/info-sleep.htm

Roberts, D. E., Foehr, U. G., & Rideout, V. (2005). Generation M: Media in the lives
of 8-18-year-olds. Henry J. Kaiser Foundation. Menlo Park, CA.

CDC Online Newsroom. Media advisory. http://www.cdc.gov/media/releases/2011/
a0926_insufficient_sleep.html

LeBourgeois, M. K., & Harsh, J. R. (2007). Racial gaps in school readiness: The
importance of sleep and rhythms? Paper presented at the Associated Professional
Sleep Societies' Annual Meeting, Salt Lake City. In Bronson, P., & Merryman, A.
Nurture shock: New thinking about children. New York, NY: Twelve, The Hatchette
Book Group.

Danner, F., and Phillips, B. (2008). Adolescent sleep, school start times, and teen
motor vehicle crashes. *Journal of Clinical Sleep Medicine* (Vol 4., no. 6) (pp. 533-
535). As reported in Bronson, P., & Merryman, A. *Nurture shock: New thinking
about children.* New York, NY: Twelve, The Hatchette Book Group

Chapter 10 - Discipline and Punishment

Thomas, A., & Chess, S. (1957). An approach to the study of sources of individual
difference in child behavior. *Journal of Clinical and Experimental Psychopathology,
18,* 347-357. (New stimuli)

Chapter 11 - Self-Discipline and Success

Dweck, C. (2007). *Mindset.* Random House. http://en.wikipedia.org/wiki/Carol_
Dweck

Kohn, A. *(1999). Punished by rewards: The trouble with gold stars, incentive plans, praise, and other bribes.* Merriam-Webster.

Bronson, P., & Merryman, A. (2011). *Nurture shock: New thinking about children.* New York, NY: Twelve, The Hatchette Book Group.

Dweck C. *Mindset.* Random House, 2007 - http://en.wikipedia.org/wiki/Carol_ Dweck

Chua, A. (2011). *The battle hymn of the tiger mother.* Penguin Group USA.

Chua A. (2011, December 24). Tiger Mom's long-distance cub. *The Wall Street Journal.*

Chapter 12 - Nurture vs. Nurture I: From Conception to Birth

Patlak, J., & Gibbons, R. (2001). Electrical activity of nerves. *Aps in nerve cells.* http:// physioweb.med.uvm.edu/cardiacep/EP/nervecells.htm. Retrieved 2009.

McDonald, A. (2007). Prenatal development: The Dana guide. In Bloom, F. E., Beal, M. F., and Kupfer, *The Dana guide to brain health.* The Dana Foundation, Inc. https://www.dana.org/news/brainhealth/detail.aspx?id=10050

Medina, J. (2010). *Brain rules for baby.* Pear Press.

Barker, D. J. (2002). Fetal programming of coronary heart disease. *Trends in Endocrinology and Metabolism. 13,* 364-368.

Levitt, N. S., et al. (2000). Impaired glucose tolerance and elevated blood pressure in low birth weight, non-obese, young South African adults: Early programming of cortisol axis. *Journal of Clinical Endocrinology and Metababolism, 5,* 4611-4618.

Welberg,, L. A., & Seckl, J. R. (2001). Prenatal stress, glucocorticoids and the programming of the brain. *Journal of Neuroendocrinology, 13,* 113-128.

Gunnar, M., & Quevedo, K. (2007). The neurobiology of stress and development. Annual Review of Psychology, *58,*145-73. Institute of Child Development, University of Minnesota. Gunnar@umn.edu. http://www.ncbi.nlm.nih.gov/ pubmed/16903808

Kinney, D. K., Miller, A. M., et al. (2008, March). Maternal stress and autism: Autism prevalence following prenatal exposure to hurricanes and tropical storms in Louisiana. *Journal of Autism* and *Developmental Disorders, 38*(3): 481-8. PMID:17619130. http://www.ncbi.nlm.nih.gov/pubmed?term=kinney%20 and%20autism

Khashan, A. S., Abel, K. M., et al. (2008, February). Maternal stress and schizophrenia: Higher risk of offspring schizophrenia following antenatal maternal exposure to severe adverse life events. Arch Gen Psychiatry. 65(2),146-52. Centre for Women's Mental Health Research, University of Manchester. http://www.ncbi.nlm.nih.gov/pubmed/18250252

Chapter 13 - Nature vs. Nurture II: Your Child is Different

Thomas, A., & Chess, S. (1957). An approach to the study of sources of individual differences in child behavior. *Journal of Clinical and Experimental Psychopathology, 18*, 347-357.

Chess, S., Thomas, A., Birch, H. G., & Hertzig, M. (1960). Implications of a longitudinal study of child development for child psychiatry. *American Journal of Psychiatry, 117*, 434-441.

Thomas, A., Chess, S., & Birch, H. G. (1970). The origin of personality. http://www.acamedia.info/sciences/sciliterature/origin_of_personality.htm

Thomas, A., & Chess, S. (1965). Your child is a person: A psychological approach to parenthood without guilt.

Rothbart, M. K., Ahadi, S. A., & Hershey, K. L. (1994). Temperament and social behavior in childhood. *Merrill-Palmer Quarterly, 40*, 2139.

Rothbart, M. K., & Bates, J. E. (2006). Temperament. In W. Damon & R. Lerner (Eds), *Handbook of child psychology* (Vol. 3, 6th ed.). Social, emotional, and personality development (pp 96-176). New York: Wiley.

Rothbart, M. K. (2011). Becoming who we are: Temperament and personality in development. *Issues for the future* (pp 248-251). New York: Guilford.

Block, J. (1971). The Q-Sort method in personality assessment and psychiatric research (pp 59). Springfield, IL: Thomas.

Caspi, A., & Silve, P. A. (2006). Personality development. In W. Damon & R. Lerner (Eds), *Handbook of child psychology* (Vol. 3, 6th ed.). Social, emotional, and personality development (pp 300-365). New York: Wiley.

Yang, N., MacArthur, D. G., Gulbin, J. P., et al. (2003). ACTNs genotype is associated with human elite performance. *American Journal of Human Genetics, 73*(3), 627-631.

Chapter15 - The Early Years II: Learning

Laliberte, R. (1997, September). Inside your baby's brain. *Parents,* 49-56.

Newberger, J. (1997, May). New brain development research: A wonderful window of opportunity. *Young Children,* 4-9.

CDC. (2011). Developmental disabilities increasing in US. CDC: 24/7: Saving Lives. Protecting People.

Chapter 16 - The Early Years III: Potential Problems

Thomas, A., Chess, S., and Birch, H. G. (1970). The Origin of Personality. http://www.acamedia.info/sciences/sciliterature/origin_of_personality.htm

National Center on Sleep Disorders Research, National Heart Lung, and Blood Institute, NIH. (2012). Sleep disorders and biological rhythms.

Schieche, M., & Spangler, G. (2005, May). Individual differences in biobehavioral organization during problem-solving in toddlers: The influence of maternal behavior, infant-mother attachment, and behavioral inhibition on the attachment-exploration balance. *Developmental Psychology, 46*(4), 293-3006.

Spencer, E. D., DuPont, R. L., & DuPont, C. M. The anxiety cure for kids: A guide for parents. www.adaa.org

Talwar, V., & Kang, l. (2008). Social and cognitive correlates of children's lying behavior. *Child Development, 79*(4), 866-881.

Shellenbarger, S. (2012, March 24). How to handle little liars. *The Wall Street Journal.*

Chapter 18 - Latent Period II: The "Tween" Years

Heifer International. https://secure1.heifer.org/gift-catalog?msource=KIK3J121480&utm_source=Bing&utm_medium=CPC&utm_term=heiferinternational&utm_campaign=heiferinternational

Chapter 19 - Adolescence I: Puberty

Herman-Giddens, (2012, November). M. Boys hitting puberty up to two years earlier. *Pediatrics.* http://www.france24.com/en/20121020-boys-hitting-puberty-two-years-earlier-study

CDC. (2010, October 22). *Drivers Aged 16 or 17 Years Involved in Fatal Crashes*: United States, 2004-2008. Morbidity and Mortality Weekly Report (MMWR), *59*(41), 1329-1334. http://www.cdc.gov/mmwr/preview/mmwrhtml/mm5941a2.htm?s_cid=mm5941a2_w

AAP, Healthychilren.org, & American Academy of Pediatrics. (2012). Talking to your children about sex.

Bernstein, E. (2011, November 15). To skip the 'talk' about sex, have an opening dialogue. *The Wall Street Journal.*

Chapter 20 - Adolescence II: The Teenage Tunnel Years

Puget Sound Educational District. (2006). Pre-k life skills. http://www.psesd.org/UserFiles/File/Special_Services/Life%20Skills%20Curriculum_Guide.pdf

Gopnik, A. (2009, January 28). What's wrong with the teenage mind? The Saturday essay, The *Wall Street Journal.*. www.edge.org.

NIH. http//science.education.nih.gov/supplements/nih3/guide/info-sleep.htm

Chapter 21 - Almost Adult

Arum, R., & Roksa, J. (2011). *Academically adrift: Limited learning on college campuses.* Chicago, IL: The University of Chicago Press.

Chapter 22 - Unhealthy Eating

Fliegal, K. M., Kit, B. K., et al. (2013). Association of all-cause mortality with overweight and obesity using standard body mass index categories. Systemic review and meta-analysis. JAMA, 309(1): 7, 71-82 doi:10. 1001/jama.2012 113090-5

CDC. (2012). Obesity rates among all children in the United States. Data and statistics, overweight and obesity. http://www.cdc.gov/obesity/childhood/data.html

Jacobson, M. (2005). *Liquid candy: How soft drinks are harming American health.* Washington, D.C.: Center for Science in the Public Interest.

Harrison, K., & Marske, A. L. (2005). Nutritional content of foods advertised during television programs children most watch. *American Journal of Public Health, 95,* 1568-1574.

Powell, L. M., Szcsypka, G., & Chaloupka, F. J. (2007). Adolescent exposure to food advertising on television. *American Journal of Preventive Medicine, 33,* S251-S256.

Kotz, K., & Story, M. (1994). Food advertisements during children's Saturday morning television programming: Are they consistent with dietary recommendations? *Journal of the American Dietetic Association, 94,* 1296-1300.

Viner, R. M., & Cole, T. J. (2005). Television viewing in early childhood predicts adult body mass index. *Journal of Pediatrics, 147,* 429-435.

Mayo Clinic. (2012). Eating disorders: Causes. http://www.mayoclinic.com/health/eating-disorders/DS00294/DSECTION=causes.

Mayo Clinic. High cholesterol: Top 5 foods to lower your numbers. http://www.mayoclinic.com/health/cholesterol/CL00002

AAP. Healthy Living. (2011). Cholesterol levels in children and adolescents. http://www.healthychildren.org/English/healthy-living/nutrition/Pages/Cholesterol-Levels-in-Children-and-Adolescents.aspx

CDC. (2012). http://www.cdc.gov/obesity/childhood/data.html

Chapter 24 - Education I: Update

Bybee, R. X., & Sage, E. (2012). No country left behind. Issues online in *Science and Technology.* The National Academies. http://www.issues.org/education.html

Chandler, M. A. (2011, September 14). SAT reading scores drop to lowest point in decades. *The Washington Post.*

Education Week. (2012). No child left behind. http://www.edweek.org/ew/issues/no-child-left-behind/

Patall, E. A., Cooper, H., & Allen, A. B. Extending the school day or school year. Review of Educational Research. Sage Journals. American Educational Research Association.

Marcotte, D. E., & Hansen, B. (2012). Time for school? Educationnext. http://educationnext.org/time-for-school/

Pool, C. (2005, February). How schools improve. *Educational Leadership, 62*(5), 96.

Chandler, M. A. (2012, January 16). In schools, self-esteem boosting is losing favor to rigor, finer-tuned praise. *The Washington Post.*

Bain, K. (2012). What the best college students do. President and Fellows of Harvard College.

Chapter 25 - Education II: Additional Educational Options and College

Council for Aid to Education. (2012). Collegiate learning assessment, 215 Lexington Ave, New York, NY.

Arur, R., & Roksa, J. (2011). *Academically adrift: Limited learning on college campuses.* University of Chicago Press.

Vanderwater, E. A., Rideout, V. J., et al. (2007). Digital childhood: Electronic media and technology use among infants, toddlers, and preschoolers. *Pediatrics,119*(5), www.pediatrics.org/cgi/content/full/119/5/e1006

Gentile, D. A., & Walsh, D. A. (2002). A normative study of family media habits. *Journal of Applied Developmental Pscyhology, 23*(2), 607-613.

Riordan, C., Faddis, et al. (2008). Early implementation of public single-sex schools: Perceptions and characteristics. U.S. Department of Education. Washington, D.C.

Chapter 26 - Exercise and Fitness

Medline Plus. National Library of Medicine, NIH. (2012). Exercise and physical fitness. http://www.nlm.nih.gov/medlineplus/exerciseandphysicalfitness.html

Archives of *Pediatrics.* (2010, September). *Journal of the American Medical Society, 9,* 9164).

CDC. (2012). How much exercise do children need? Physical Activity for Everyone. http://www.cdc.gov/physicalactivity/everyone/guidelines/children.html

National Association for Sport and Physical Education. http://www.aahperd.org/naspe/standards/nationalGuidelines/

Chapter 29 – Bullying and Other Violence

National Institute of Mental Health (NIMH), NIH. National Comorbidity Survey Adolescent Supplement (NCS-A). 2013.

World Health Organizaion (WHO). (Depression and disability)

American Academy of Child and Adolescent Psychiatry. The depressed child. http://www.aacap.org/cs/root/facts_for_families/the_depressed_childhttp://www.aacap.org/cs/root/facts_for_families/the_depressed_child

Minino, A.M., Herron, H.P., & Smith, B.L. (2006). Deaths: Preliminary data report for 2004. National Vital Stat Rep., 54(19): 1-49.

CDC. Web-based injury statistics query and reporting system. Jun 14, 2010. www.cdc. gov/injury

Eaton D.C., Kann L, et al. CDC. (2008). Youth risk and surveillance: United States, 2007. MMWR Surveillance Summary, 57(4): 1-131.

National Adolescent Health Information Center. 2007 fact sheet on violence: Adolescents & young adults. San Francisco, CA: University of California, San Francisco, CA. http://hahic.ucsf.edu/downloads/violence.pdf

Bushman, J.B., Jamieson, P.E., et al. (2013). Gun Violence Trends in Movies. *Pediatrics*.

Council on Communications and Media. (2009, October). Media violence. Pediatrics, 124-1495.

Kuntsche, E., Pickett, W., et al. (2006). Television viewing and forms of bullying among adolescents from eight countries. Journal of Adolescent Health, 39, 908-915. http://www.jahonline.org/article/S1054-139X(06)00250-3/abstract

Huston, A.C., Donnerstein, E., et al. (1992). Big world, small screen: The role of television in American society. Lincoln, NE: University of Nebraska Press.

DeBenedittis & McCannon, B. Television violence and our kids. http://www.medialiteracy.net/pdfs/tv_violence.pdf.

Federman, J., (Ed). (1998). National television violence study (Vol. 3). Thousand Oaks, CA: Sage Publications.

Yokata, F., & Thomspon, K.M. (2002). Violence in G-rated animated films. JAMA, 283(20); 2716-2720.

Baselon, E. (2013). *Sticks and stones*. New York: Random House.

Olweus, D. *Bullying at school: What we know and what we can do* (pp 1093). Oxford: Blackwell.

Laner, L. (2012). Report: Average U.S. teenager sends/receives 60 texts per day. Pew Research Council.

Rich, M., Woods, E.R., Goodman, E., et al. (1998). Aggressors or victims: Gender and race in music video violence. Pediatrics, 101(4) part 1: 669-674.

Biebl, S.J., & DiLalla, L.F. Early temperament as a risk factor for physical and relational bullying. Education.com http://www.education.com/reference/article/temperament-bullying-risk-factor/

HealthyChildren.org. AAP. (2012). Safety & prevention: Bullying—it's not okay. http://www.healthychildren.org/English/safety-prevention/at-play/Pages/Bullying-Its-Not-Ok.aspx

Index

F
Facebook, 215-216
fact/fantasy distinction. See reality/fantasy distinction
failure
    as component of success, 19-20, 36, 90-91
    parental role, 111, 163-165
    Peter Principle, 93
family communication meetings, 18-19, 56, 63-64
family dinner, 18-19, 56, 133, 178
family size and spacing, 15, 35-37
fantasy/fact distinction. See reality/fantasy distinction
FAS (fetal alcohol syndrome), 99
FASD (fetal alcohol spectrum disorder), 99
fast food, 169
fatherhood
    benefits of co-parenting, 31-32
    bonding with child, 109-110
    changing face of, 25-28
    and child's self-esteem, 26
    hormonal changes, 26, 27, 42
    newborns, 26-27, 30-31, 123
    paternal disharmony, 41-42
    paternal participation, 26
    role in child development, 26-27
    stay-at-home dads, 32-33
    substitute fathers, 28
    traditional, 25-27
    value of fathers, 27-28
fatherless homes, 25, 27, 28, 34-35
favorite children, 36-37
FDA (Food and Drug Administration), 100
Fearlessness. See risk-taking
Fears, early years, 127
Federal Trade Commission (FTC), 51-52
fetal alcohol spectrum disorder (FASD), 99
fetal alcohol syndrome (FAS), 99
"fetal programming," 98
firstborn children, 36-37
fitness. See exercise and fitness
food. See eating
Food and Drug administration (FDA), 100
forgiveness, 43
Franklin, Benjamin, 3-4
Freud, Sigmund, 102
friends. See peers

M

manners. See courtesy and manners

marijuana use

    and addiction, 225-226

    detecting, 60

    and family dinners, 19

    first experiences, 227-228

    history, 225-228

    leading to harder drugs, 228

    stages, 228

    strength of marijuana, 226

marriage. See also co-parenting; stepparents

    choice of life mate, 161-162, 163

    v. cohabitation, 34

    disharmony, 40-41

    gay marriage, 35

    importance of balance, 11

    mother-in-law-it is, 163

meals. See eating

meaningful life. See purpose-driven life

media. See also television

    adolescence, 146

    and alcohol addiction, 222

    children's viewing time, 47-48, 56, 190

    as conversation starter, 203

    do's and don'ts, 55-58

    early years, 114-115

    and eating habits, 169-170

    educational television, 51-52

    entertainment, 50

    exercise and play, 193

    family movie night, 72

    history, 48

    and illicit drug use, 227

    influence on education, 190

    latent period, 134

    learning, 50

    media literacy, 48-49

    messages, 49-50

    negative aspects, 24, 51

    news, 50-51

    parental portrayal, 51, 56

    as parents, 47-58, 137

    positive aspects, 50

    rating systems, 52-53, 216-217

for mothers, 24
religion as a basis for, 5-6
purpose-driven parenting
communicating, 13-20
happiness and success, 7-11
morality and building character, 1-6

Q
quality time, 72-73
quitting, 93, 138-139

R
rap music, 211
rape, 195-196, 200
reading, 119
Reagan, Nancy, xii, 226
Reagan, Ronald, 60, 97, 178
reality/fantasy distinction
early years, 112-113, 128
fears, 127
latent period, 131-132
media literacy, 114-115, 129
teasing, 113-114
reasoning, 105-106
reconciliation, 43
religion
belief in God, 2-3
morality and building character, 5-6
parochial schools, 6, 186
and sexual activity, 198-199
REM sleep, 68
restrictions, disciplinary, 80-81
rewards, disciplinary, 75-76, 78, 82-83
risk-taking, 91-92, 122, 144, 219-220
Roksa, J., 189
role models
alcohol and drug use, 220
dining habits, 177-178
latent period, 136
reading, 119
single-parent families, 45
teenage sexuality, 198
television viewing, 56
violence prevention, 213-214
rules, disciplinary plan, 75-76